Chicago
Churches and
Synagogues

Chicago Churches and Synagogues

An Architectural Pilgrimage

By George A. Lane, S.J.

Photographs by
Algimantas Kezys
and George Lane

Loyola University Press
Chicago   60657

Ad majorem Dei gloriam

This book is jointly distributed by

Loyola University Press
3441 North Ashland Avenue
Chicago, Illinois   60657

and

The University of Chicago Press
5801 South Ellis Avenue
Chicago, Illinois   60637

UCP Order No.:   49560-4

Design by Mary Golon

Photo credits appear on page 254.

Quotations from *An Autobiography* by Frank Lloyd Wright © 1977,
reprinted by permission of the publisher, Horizon Press, New York

The color illustration, "The Presentation of Christ in the Temple,"
reprinted by permission of *STAINED GLASS* magazine

Library of Congress Cataloging in Publication Data

Lane, George, 1934-
   Chicago churches and synagogues.

   Includes index.
   1. Chicago (Ill.) — Churches — Guide-books.
2. Chicago (Ill.) — Synagogues — Guide-books. I. Title.
NA5235.C4L3   726'.3'0977311   81-8240
ISBN   0-8294-0373-6   AACR2

To my mother, Jewel K. Lane,
who loves Chicago and its people,
Christians and Jews, blacks and whites,
my brothers and sisters, their families,
and me.

*Detail, faceted rock glass
and opalescent glass
Louis C. Tiffany
Second Presbyterian Church*

Entrance canopy, Holy Trinity Cathedral. Louis H. Sullivan, architect

Contents

Chancel area, St. Paul Catholic Church. Henry J. Schlacks, architect

Preface

The architectural pilgrimage which culminated in this book began in the fall of 1979 when my friend Henry Tabor and I began our Sunday morning visits to churches and synagogues. For me the pilgrimage continued almost every Sunday for fourteen months with many sorties during the week. It proved fascinating, full of surprises and discoveries, and personally enriching.

On one of the first Sundays, Henry and I visited *Jackowo*, St. Hyacinth Church, in the Avondale neighborhood. Turning into George Street that morning, we saw a crowd of people on the sidewalk outside the church. The doors were open. "Between services," I thought, "or maybe the people were just attending casually from a distance." But then the men and women knelt down on the sidewalk and on the front steps. It was the consecration, the most solemn part of the mass. We parked our car and approached with reverence. The church was full, wall-to-wall people; even the two balconies were full. So Henry and I just stood outside and listened with awe and amazement to the singing, in Polish, that filled the huge church and the area around it.

On another Sunday we visited Holy Trinity Orthodox Cathedral on North Leavitt Street. We came in the middle of the service and stood near the back. It was thoroughly Eastern and profoundly captivating. Clouds of incense filled the small church. Candles flickered before the shrines. Richly adorned icons abounded. *A cappella* singing between celebrant and choir, in English and Old Slavonic, sounded like something from heaven itself. A touch of Holy Russia in Chicago.

Another Sunday we visited Quinn Chapel at 24th and Wabash, the oldest black congregation in the city. We were warmly greeted and invited to participate in the service which was about to begin. We admired the bright, simple sanctuary, heard about the history of the church from State Representative Corneal Davis, listened to the choir, and then proceeded on our pilgrimage.

Visiting St. Paul's on 22nd Place and Hoyne Avenue is all the world like visiting a cathedral in northern France. St. Paul's is a scaled down French cathedral in American brick. And the mosaics in the church are breathtaking.

An authentic Japanese temple can also be found in Chicago, the Midwest Buddhist Temple in the Old Town neighborhood on the Near North Side.

And Yugoslavia too. On the far Southeast Side of Chicago, one can find an exact replica of a fifteenth century Serbian monastery church in St. Simeon Mirotocivi on East 114th Street.

And on and on. There is an incredible variety and richness in the churches and synagogues of Chicago. Most every architectural style can be found, from the ancient Christian basilica through the round-arched Romanesque and the noble Gothic, from Byzantine to modern styles. Fine examples of each can be discovered within the city.

But visiting a church can be a personal pilgrimage as well. While I was photographing the great murals in St. Adalbert's one Saturday afternoon, a middle aged couple came in with their teenage son and daughter. I visited with the youngsters in the balcony of the church. This is where their parents were married. The family now lives in the suburbs and the youngsters had never seen this magnificent church before. They could hardly believe its size and grandeur.

And there is a majesty and dignity about the old churches too. Father Daniel Sullivan told me how a group of high school students had come to St. Mel-Holy Ghost from a suburban church which had a multi-purpose room for Sunday services. They had come with guitars and Father told them they were welcome to practice for the liturgy until the rest of the group arrived. "We can't practice in here, Father," came the reply, "this is a church."

But as many of the buildings are treasures, like Second Presbyterian, many more are humble places of worship, and all of them are witnesses of faith and fellowship.

I hope that this book may serve as a guide to the churches and synagogues of Chicago, so that many more people will make the pilgrimage that I did and rediscover the treasures in wood and stone and glass that exist in these buildings. But while visiting these witnesses of former faith, the modern pilgrim will discover that the same faith is alive and well and living in the churches and synagogues today, that there is warmth and welcome here, and an abundance of fellowship. Sunday mornings are the best time to visit, for the churches are open then and the purpose for which they were built can be experienced first hand. "For my house," says the Lord, "shall be called a house of prayer for all the peoples." *Is. 56, 7.*

Ark and bema, K.A.M. — Isaiah Israel Temple. Alfred S. Alschuler, architect

Acknowledgments

The original inspiration for this book came to my good friend Henry Tabor while he attended a wedding in Holy Name Cathedral. As Henry admired the beautiful ceiling in the church, he said to himself, "Someone should write a book about Chicago's churches."

Henry shared his idea with his friends Jim and Sally Unland, who formulated the concept and proposed it to me. I found Algimantas Kezys, S.J., willing and eager to photograph the churches. Richard Walsh encouraged me to write the book and I proposed the project to Rev. Vincent C. Horrigan, S.J., then Director of Loyola University Press. He approved the proposal in September 1979 and the research, writing, and fieldwork was under way. I am especially grateful to each of these people, including the late Father Horrigan, for their confidence in me and their continued support and encouragement of the project.

Rev. Daniel L. Flaherty, S.J., Director of Loyola University Press, and all the people at the Press were very helpful and supportive as the work progressed.

I am deeply grateful to the pastors, rabbis, and administrators of the churches and synagogues who responded to my questionnaires. These responses together with the parish anniversary and dedication books which they gave me provided the principle resource material for this book.

At the beginning of my research, I met with Bill Jacobs and Steve Heinz who had conducted church tours for the Chicago Architecture Foundation. They generously shared their notes, knowledge, and enthusiasm with me. Others who shared their expertise with me included Melvyn Skvarla and Sally Chappell, presidents of the Chicago Chapter of the Society of Architectural Historians, and Dr. Robert Irving, Dean of Humanities at Illinois Institute of Technology and consultant to the Chicago Architecture Foundation and member of the advisory committee, Chicago Landmarks Commission. Special thanks also go to Robert Piper of the Landmarks Preservation Council, William Hinchliff, Philip Pecord, Michael Kocolowski, William Bollin, and Rev. Menceslaus Madaj, Archivist for the Archdiocese of Chicago.

John Hern at the Chicago Commission on Historical and Architectural Landmarks gave me valuable leads and directives. Tim Samuelson helped me with information about the works of Adler and Sullivan, and Anne Royston shared with me her research on the churches of Chicago.

I am also indebted to Rev. Michael E. Komechak, O.S.B., of St. Procopius Abbey, Lisle, and Rev. Edmund J. Siedlecki, Chairman of the Liturgical Advisory Board of the Archdiocese of Chicago, for the information and directives which they gave me.

Several people proved to be valuable resources on groups of church and synagogue buildings. Dr. James E. Landing at the Chicago Circle Campus of the University of Illinois shared his research with me on the Eastern Churches in Chicago. Roderick Dibbert, former Historiographer of the Episcopal Diocese of Chicago, was my principle guide to the Episcopal churches. Rachel Heimovics, author of *The Jewish Resource Book*, directed my attention to several significant synagogues that I had not been aware of. The research work of Charles Gregersen greatly contributed to my treatment of the churches designed by Solon S. Beman. The publications and displays of Marya Lilien and Lester and Malgorzata Ejsmont were very helpful to me in my accounts of the Polish Catholic churches in Chicago.

Preparation of a book like this would not be possible without the gracious assistance of libraries and librarians. I am especially grateful to Daphne C. Roloff, Director of Libraries, John Zukowksy, Architectural Archivist, and Cecilia Chin, Associate Librarian, at the Burnham Architectural Library of The Art Institute of Chicago. Dorothy Lyles, Curator of the Harsh Collection at the Charles C. Woodson Regional Center of the

Acknowledgments

Chicago Public Library, was very helpful to me. Grant T. Dean and Janice Soczka, Assistant Curators of the Printed Collections at the Chicago Historical Society, Roy Fry at the Cudahy Memorial Library of Loyola University, and the newspaper microfilm librarians at the Main Branch of the Chicago Public Library were all most kind and cooperative in making their resources available. Mrs. Jean Baue at the Concordia Historical Institute in St. Louis was also very helpful to me, as was Robert Johnson of the Christian Science Committee on Publications in Chicago.

A number of practicing architects generoulsy shared their time and knowledge with me. Among them were Alfred S. Alschuler, Jr., Gerald Barry, Peter Camburas, Christopher Chamales, Thomas E. Cooke, Michael Gaul, Radoslav Kovacevic, William Lavicka, Irving Moses, Norman Schlossman, Harold A. Stahl, and Paul Straka.

In the area of stained glass windows, I learned much from Sharon Darling, Curator of Decorative Arts at the Chicago Historical Society and author of *Chicago Ceramics and Glass*. Through Sharon I was privileged to meet Erne R. and Florence Frueh who shared with me their enthusiasm for stained glass and at my request wrote the fine essay, "Ecclesiastical Stained Glass in Chicago," which appears in this book. Thanks also to Frank Drehobl of Drehobl Bros. Art Glass Co. and Lubomyr Wandzura of Giannini and Hilgart and Nick Wenz of Wenz Art Glass Co.

In the area of pipe organs, I am grateful to Frank Pellegrini for writing the essay on organs which appears in this book. I was assisted in my research on organ installations by Ronald Sauter, Daniel Bogue, and by David McCain of *The Diapason* magazine.

Three reference works were especially helpful to our research. The first was the two volume *History of the Parishes of the Archdiocese of Chicago* edited by Rev. Msgr. Harry C. Koenig and published by the Archdiocese in September 1980. A second very helpful volume was *Faith & Form, Synagogue Architecture in Illinois,* published by Spertus College Press in 1976. A third source was A. T. Andreas' three volume *History of Chicago* published in 1885.

Most of the photographs in this book were taken by Algimantas Kezys, S.J., and myself. I am especially indebted to Al for generously contributing his time and energy to this project. Jim and Sally Unland helped to fund the photography.

The reproduction of color plates in this volume was made possible by a generous grant from the Graham Foundation for Advanced Studies in the Fine Arts. I would like to thank its director, Carter H. Manny, Jr., for his continued support and interest in this publication.

A special word of thanks to my friend Mary Golon who designed this book.

I was extremely fortunate to be able to engage the help of Ellen Skerrett as research assistant and editor for this book and Tim Barton, a writer and researcher for the Chicago Landmarks Commission, who read the manuscript for architectural description and made many helpful editorial suggestions.

Many centuries ago the Psalmist wrote, "Unless the Lord build the house, in vain do the builders build it." The acknowledgments cited above clearly indicate that the "building" of this book has had the Lord's abundant blessing. *Deo gratias.*

Introduction

Chicago is a city of churches. No resident or visitor has to travel more than a few blocks before finding a church or synagogue. Someone has estimated that there are more than two thousand churches in Chicago. They range from massive architectural monuments to humble storefronts. The motorist on the Chicago expressways sees a skyline of steeples. From the lakefront on the east to the city limits on the west, each neighborhood has more than a few houses of worship.

When Americans travel abroad, their itineraries invariably lead to the churches and cathedrals of the lands they visit. When at home, however, they rarely take a sensitive look at their own churches, even the ones in which they worship. But recently there has been a growing interest in the churches of Chicago. More people are asking, "What is that yellow brick church I see from the expressway on my way downtown?" And more people are visiting the churches and synagogues and bringing their children to visit the places where they were baptized, made their first communion, bar/bat mitzvah, or where they were married.

Principle of Selection

The principle of selection for the churches and synagogues in this book was architectural significance, first of all, and then a consideration for the historical and social importance of a building or congregation.

The original list consisted of about forty buildings. It was critiqued and augmented by experts in the field, and then grew gradually as additional fascinating or noteworthy buildings were discovered, or as friends and acquaintances would say, "Have you seen St. _____ Church on the South Side? It has magnificent windows."

There are 125 buildings described in this book. There are many more fine houses of worship which might have been included but were not because of lack of time and space.

The churches and synagogues included here are all located within the city of Chicago, with four notable exceptions: Unity Temple in Oak Park, Baha'i Temple in Wilmette, North Shore Congregation Israel in Glencoe, and the St. Procopius Abbey Church in Lisle, Illinois.

Listings

The churches and synagogues are listed chronologically from the oldest functioning church, St. Patrick's, to those of recent construction. Each entry is followed by two dates; the first, that which appears on the cornerstone, and the second, the year in which the church or synagogue was dedicated.

The addresses which follow each listing indicate the location of the front door or principal facade of the building. Mailing addresses, often designating rectories or church offices, can be found together with telephone numbers in the alphabetical index at the back of the book.

The address of each building is followed by a directional coordinate so the reader or architectural pilgrim can tell just where the church or synagogue is. For instance, St. Patrick's is listed at 140 South Desplaines Street (700 West). The front doors of the church face Desplaines Street, a north-south street, which is 700 or seven blocks west of State Street. This locates the church just about two blocks south of Madison Street and seven blocks west of State Street, State and Madison being the principal coordinates of the city. So the church is on the Near West Side.

After the address comes the name of the architect. If the designer of the building was a member of an architectural firm, the firm name is given and the design partner is credited within the body of the account.

Then comes landmark designations, if any, the architectural style of the building, and then the seating capacity which gives a general notion of the size of the structure.

Architectural Styles

The churches and synagogues of Chicago represent all the major architectural styles of Eastern and Western Europe. There are oriental buildings too, as well as many fine examples of modern and contemporary architecture. When surveying many buildings and trying to describe the architectural character of each, the categories of historical styles are helpful. Some buildings fit easily into these traditional categories, others do not. But even when a building is designed within a traditional style, there is always the individual element of the architect's own treatment of the project. And so there is a great variety.

Since the designation of style is useful in many cases, we will offer a thumbnail sketch of some traditional styles, a few of their distinguishing features, and in the index at the back of the book, we will list where examples of these styles may be found in Chicago churches.

Basilica

The basilica is an ancient style of building used by the Greeks and Romans for courts of law and for markets. It is rectangular in plan, has three aisles divided by columns, a flat roof, and the columns often support a clerestory. The basilica has an apse at one end and a narthex or vestibule at the other. It was the Roman basilica in the early fourth century that the Christians adopted for their first places of public worship. St. Paul's Outside the Walls, built in 380 A.D., is the archetype of the Christian Roman basilica.

Byzantine

The Byzantine style of architecture originated in the sixth century in Constantinople during the reign of the Emperor Justinian. The distinguishing characteristic of the Byzantine style is the great hemispherical dome supported on pendentive vaults over a square base. The most famous example of this is the church of *Hagia Sophia*, 532-37 A.D., whose dome spans 103 feet and its apex is 163 feet above the floor. The popularity of this style radiated from Constantinople and flourished for nearly a thousand years with periods of conspicuous creativity in the sixth and ninth centuries. In Chicago it enjoyed a revival in the 1920s.

Romanesque

The Romanesque style of architecture emerged in northern Italy in the eleventh century. It is characterized by the round arch. The style subsequently spread to southern France, Spain, and central Europe. Arcades of round arches are found resting on columns or masonry piers. Romanesque churches have barrel or tunnel-vaulted ceilings. The eleventh century Cathedral of St. Mary in Speyer, Germany, is considered one of the finest examples of Romanesque architecture in Europe. The famous nineteenth century Boston architect Henry Hobson Richardson led a Romanesque revival in the United States after 1870.

Gothic

The pointed arch, the ribbed vault, and flying buttresses are among the salient features of Gothic architecture. The desire was to create churches that were higher, lighter in structure, and spiritually uplifting. Verticality became the ideal, slenderness of members, balance, and unity.

The origin of the Gothic style is commonly attributed to Abbot Suger when he reconstructed the Abbey Church of St.-Denis in Paris in 1132. The style flourished in northern France, England, and Germany throughout the Middle Ages. The Cathedral of Chartres is perhaps the definitive expression of the French Gothic style. A simplified Victorian Gothic was popular in the United States in the 1870s and 1880s. Around the turn of the century and later, Ralph Adams Cram led a Gothic revival in church architecture in the United States. This revival adhered closely to the ideals of the English Perpendicular Gothic.

Renaissance

The Renaissance style of architecture originated in Florence, Italy, in the early fifteenth century. Its popularity spread through the Italian peninsula and by 1700 it pervaded most of Europe. The aim of the Renaissance was a rebirth or revival of classicism. In architecture, this resulted in the widespread use of Greek and Roman forms and ornament; for example, the column, the round arch, and the dome. Harmony and proportion of elements were the controlling ideals. The basic element of design was the classical order, a system of architectural units, of which there were five: the Tuscan, Doric, Ionic, Corinthian, and Composite. St. Peter's Basilica in Rome is considered to be the finest example of Renaissance architecture.

The Greek Revival style of architecture dominated the Columbian Exposition of 1893 in Chicago and was subsequently used by Solon S. Beman for Christian Science churches. The Renaissance style became popular in Chicago church and synagogue construction after the turn of the century up until the time of the Depression.

Modern

Frank Lloyd Wright, William Drummond, and Francis Barry Byrne all rejected traditional styles of architecture and devised new forms for houses of worship. Because of these innovations their churches in the Chicago area appear on the National Register of Historic Places. Wright rejected all traditional symbolism. Drummond followed this pattern. And Byrne's St. Thomas the Apostle Church in Hyde Park was the first modern-style Catholic church in America. The simplified interior was designed to focus attention on the altar. The high ceiling once had the largest span in the world unsupported by arches or pillars.

International

The chief proponent of the International style of architecture, Ludwig Mies van der Rohe, came to Chicago from Germany in 1938. He designed the Saint Saviour Chapel on the campus of IIT. This small building with its rectangular lines, steel frame roof, and glass facade exemplifies the simplicity and spartan qualities of the International style. The principles of this style were so pervasive that they influenced the design of many churches built after 1950.

Liturgy and Architecture

Throughout history the building of churches and temples has been man's highest form of architectural expression. Bill Jacobs, a docent with Chicago's ArchiCenter, has called our churches and synagogues "frequently our best, most splendid buildings." But architecture is not an art that is practiced for its own sake. Ecclesiastical architecture serves worship. Form follows function, and the function of a church or synagogue is to be a place of assembly for prayer and worship.

Church architecture over the centuries has been determined by how people worship, what they do during religious services, and what the demands of the liturgy might be.

Jewish worship, for instance, consists of readings from the Torah, explanations of the Scripture, responsive singing, and sermons by the rabbis. There is no one architectural style that is distinctively Jewish. Romanesque and Moorish Revival styles were used by synagogue designers in Chicago from 1870 to 1900. Gothic Revival was used for a short time. Renaissance styles became popular between 1900 and the First World War, and a Byzantine Revival came in during the 1920s. The International style has been influential since World War II.

But whatever the style of the building, Jewish services require an auditorium with seats facing a platform in the front which contains the ark where the scrolls are kept, seats for the rabbis and cantors, and a pulpit or reading stand.

Introduction

Early Christian services evolved from the Jewish synagogue service. Sacred Scripture was read and explained, prayers were offered, a sermon was given, and this was followed by the Eucharistic meal, the sharing of the sacred Bread and the Cup as the Lord had commanded at the Last Supper—"Do this in memory of Me." Until the fourth century A.D. these services took place in private homes or in catacombs where small groups of Christians would gather.

When Constantine allowed Christians to practice their religion in public in 313 A.D., they began to gather in larger buildings and to build churches. In the large cities, such as Rome, they used basilicas for worship.

Using larger, more formal buildings for their assemblies had the effect of making the services more formal too. Once the Church had gained political and social status, the mass picked up certain aspects of Roman and Byzantine court ceremonial. Such things as the use of incense, bowing and genuflections, the kissing of cruets and the Scriptures, the elaborate vestments and so on, all came into the mass during the late Roman period. These formalities made the service something of a spectacle and somewhat remote from the common people.

Early Christian services were always conducted in the language of the people; that is, in Greek or Latin. But as time went on and the romance languages developed in Western Europe, the Christian liturgy remained in Latin and gradually became less and less intelligible.

As the services became more formal and less comprehensible to the people, this "remoteness" came to be reflected in the architecture. Altars were elevated and moved back into apses or chancels, rood screens appeared, and communion rails proved to be something of an unintended barrier between the high altar and the congregation. The service, in fact, got so far from the family meal of the Christian community which Jesus intended that the Second Lateran Council in 1215 made it a law that everyone had to receive Communion at least once a year at Easter time. The people had become more spectators than participants in the sacred liturgy and they felt themselves unworthy to share the sacred meal.

Probably as an unconscious compensation for the remoteness of the liturgy, devotion to the saints grew. A multitude of shrines and statues appeared in the churches, and the practice of private devotions, such as saying the rosary, became the only really intelligent way for people to worship in church. The liturgy of the mass itself had become quite unintelligible to the people in the pews. It was against all of this, of course, and other things as well, that Luther revolted in 1517.

Protestant worship called for a simplification of furnishings and ornament within the church, a focus on the reading of Sacred Scripture, on prayers, congregational singing, and on the preaching of the Word of God—all in the language of the people. Whatever seating arrangement helped the people hear the Word of God was the best. So amphitheater seating was introduced, the Akron plan was adopted in many churches. The center of the service became the Word and the Sacrament of the Lord's Supper.

Some of the excesses and many of the abuses in Catholic worship were corrected by the Council of Trent in the sixteenth century. But the mass as offered in Latin and "removed" in various other ways from the people was perpetuated for the next four centuries. The situation in which the practice of private devotions at mass, saying the rosary or praying to the saints, continued to be the only meaningful method of worship for most of the people most of the time.

But all this was changed by the Constitution on the Sacred Liturgy of the Second Vatican Council in 1963. The Council required the use of vernacular languages, brought the altar close to the people, replaced communion railings with communion stations, and made one altar the focal point of the church. These reforms can clearly be seen in the furnishing and decoration of any Catholic church built or renovated since 1965.

Ethnic Churches and National Parishes

The giants of commerce and industry in Chicago built skyscrapers in the central business district. In the neighborhoods of the city the little people, the immigrants, the ethnic minorities, built houses of worship as symbols of their identity and their ethnic pride. The church or synagogue was always the finest building the congregation could afford. It was often a symbol of continuity with the past, a link with the Old World, as well as being a center of social life and worship. Here the ethnic languages were spoken and the national traditions were preserved. Here the patron saints of the people were honored and the great events of their religious history were called to mind in marble, glass, or mural painting.

The churches and synagogues of Chicago document the places of origin and the movements of ethnic groups within the city. In each of the accounts which follow, we try to indicate who built the church, when, and who the people are who are worshiping there now. The churches are repositories of history and heritage. They are the noble landmarks of people. They are storehouses of tradition as well as being monuments of faith.

And often enough, these treasured buildings have been handed on to new worshipers as people move from one neighborhood to another. The synagogue has become a Baptist church. The Greek Orthodox church has become a mosque. The Irish parish has become black or Latino. The Catholic church usually remains as the neighborhood undergoes racial change and the buildings begin to serve other groups of people who profess the same faith.

Before the promulgation of canon law in 1918, the Catholic Church established territorial parishes for English-speaking Catholics and nonterritorial or national parishes for Catholics who spoke foreign languages. For instance, in 1846 St. Patrick's was founded for English-speaking Catholics, mostly Irish, on the West Side. In the same year both St. Peter's and St. Joseph's were organized for German-speaking Catholics who lived in the center of the city and north of the river respectively.

Although mass was offered in Latin in all of the national parishes, the sermons, bulletins, devotions, and social life in these parishes would be conducted in the mother tongue. In the ethnically diverse Bridgeport area, for example, one can find as many as twelve Catholic churches within a small area. St. Anthony and Immaculate Conception were founded for Germans, St. Jerome for the Croatians, St. Maria Incoronata for Italians, St. John Nepomucene for Bohemians, St. Mary of Perpetual Help and St. Barbara for the Polish, and St. George for the Lithuanians. St. Bridget, All Saints, St. David, and Nativity of Our Lord were all founded as territorial parishes for English-speaking people, mostly Irish.

Although few national parishes were formed after 1918, the needs of new Catholic immigrants were met by older ethnic parishes, such as St. Francis of Assisi on Roosevelt Road. This parish was founded by German Catholics in 1853 but it has been a Mexican parish since 1925. Today all the services are conducted in Spanish and St. Francis of Assisi continues to serve thousands of Mexican Catholics in Chicago. Other ethnic parishes with sizeable concentrations of foreign-language parishioners will usually have different services in different languages; for instance, St. Stanislaus Kostka on Noble Street has masses in English, Spanish, and Polish.

It will be good to note here that most of the Catholic parishes in Chicago are conducted by the diocesan clergy, that is, by priests who are appointed by and answer directly to the Catholic archbishop. Some of the parishes, however, are conducted by religious order priests, by Jesuits, Augustinians, Claretians, Dominicans, Franciscans, Redemptorists, Resurrection fathers, Servite friars, Viatorians, Vincentians, and others. These priests are appointed by and answer directly to their religious superiors who in turn work cooperatively with the archbishop. So Holy Family Church on Roosevelt Road will be cited in the text as a Jesuit parish, whereas St. Patrick's on Desplaines Street is conducted by diocesan priests.

The churches and synagogues of Chicago are witnesses of faith. In some instances they are monuments of architecture. In many instances they contain veritable treasures of painting, wood carving, and stained glass. But these buildings are not museums or art galleries. Each one is a functioning house of worship. Rev. Elam Davies, pastor of the Fourth Presbyterian Church, has said, "Buildings, however beautiful, must symbolize a living temple of concerned men and women." The ultimate purpose of the buildings and the ultimate criteria by which they must be judged is how well they inspire faith, how well they foster fellowship, and how well they instill compassion for fellow men and women.

"The Madonna of Mannheim." Lunette. F.X. Zettler Royal Bavarian Art Institute, Munich. St. Boniface Church

19

Chancel area, St. Mary of the Lake Church. Henry J. Schlacks, architect

1852-1899

Heralding Angel, bronze
Frederic C. Bartlett, sculptor
Second Presbyterian Church

**Old St. Patrick Church
1852-56
140 South Desplaines Street
(700 West)**

Architects: Carter and Bauer
  Chicago Landmark, 1964
  National Register of
  Historic Places, 1977
Style: Romanesque
Seating: 800

The oldest church building in Chicago, rich in Irish imagery and heritage.

"Constructed during the period 1852 to 1856, St. Patrick's is the oldest church building in Chicago and one of the few buildings which survived the Great Fire of 1871." Thus the Chicago City Council under Mayor Richard J. Daley designated St. Patrick's an historic landmark on March 10, 1964.

Founded in 1846, St. Patrick's was the second Catholic parish in Chicago following St. Mary's, 1833. It was established to serve the growing English-speaking immigrant population, mostly Irish, who were settling west of the Chicago River.

The church, 64 by 124 feet, is constructed of Milwaukee common brick with Lemont stone base and trim. A great bronze cross ten feet high and rich in Celtic ornament stands outside near the base of the south tower and proclaims the church to be "St. Patrick's." The building was raised eight feet and a basement was added in 1871. The octagonal towers on the front of the church were completed in 1885. The south tower with a tall Roman spire represents the church in the West. The north tower with a rounded onion dome of Byzantine style represents the church of the East. The two towers together symbolize the universality of the Catholic faith.

St. Patrick's is noted for its interior decoration based upon the illumination in the ancient Irish Book of Kells. The magnificent stained glass windows were designed by the Chicago artist Thomas A. O'Shaughnessy and executed under his direction in the studios of the Kinsella Art Glass Co. of Chicago. These windows, installed in 1912, depict the great saints of Ireland—Patrick, Bridget, Finbarr, Colman, Sennan, Columbanus, Attracta, Columbkille, Brendan, Carthage and Gall.

The whole church is richly ornamented with the symbols and designs of ancient Gaelic art. The *Window of Faith*, a triptych in the center of the east facade, contains 250,000 pieces of glass. The stained glass canopy over the main altar carries symbols of the four evangelists. The mosaic work around the baptistry at the rear of the church is especially fine. The carved walnut statues, the communion rail, the pulpit, and the hand-carved decoration on the main altar are also noteworthy.

St. Patrick's is a friendly parish which has undergone many changes. It now serves travelers, downtown workers, and Irish-Americans who return to visit this bit of Ireland in Chicago where their parents and grandparents worshiped.

The Cathedral of St. James
1856-57, 1875
65 East Huron Street
(700 North)

Architect: Edward J. Burling
  Reconstruction, 1875,
  Burling and Bacchus
Style: Victorian Gothic
Seating: 700

The oldest Episcopal church in Chicago; the cathedral parish since 1955.

The Cathedral of St. James at the corner of Wabash and Huron streets is the oldest Episcopal church in Chicago and one of the oldest in Illinois.

Father Isaac Hallam, at the request of the John Kinzie family, organized St. James parish in November of 1834 among the early settlers around Fort Dearborn. This parish was responsible for the organization of many other Episcopal churches in Chicago, among them Trinity Church at 26th and Michigan in 1842, the Church of the Ascension on La Salle Drive in 1857, and St. Chrysostom's on Dearborn Parkway in 1894.

Parts of the present Joliet limestone church, principally the walls and bell tower, date from 1857 before the building was gutted by the Chicago Fire of 1871. The church was then rebuilt according to the original plans and completed in 1875. Joliet limestone was widely used for church construction in the 1870s and 1880s. It remains bright and clean because the rain washes away the surface of the stone.

The vertical lines of the cathedral are accentuated by sturdy pinnacles. These are functional as well as ornamental; they give additional weight and strength to the buttresses.

Inside the front doors of the church at the north end of the narthex is a tablet which commemorates a visit by Abraham Lincoln to St. James in 1860, the day after he was elected president of the United States.

Also at the north end of the narthex is a memorial altar erected "In honor of those who fought—in memory of those who fell" in the Civil War. The altar survived the Fire, and when the rubble had been cleared away, it served as the principal altar in a temporary chapel built in the narthex until the church itself could be reconstructed.

At the entrance to the nave is the Paul C. Popp memorial baptistry. The font, a gift to the cathedral in 1875, was restored and placed in its present location in 1975. It is

St. James has a variety of stained glass windows installed at different times and representing a number of styles of American and English art glass. At the rear of the cathedral is the Randall memorial window, installed in 1963 by Charles J. Connick Studios of Boston, depicting Christ the King reigning in glory from the cross in traditional priestly vestments.

The organ in St. James is a 45-rank Austin organ installed in the 1920s and complemented in 1961 by a 15-rank choir organ in the north transept.

Perhaps the most widely known feature of the cathedral is the Chapel of St. Andrew, for it was here that the Brotherhood of St. Andrew was founded by James L. Houghteling and his Bible class in 1883. The brotherhood is now an international organization with hundreds of chapters and thousands of members dedicated to bringing young men to Christ and his church. The chapel was designed by Bertram G. Goodhue and is modeled after an ancient abbey chapel in southern Scotland.

one of the finest examples of Italian marble sculpture in Chicago.

Supporting the roof of St. James is a sturdy system of hammer-beam trusses and wooden vaulting.

The focal point of the cathedral is the marble high altar with its great cross and candlesticks. The Holy Eucharist is offered here. On the left side of the sanctuary is the *cathedra* or bishop's chair, the symbol of his authority. It is from this chair and the fact that this is the bishop's church, that we have the word "cathedral." St. James was designated a cathedral in 1955.

Holy Family Church
1857-60
1080 West Roosevelt Road
(1200 South)

Architects: Dillenburg and
Zucher
    Tower and interior,
    John Van Osdel
Style: Gothic
Seating: 1,000

The original Jesuit church on
Twelfth Street, constructed like a
European cathedral on the
Illinois prairie.

When Rev. Arnold Damen, S.J., began building Holy Family Church in 1857, it was known as the church on the prairie. The land to the south and west was virtually uninhabited. Nevertheless, when the building was dedicated in 1860, it was one of the largest churches in the country.

Holy Family is the first Jesuit parish in Chicago. It is also the second oldest church building in the city, and like St. Patrick's, it survived the Chicago Fire of 1871, miraculously, it is believed, in answer to a vow by Father Damen that if the church were spared, seven lights would always burn before the shrine of Our Lady of Perpetual Help

in the east transept. The lights are burning to this day.

Holy Family parish grew dramatically and by 1890 it had become the largest English-speaking parish in the United States serving 25,000 people. It had five grade schools with 5,000 students, a high school, St. Ignatius, and a college which would become Loyola University of Chicago.

Different parts of the huge church were built at different times. The original building, constructed of brick with Illinois cut stone trim, was 146 feet long and 85 feet wide. In 1862 the transepts were added increasing the width to 125 feet. In 1886 the

nave was extended 40 feet to the south to the present length of 186 feet.

The main pillars of Holy Family, curiously, slant outward and are 18 inches off plumb. But several structural surveys in recent years have shown that the pillars are not moving and apparently have had this inclination for many, many years.

John Van Osdel, the foremost architect in Chicago before the Civil War, is credited with the design of the 226-foot tower and the interior of the church. The tower, constructed of wood with a sheet metal finish, was not completed until after 1874.

26

The high altar is surmounted by a 52-foot reredos of hand-carved walnut enclosing a picture of the Holy Family, a copy of a Murillo by a Flemish Jesuit painter. The altar, all the statues on the reredos, and the confessionals around the church were carved by Anthony Buscher. The Last Supper scene on the front of the high altar was carved by Sebastian Buscher, Anthony's nephew, and is a reproduction in wood of Da Vinci's *Last Supper*.

The communion rail is a masterpiece of wood carving done by Louis Wisner, a Lutheran who lived in the

parish. It was installed in 1866. A eucharistic theme is carried throughout the 17 panels that span nearly the whole width of the church.

The stained glass windows in the nave of the church were done in the German baroque style and depict scenes from the lives of Jesuit saints. The windows near the side altars at the front of the church portray the Nativity on the west side and the Annunciation on the east. These beautiful windows were made and installed by the Von Gerichten Art Glass Co. of Columbus, Ohio in the parish's jubilee year of 1907.

The original great organ of Holy Family Church was built in 1870 by Louis Mitchell &

Son Co. of Montreal with pipes and reeds imported from Paris. The organ had 64 stops, 3,944 pipes, was acoustically perfect, and was considered to be one of the musical masterpieces of its time. It was rebuilt in 1890 by Frank Roosevelt of New York and again in 1923 by the Tellers-Kent Organ Co. It was then enlarged to 72 stops and 5,142 pipes. A new Austin organ was installed in 1949.

The organ front on the second balcony of the church is of carved walnut in Gothic style surmounted by dozens of carved angels each with a musical instrument. The

front is all that remains of the great organ as it was sold in 1971 and is now housed in St. Peter's United Church of Christ in Lake Zurich, Illinois.

The new altar platform and the free-standing altar were built in 1979. The altar was constructed from pews that were removed to make room for the platform.

The statuary and art work within the church reflect the different ethnic groups which the parish has served over the years. St. Patrick, the first of over 100 statues, stands for the Irish who built the church and worshiped there for almost a century. Italian immigrants began coming in 1890 and became a majority in the parish by 1920. A statue of St. Francis Xavier Cabrini stands near the sanctuary on the left side. She lived in the parish and worshiped here while she was establishing Columbus Extension, now Cabrini Hospital, on Lytle Street. During the 1940s the parish population included Slavs and Mexicans as well as Irish and Italians. The painting of the Black Risen Christ by James Hasse, S.J., over the east side altar and the picture of Our Lady of Guadalupe over the west side altar represent the black and Mexican-American people whom the parish serves today.

St. Michael Church
1866-69, 1873
455 West Eugenie Street
(1700 North)

Architect: August Wallbaum
Style: Romanesque
Seating: 1,600

Once a German church and neighborhood, the great tower of St. Michael's now identifies the historic Old Town Triangle district.

Historic St. Michael's has been called "Chicago's best kept secret." The parish was founded in 1852 as more and more German immigrants came to Chicago and settled north of the river in an area known until the 1940s as North Town. Land for the new church was donated by Michael Diversey of the Diversey and Lill Brewery and the church was named for his patron saint. Diversey Avenue also commemorates this early Chicago brewer.

The Redemptorist fathers took charge of St. Michael's in 1860 and the cornerstone for the new church was laid in 1866. Constructed of red brick with elaborate limestone trim in a Romanesque style,

St. Michael's was 190 feet long and 80 feet wide, cost $131,000, and was completed and dedicated in 1869.

The Great Fire of 1871 destroyed the whole North Town neighborhood and gutted St. Michael's leaving only the walls of the church and part of the tower standing. The *Daily Tribune* reported St. Michael's to be "the most imposing ruins on the north side." But the industrious parishioners soon rebuilt the church and it was rededicated on October 12, 1873.

The five great bells, weighing between 2,500 and 6,000 pounds each, named for St. Michael, St. Mary,

St. Joseph, St. Alphonsus, and St. Theresa, were blessed and installed in 1876. Local tradition has it that anyone who can hear the bells of St. Michael's is a resident of Old Town.

The tower of St. Michael's with its illuminated four-sided clock is a landmark on the Near North Side. It rises 290 feet above Old Town, was completed in 1888, and is visible for miles around. The cross on the top of the steeple is 24 by 9 feet and weighs 2,235 pounds.

The interior of St. Michael's has been redecorated many times, but always with the off-white, gold, and light blue motif characteristic of Bavarian baroque church interiors. Five altars, including the permanent altar with its 56 foot high reredos, were built and installed by Hacker and Son of La Crosse, Wisconsin in 1902. High above the permanent altar a statue of St. Michael stands in conquest over the fallen angels.

The altar on the west side of the church in honor of Mary, Mother of Perpetual Help, enshrines a painting that was entrusted to the Redemptorist fathers by Pope Pius IX in 1865. This picture is said to have miraculously survived the Fire of 1871 and it is especially dear to the parishioners.

The exceptionally tall stained glass windows of St. Michael's were supplied by Mayer & Company of Munich in 1902.

A three-manual Kilgen organ with 37 ranks and 2,236 pipes was installed in 1925.

St. Michael's Church is still the center and its tower the identifying mark of the Old Town neighborhood which has enjoyed a revitalization that began in the 1930s and continues to this day.

The main facade of this church is on Eugenie Street. Its gabled, three-portal main entrance recalls the cathedrals of Europe and like them represents the three persons of the Blessed Trinity. The tripartite theme is carried through on the facade by the three large window openings above and behind the main entrance. A nine-foot statue of St. Michael, sent to the parish in 1913 by a Bavarian stonecutter, is located above the central arch and is flanked by Corinthian columns. Brick corbelling with limestone trim beneath and limestone eaves above completes the main portion of this north elevation.

First Baptist Congregational Church   1869-71
60 North Ashland Avenue (1600 West)

Architect: Gurdon P. Randall
Style: Gothic
Seating: 1,500

A classic Victorian church, a reminder that Chicago's elite once lived on Ashland Avenue.

The sharply pointed spire rises 175 feet above Ashland Avenue on the Near West Side. The picturesque Lemont limestone church stands as a reminder of the days when Chicago's best homes and gardens clustered around Union Park across the street. The Union Park Congregational Church built this building in 1869 as is attested by a large plaque on the north wall of the tower. The First Congregational Church, founded in 1851, merged with the Union Park congregation and moved to this site in 1910. The First Baptist Congregational Church acquired the building in 1970.

In the dark days after the Chicago Fire had burned down much of the city in 1871, the Mayor's Office, the City Council, and the General Relief Committee were temporarily located in this church.

The church is almost square in plan, except for shallow transepts which emerge a few feet to the north and south. The wide expanse of the handsome timbered ceiling is hung from a large free-span wooden truss system; some of the beams are as large as two feet square. These beams were reinforced in 1927 when much of the building was restored and renovated.

With a view to the sermon-centered Congregational service, Gurdon Randall designed the auditorium in amphitheater style. He is often credited with originating this widely-imitated seating design. A gracefully shaped curving balcony is cantilevered out from the exterior walls on all four sides; it is further supported by cast iron columns. The carved oak balcony railing moves from the choir area behind the pulpit up and around in a broad oval.

The pulpit furniture dates from the 1851 First Congregational Church, and

it is reported that every president of the United States from Abraham Lincoln to John Kennedy stood behind this pulpit.

The interior of First Baptist Congregational is dominated by the Andrew R. Dole Memorial Kimball organ, reputed to be the largest enclosed pipe organ ever made. It was installed in 1927 at a cost of $250,000. It is a four-manual and pedal organ containing 117 ranks and 5,466 pipes, ranging from the 32-foot Bombarde and Diaphones to the small high tones of the mixture ranks whose speaking length is about one-half inch. Two rooms were constructed on either side of the organ case to accommodate the great size of the instrument and additional chambers were provided in the balcony for the echo and antiphonal organs.

The auditorium is lighted by six chandeliers, ten lancet windows, and three large Gothic-arched windows. The windows are made of opalescent glass imported from Italy. They continue from the main floor, through and behind the balconies, and upward.

The First Baptist Congregational Church is an active, thriving Christian community under the direction of Rev. Arthur D. Griffin. It has six choirs, four organists, pre-school, primary school, and young adult Christian education programs, a band, a concert orchestra, a full complement of ministers, deacons, and deaconesses, and a missionary program. The church is in excellent physical condition and as functional for worship and organizational purposes now as it was a century or more ago.

**Second Presbyterian Church
1872-74
1936 South Michigan Avenue
(100 East)**

Architect: James Renwick
  Interior restoration, 1900,
  Howard Van Doren Shaw
  National Register of
  Historic Places, 1974
  Chicago Landmark, 1977
Style: English Gothic
Seating: 1,000

This landmark church on South
Michigan Avenue contains
veritable treasures of stained
glass and decorative art.

James Renwick (1818-95) was
one of the foremost American
architects of his day. His
designs, especially that for
St. Patrick's Cathedral in New
York, made him one of the
leaders of the Gothic Revival
movement in American
architecture. Renwick had
been the architect for the
previous Second Presbyterian
church which was built in
1851. That church stood at
the corner of Wabash and
Washington streets and was
destroyed in the Chicago Fire
of 1871. The parishioners
sought Renwick again to
design their new church
at 20th Street and South
Michigan Avenue. These
people, the Armours, Swifts,
Fields, Kimballs, Pullmans,
Crerars, Ishams, Shaws,

and others who lived on or
near Prairie Avenue were
accustomed to the best.
Their confidence in Renwick
was not misplaced.

The architect designed an
impressive edifice modeled
after the style of English
Gothic churches of the early
fifteenth century. Second
Presbyterian was constructed
with rusticated Illinois
limestone with cut stone trim.
The limestone has a blotched
appearance because of black
bituminous deposits in the
quarry from which it was dug.
The previous Second Church,
built with stone from the same
quarry, had been known as
the Spotted Church.

The facade of Second
Presbyterian has a massive

wall with buttresses and
pinnacles, relieved by
Gothic-arched windows,
horizontal bands, and four
large sculptured medallions
symbolizing the four
evangelists: Matthew as a
young man, Mark as a lion,
Luke as an ox, and John
as an eagle.

A square crenellated tower,
complete with gargoyles and
blind arcading, stands at the
southeast corner of the
building. Each side of the
tower has a large pointed arch
into which is set a sculptured
angel and two smaller arches.
These smaller arches are
supported by graceful granite
columns with foliate capitals.
The tower once had a spire.
But this was blown down in

a storm in 1959 and was not replaced.

Heavy buttresses and large windows divide each side of the church into six bays. There is a band of clerestory windows above. An oriel on the south elevation, where the church joins the parish hall, has a medieval flavor about it.

Inside, Second Presbyterian is warm, majestic, and reverent with an atmosphere quite unlike any other church in Chicago. The prominent Chicago architect Howard Van Doren Shaw and the mural painter Frederic C. Bartlett collaborated in restoring and decorating the interior of the church after it was destroyed by fire in 1900. The warmth of the church comes from the extensive use of oak paneling, the soft greens, golds, and browns in the murals, and the stained glass windows.

Behind the beautiful organ screen is Bartlett's 30-by-40-foot Tree of Life mural, with the Rainbow of Hope, and above that a choir of angels in a star-studded heaven. On top of the organ screen stand four bronze heralding angels, Michael, Gabriel, Uriel, and Raphael.

There is a balcony around three sides of the auditorium. It is reached by way of handsome wooden staircases near the back of the church. The ceiling rises to a height of 60 feet and the great clear-span vault is paneled with alternating plain and scrolled panels. At the intersection of the beams there are small plaster animals painted in bright colors, turtles, salamanders, birds, snakes, bats, and squirrels.

The organ in Second Presbyterian was originally built by Hutchings-Votey in 1904 and had three manuals. It was rebuilt by Austin in 1917 and a fourth manual was added. The organ now has 50 stops and 2,524 pipes.

But the greatest treasures in Second Church are the stained glass windows by Louis C. Tiffany, John LaFarge, Louis J. Millet, and two in the vestibule by the English Arts and Crafts leaders, Sir Edward Burne-Jones and William Morris. The windows must be seen to be appreciated. A listing of subject matter and date of installation must suffice here.

From the northwest corner clockwise around the church: Tiffany's *Pastoral Window*, installed about 1918; Millet's *Cast Thy Garment About Thee and Follow Me*, between 1895 and 1900; Tiffany's *Behold the Lamb of God*, between 1891 and 1895; John LaFarge's *Angel in the Lilies*, 1893; Tiffany's *Jeweled Window*, 1895, from the First Presbyterian Church, installed here, 1913; and the Arts and Crafts window designed by Shaw. On the east wall of the church, Tiffany's *Ascension*, four inches thick in places and weighing over four tons, and below, *The Five Scourges*, all installed in 1919. On the south wall of the church, Tiffany's *Christ Blessing the Little Children*, from the First Presbyterian, 1893, installed here in 1913; Tiffany's *Angel at the Open Tomb*; Tiffany's *Peace Window*, 1890; Tiffany's *Mount of the Holy Cross*, between 1891 and 1895; McCully & Miles's *Beside the Still Waters*, 1910; and Tiffany's *St. Paul Preaching to the Athenians*, from First Presbyterian, 1895, installed here, 1913.

Most of the mansions of Prairie Avenue are long gone. Second Presbyterian, however, remains. Its current membership is about 40 percent white, 40 percent black, and the rest are Spanish-speaking, Chinese, and Japanese. Rev. Joe Francis, pastor since 1966, and his congregation are holding on in faith and hope and still worshiping every Sunday in this magnificent church on Michigan Avenue.

Trinity Episcopal Church
1873-74
125 East 26th Street

Architects: Lloyd & Pearce
    Interior, 1920,
      Tallmadge & Watson
Style: English Gothic
Seating: 300

Trinity, the second oldest
Episcopal parish in Chicago,
worships in an authentic
fourteenth century English
Gothic chapel.

Trinity Church was founded
from St. James' by a small
group of Episcopalians in
1842. They built a frame
church on Madison Street
between Clark and La Salle
in 1844. In 1861 the
congregation built a large
stone church on Jackson
between Wabash and
Michigan. This building was
destroyed by the Chicago Fire
in 1871. The parishioners
then moved south to 26th and
Michigan and there built a
large limestone church with
cut stone trim. The church
faced Michigan Avenue and
had a chapel adjoining it to

the east. In 1894 the Blair
family erected a parish house
immediately east of the chapel
for Sunday school and
guild meetings.

On January 7, 1920 the large
stone church was totally
destroyed by fire, but the
chapel survived and its
interior was subsequently
remodeled according to the
plans of Tallmadge & Watson
in authentic fourteenth
century Gothic style.

The altar railing was
preserved from the old
church, whereas the altar and

reredos were new. The great
bronze angel lectern was
removed from the rubble and
beautifully restored for the
new church. This lectern had
been exhibited at the World's
Columbian Exposition in 1893
by the Gotham Ecclesiastical
Goods Co. of New York,
received a first prize, and was
subsequently purchased and
donated to Trinity by one of
its parishioners.

Trinity Church is longitudinal in plan. Three steps lead up from the pews to the choir area in front, and then to the sanctuary. There is a high, open-truss wooden ceiling with a fine rood cross and clerestory windows. The stained glass windows in the chancel and on the north facade of the church were designed by the original architects and executed by Wells Bros. of Chicago.

This church, under the direction of Rev. Henri Stines, has a communion service at eight o'clock on Sunday mornings and the parish Eucharist at eleven. Social hours follow the services and a warm welcome is extended to visitors.

Holy Name Cathedral
1874-75
735 North State Street

Architect: Patrick C. Keely
　Renovation, 1968-69
　C. F. Murphy Associates
Style: Victorian Gothic
Seating: 1,520

The Catholic cathedral of Chicago, a Victorian Gothic church which has undergone a tasteful modern renovation.

A cathedral is so named because it contains a *cathedra*, the official chair of a bishop. Holy Name Cathedral is the Catholic bishop's church, the principal church of the Archdiocese of Chicago.

Holy Name is a venerable old building which has undergone a modern renovation incorporating some of the best elements of the old and the new. The marble columns date from an 1890-93 renovation when the steeple was replaced, the foundations rebuilt, and a limestone clerestory and turrets were added on the outside. Major James R. Willett and Alfred F. Pashley directed this renovation

which included an elegant water-pegged black walnut ceiling, probably unique in the Chicago area.

In 1914, architect Henry J. Schlacks conceived an unusual plan to enlarge the sanctuary of Holy Name Cathedral. The apse was sliced off the church and moved 15 feet to the east onto new foundations. New walls, roof, and floor then closed the gap. The cathedral is now 233 feet long, 126 feet wide at the transepts, 70 feet high inside, and the spire rises 210 feet above the street.

Holy Name Cathedral was designed by the prolific Brooklyn architect, Patrick C. Keely, who is reputed to have designed six hundred

churches and sixteen cathedrals, mostly in the eastern United States. In Chicago, he also designed St. James Church on South Wabash Avenue and St. Stanislaus Kostka on North Noble Street.

The present cathedral replaced a large Gothic-style brick church which stood on the southeast corner of State and Superior and was burned down in the Great Fire of 1871. The dedication of the present church in 1875 brought out the largest civil and ecclesiastical procession the city had ever seen: 5,500 men and women, 18 bands, 5 bishops, 57 priests, a 25-voice

The stained glass windows, abstract in design and progressively brighter toward the front of the church, were created in Milan. The cathedral doors were designed by Albert Friscia. They are bronze, each weighs over 1,200 pounds, yet they open at a touch with the help of a unique hydraulic power system.

Holy Name is a vital parish serving comparatively few families, but many young adults, business people, and senior citizens. The parish encompasses the wealthiest neighborhood in the city as well as one of the poorest. A large proportion of the daily worshipers are business people and commuters who attend their home parishes on weekends. Every Sunday there are six masses in the morning and one in the evening. The cathedral operates a grade school and a high school. The Sisters of Charity, B.V.M., are responsible for both.

Visitors to the cathedral looking toward the ceiling high above the sanctuary will see three wide-brimmed red hats, called *galeros*. They belonged to the three previous cardinal-archbishops of Chicago, Mundelein, Stritch, and Meyer. Upon the death of each cardinal, his official hat is suspended from the ceiling of his cathedral church, a custom which has prevailed since the thirteenth century.

priest choir, and a 20-piece orchestra. The parade lasted an hour and a half.

Since that time, Holy Name has not been without momentous celebrations. In 1926 when the International Eucharistic Congress convened in Chicago, more than one million people in a five-day period came to Holy Name to honor the Blessed Sacrament. And when Pope John Paul II came to Chicago in 1979, he visited the cathedral twice, was greeted with performances by Luciano Pavarotti one night and the Chicago Symphony Orchestra the next, by huge crowds of people both inside and

outside the church, and an enormous television audience all over the United States.

A major reconstruction of the Lemont limestone cathedral was carried out by C. F. Murphy Associates in 1968-69. The foundations had to be rebuilt again; the building was completely gutted and renovated according to the liturgical norms of the Second Vatican Council. The internal furnishings of the church were supplied by the International Institute of Liturgical Art, Rome. A new free-standing granite altar designed by Eugenio de Courten became the focal point of the church. It stands near the intersection of nave

and transepts beneath a great wooden crucifix which is suspended from the ceiling. The tabernacle for the Blessed Sacrament no longer rests on the main altar but is kept in a shrine on the left side of the sanctuary. The new bishop's chair, the *cathedra*, was simplified, made without a canopy, and located on the back wall of the sanctuary.

The five bronze panels on the rear wall of the sanctuary celebrate the Holy Name of Jesus and were designed by the acclaimed sculptor Attilio Selva. The new stations of the cross cast in bronze and bordered in red marble are the work of Goffredo Verginelli.

Olivet Baptist Church
1875-76
3101 S. Martin Luther King Drive   (400 East)

Architects: Willcox & Miller
Style: Victorian Gothic
Seating: about 1,400

Built by the First Baptist Church of Chicago, this church is an elegant example of Victorian Gothic architecture.

The inscription on the front of the church on the southeast corner of 31st Street and King Drive reveals that this building was erected by the First Baptist Church of Chicago. It provides an excellent example of nineteenth century Protestant church construction.

The First Baptist Church was organized in October of 1833 and used the Chicago Temple near the corner of South Water and Franklin streets for its worship services. A. T. Andreas recounts that this building, a log cabin, had been the first house built for religious worship in Chicago and was used by the Methodists, Presbyterians, and Baptists alike.

Just previous to the 31st Street location, the First Baptist Church had been on Wabash Avenue downtown. That church escaped the Great Fire of 1871 only to be destroyed in the fire of July, 1874.

The present building is constructed of Illinois limestone with cut stone trim. The auditorium measures 98 by 70 feet, and the seats are all arranged so as to face the pulpit on the east side of the room. There is a gallery extending around the other three sides of the auditorium. The church is beautifully maintained and is in excellent physical condition.

Just behind the pulpit platform is a large tank used for immersion baptisms. Also behind the pulpit, but above the baptistry, is a large three-manual Möller pipe organ installed in 1924.

The interior of the auditorium is very handsome, especially the pulpit area, with its dark polished woodwork and red upholstery. The pulpit furniture is hand carved as are the capitals of the columns, the ends of the pews, and the corbels for the ribs which support the balcony.

Some time ago the ceiling of Olivet Baptist Church, originally 50 feet high, was lowered. It is now acoustical tile. The new steeple was added in 1978.

The Gothic-arched stained glass windows beind the balcony on three sides of the auditorium are made of amber-colored opalescent glass with simple ornament around the edges. The windows illumine the church with a warm bright glow, especially at sunset.

Olivet Baptist Church traces its origins to 1853 when the Zoar Baptist Church began in Chicago. Zoar merged with Mt. Zion Baptist Church on December 22, 1861 and the two became the Olivet Baptist Church. Olivet acquired this building in 1917.

Olivet today is a thriving congregation with a large membership and a large Sunday school under the direction of Dr. Joseph H. Jackson, D.D.

St. James Church
1875-80
2940 South Wabash Avenue
(50 East)

Architect: Patrick C. Keely
   Restoration, 1974-76,
   Paul Straka
Style: Victorian Gothic
Seating: 500, originally 1,200

Victorian Gothic with a modern interior, the mother church of South Side Catholic parishes.

St. James is a phoenix. The bright, reverent, attractive space found in the church today rose from ashes through the determination, loving persistence, and hard work of the people of St. James. The priests, nuns, parishioners, and architect all worked together.

The fire began under the sacristy in the middle of the night, December 22, 1972. It burned mostly under the floor, but into the church too, from 3 A.M. until 11 the next morning. Fire fighters broke out stained glass windows and filled the church with foam to smother the fire. They saved the church, but left a cold, wet, charred ruin with wind blowing through where the windows used to be.

But even that first morning a woman handed Rev. Patrick O'Malley a check for one hundred dollars to help rebuild the church. "We need the church," the people said. A committee was formed, an architect was chosen, and months of planning and work began. Friends and neighbors removed debris. Parishioners stripped one hundred years of varnish and wax off the old black pews to reveal the beautiful white oak and walnut seen today. The old marble altars had crumbled in the heat of the fire.

Focus and simplicity controlled the new design. Some elements of the old, like the pews, were retained for continuity with the past. But everything was incorporated into the new plan with a view to serving the liturgy. Paul Straka, the restoring architect, believes that a church is for liturgy. It is the worship that is most important. The architecture creates the environment for worship, and so everything must focus upon the center of the liturgical action, the altar table. The priest, the people, and the prayer are the main thing; nothing else must get

in the way. The pews are arranged so that everyone is nearby, gathered around the altar, facing it, aware of other worshipers around them, but not looking directly into anyone else's face.

With fewer pews close to the altar, a spacious meeting and greeting place was provided in the back part of the church. Coffee and rolls are served here after Sunday masses. This space is especially welcome to people who live in small apartments.

In the center of this space near the entrance of the church is the beautiful font, a symbol of entry. It is used both for baptism and for holy water. Baptisms are performed at Sunday liturgies in which everyone welcomes the new member who is entering the community of believers for the first ime.

The organ of St. James, built in 1891, is a Roosevelt tracker-pneumatic organ, one of the few such instruments in the United States. It was awarded first prize at the Columbian Exposition of 1893. The organ plays now, but is in need of repair.

The great tower of St. James, 160 feet high, houses a 20-bell carillon installed in 1895 and considered one of the finest in the country. The bells range from the big St. James bell which weighs five tons to the smallest one weighing one hundred pounds. The bells have been out of order in recent times, but are being repaired now.

Old St. James, the parish's official title, was the eleventh Catholic parish in Chicago, founded in 1855. Because of its mission churches of St. Thomas the Apostle in Hyde Park, St. Anne at 55th and Wentworth Avenue, and St. Patrick in South Chicago, St. James was known as the mother church of the South Side Catholic parishes.

St. Stanislaus Kostka Church
1877-81
1327 North Noble Street
(1400 West)

Architect: Patrick C. Keely
Style: Renaissance
Seating: 1,500

The mother church of all Polish Catholic parishes in Chicago, once the largest Catholic parish in the United States.

Just north of Division Street, the Kennedy Expressway swings around a huge basilica-like church with twin towers, and only one cupola. This is St. Stanislaus Kostka Church. The south cupola was struck by lightning and destroyed in 1964.

St. Stanislaus Kostka, founded in 1867, is the first and mother church of all the Polish Catholic parishes in Chicago. The present church, the second on this site, was begun in 1876. It is modeled after a church in Krakow, is 200 feet long, 80 feet wide, and its tower rises 200 feet above street level. The building is of brick

construction. A stucco veneer was added in 1923 and a new entrance was built which enclosed the front stairs in that same year.

Inside, St. Stanislaus is spacious and majestic like an old world cathedral. Interior decorating was last done by the Daprato Studios in 1942. Oak pews fill the church. The main aisle leads up to an elaborate baroque altar surrounded by beautifully carved oak choir stalls. Immediately above the altar is a painting of Our Lady placing the infant Jesus in the arms of the young Stanislaus Kostka telling him that he must join the Society of Jesus. The sixteen-year-old Polish nobleman subsequently

walked 450 miles from Vienna to Augsburg and then another 800 miles to Rome to join the order. He died a Jesuit novice in Rome on the feast of Mary's Assumption, August 15, 1568.

The huge painting on the sanctuary dome by the Polish painter Thaddeus Zukotynski shows the risen Christ in the company of the saints in heaven. The Latin inscription reads: "I am the Resurrection and the Life. Alleluia. And on the third day He arose as He said. Alleluia."

In 1871 Bishop Foley placed the Resurrection fathers in charge of St. Stanislaus Kostka parish and all the Polish missions in the diocese

of Chicago. Between that year and 1900, they founded twelve parishes in the city, and today they staff seven parishes on the Northwest Side. Rev. Vincent Barzynski, C.R., built St. Stanislaus Church and was pastor from 1874 until his death in 1899. It was during his pastorate that St. Stanislaus became the largest Catholic parish in the United States, numbering over 8,000 families, 40,000 people in 1897. On any given Sunday there were six masses in the lower church and six in the upper church.

The chandeliers on each side of the nave are said to be from the studios of Louis C. Tiffany of New York. The stained glass windows by F. X. Zettler of the Royal Bavarian Art Institute, Munich, portray the mysteries of the Rosary and were installed in 1903.

The building of the Kennedy Expressway in the late 1950s forced many parishioners to move out of the area. Today there are 850 families in the parish: some Polish people who remain, others of various ethnic backgrounds, and a large Mexican-American community.

The Greenstone Church
Pullman United Methodist Church 1882
11201 S. St. Lawrence Avenue (600 East)

Architect: Solon S. Beman
Style: Romanesque
Seating: 600

The church designed by Solon S. Beman in the historic town of Pullman.

George M. Pullman, founder and president of the Pullman Palace Car Company, built the town of Pullman in 1880-81. It was an economic and social experiment, the largest and most complete nineteenth century planned industrial community. The railroad car magnate engaged Solon Beman as architect and Nathan Barrett as landscape designer to plan the town. They developed what was to be one of the greatest achievements of both their careers. Pullman today has both city and national landmark designation.

George Pullman felt that no American community would be complete without a church. So the Greenstone Church was built and dedicated in 1882. Pullman intended the building to house a community church where all the residents would worship together. But when meetings were held, each denominational group wanted its own minister and each went its own way. No group alone was large enough to afford Pullman's rent for the building. The Presbyterians rented the church for occasional services, but for the most part it remained empty until it was sold to the Methodists in 1907.

The Greenstone Memorial Church was built with large blocks of serpentine limestone quarried in West Chester, Pennsylvania. The main body of the church has a high gabled roof. The windows,

doorways, and openings in the tower all have round arches. The bell tower with its lofty, pointed steeple gives the church a distinctive appearance and complements the lovely park across the street. A parsonage, Sunday school classrooms, and other community space adjoin the church proper to the south.

The stained glass windows in the Greenstone Church are patterned in geometrical rather than pictorial designs. The large rose window on the west facade was recently restored. The original Steere & Turner tracker-action pipe

organ located behind the altar on the east wall of the church was restored in 1966. The woodwork in the sanctuary, the pews, and the open-timbered ceiling give the church a warmth and attractiveness that is admired by parishioners and visitors alike.

The Greenstone Church, like the whole Pullman district, is undergoing gradual restoration and redevelopment.

All Saints Episcopal Church
1882-84
4552 N. Hermitage Avenue
(1734 West)

Architect: John C. Cochrane
Style: Shingle
Seating: 250

A village church in the city, perhaps the oldest frame church in Chicago.

The All Saints parish history begins, "Ravenswood was a little village with wooden sidewalks and open ditches, several miles beyond the limits of Chicago, when on January 15, 1882, the first services of the Episcopal Church were held in the Ravenswood Methodist Church, borrowed for the occasion. Bishop McLaren was the officiant and the choir came from the Church of the Epiphany. On March 2, 1884, the church building was completed and used for the first time."

The church itself is a frame building, perhaps the oldest frame church still in use in Chicago. It is 97 by 41 feet, with stucco part way up the outside walls, then wooden shingles, and a steep gabled roof. The church was recently painted, bright yellow with brown trim. At the northeast corner of the building stands a quaint, very distinctive bell tower. For years after its installation in 1885, the bell was used both to call the faithful to worship and to call the volunteer fire department to fight fires.

Another story about the bell tower recounts how the rector barricaded himself in the tower to protest the movement for women's suffrage. (Food was sent up to him in baskets by the *women* of the parish.)

Inside, All Saints is longitudinal in plan, has a high open-truss ceiling, and is furnished with oak pews. Carl Sandburg, who lived one-half block north on Hermitage, sat in the third pew from the front on the north side of the aisle. The stained glass windows are original, with simple geometrical designs and bright colors.

The chancel of the church has two altars. A simple free-standing altar now occupies the area close to the congregation. The organ console is to the right of this altar; the pipes of the two-manual Hall organ are to the left. One step up and behind this area is the permanent altar located against the west wall of the church.

There have been some structural problems over the years. Tie rods hold the side walls of the church from further expansion under the weight of the roof. Some of the ceiling fell in 1967. Apart from this, the church is in remarkably good condition as it approaches one hundred years of service.

All Saints has four services on Sunday mornings, two masses in English, one in Malayalam, and one in Spanish. The parish is deeply involved with the neighborhood. It sponsors a day care center, an alternative, fully-accredited high school, a Native American educational center, and a program to teach English to the Spanish speaking.

All Saints is a village church which has been surrounded by a city. It has adapted itself to its changing neighborhood, and it looks forward to its future with faith and hope.

Church of the Ascension
1882-87
1133 North LaSalle Drive
(150 West)

Architects: Albert Wilcox
and John Tilton
Style: French Gothic
Seating: 250

This histroic church led the
Anglo-Catholic Movement in the
United States from 1869 on.

The French Gothic, Lemont limestone church at the southeast corner of Elm and LaSalle has a history as interesting as its architecture. Founded in 1857 from St. James Episcopal Church, Ascension was in the forefront of the Anglo-Catholic Movement in the United States from 1869 on. This was the American counterpart of the Oxford Movement which began in England in 1833. The early clergy and parishioners of Ascension were engaged in a long feud with the diocese of Illinois and were under attack by the newspapers of Chicago for introducing elements of the Catholic tradition such as solemn mass, ornate vest-

ments, candles, and the *sanctus* bell. But the parish flourished. Before he left for New York in 1884, Rev. Arthur Ritchie at Ascension officiated at the first benediction of the Blessed Sacrament in the entire Anglican Communion since the sixteenth century. Succeeding rectors of Ascension continued these practices and even added others. But they were also able to establish more amicable relations with the bishop and the diocese.

The present church building was begun in 1881 with a design by Albert Wilcox. The walls went up 18 feet, construction was delayed, and services were held in a chapel

at the east end of the building. The church was finally completed in 1887 as designed by John Tilton.

For the most part, the exterior of Ascension Church has retained its original appearance. The crucifix on the west facade was formerly the rood cross inside and dates from 1887. It was moved outside when the central entrance was closed and a porch removed for the widening of LaSalle Street in 1930.

In the narthex is a baptismal font dating from the 1860s. The font survived the Fire of 1871 which destroyed the previous frame church and all the homes of the parishioners.

46

Entering the nave, one finds that the reddish tile floor, the dark oak pews and wainscoting, the red brick on the walls, and the dark wooden ceiling give the church a subdued atmosphere which focuses one's attention on the beauty of the high altar and the stained glass windows.

The high altar with its tall Gothic spire is made of American statuary marble and was designed by John Stout in 1894. The adoring angels on either side of the altar are alabaster and were carved in London. The six beautiful mosaic panels on the front of the altar were made in Venice and are replicas of mosaics on the high altar of St. Mary's Church in Cologne, Germany.

The delicate iron rood screen and its figures were also designed by John Stout in 1894. The dark Georgia pine ceiling of Ascension rises steeply to a height of 70 feet on open hammer-beam trusses. The beautiful polychrome work on the principal rafters was done in the 1960s.

The stained glass windows on the Elm Street side of the nave present the mysteries of the rosary. The window closest to the entrance was created by Reynolds, Francis and Rohnstock of Boston in 1925. The remaining four windows were done by the Willett Studio in 1966 and 1967.

In the choir loft above the narthex is a fine 64-rank Schlicker pipe organ installed in 1964. Ascension and its choir have a reputation for exceptionally fine sacred music.

The Church of the Ascension has a full schedule of religious services including solemn mass, evensong, and benediction on Sundays, daily mass, and recitation of the divine office every morning and evening.

LaSalle Street Church
1882-86
1136 North LaSalle Drive
(150 West)

Architect: Christian O. Hansen
Style: Gothic
Seating: 350

A noteworthy Gothic structure with trinitarian decorative motifs.

The brick church with the Illinois limestone facade at the southwest corner of LaSalle and Elm streets currently houses an independent, non-denominational evangelical congregation. But the building was erected between 1882 and 1886 by the English-speaking Evangelical Lutheran Church of the Holy Trinity (now at Magnolia and Addison). Holy Trinity, founded in 1855, was the first English-speaking Lutheran church in Chicago. Between 1914 and 1935 the building was owned by the Christ Church of Deliverance. In 1936 it was purchased by the Moody Church and operated as the Moody Italian Mission. The church was renamed the Elm-LaSalle Bible Church in the early 1960s. By the early 1970s, the congregation changed its name to the LaSalle Street Church, became independent of the Moody Church, and purchased the building from Moody in December of 1973.

Over the years the congregation has consisted of neighborhood people and there has always been a very active Sunday school and neighborhood outreach.

The basic style of this church is Gothic. Gothic arches abound, from the 50-foot vault of the nave, the rib vaulting above the windows, the window shapes themselves, the molding above the altar, the designs in the wooden sacristy screens, as well as the end pieces of the pews.

In keeping with the name of the original congregation, the decorative motif of this church is trinitarian. Trinitarian symbols may be found throughout the church, trefoils, triangles, fleur-de-lis, three-leafed plants, even the

shape of the "rose" window above the altar.

All the furniture in LaSalle Street Church is made of golden oak; and except for the altar, reredos, and chancel furnishings, it is original to the building. The latter were removed in 1914 when the Lutherans sold the church. But in 1969 when First St. Paul's at LaSalle and Goethe rebuilt their church, LaSalle Street Church received their "old" altar, reredos, pulpit, and lectern—all in the same golden oak!

The stained glass windows in this church, which date from the 1880s, are particularly rich and colorful. The basic designs are wonderfully

worked patterns of flowers, leaves, and trinity symbols. The Good Shepherd window on the east facade depicts Christ in the central panel surrounded by a delightful collage of floral and geometrical designs. There are five double-paneled windows on each side of the nave, and a "rose" window in the shape of a triangle above the altar.

The bell tower of LaSalle Street Church rises 100 feet above the street. A small ornamental turret opposite the tower was destroyed by fire in the 1930s. The present congregation hopes to restore it.

**Assumption B.V.M. Church
1884-86
319 West Illinois Street
(500 North)**

Architect: Giuseppe Beretta
Style: Renaissance
Seating: 500

The first Italian Catholic church in Chicago.

The church on Illinois Street just behind the Merchandise Mart was the first church built by and for the Italian Catholics in Chicago. It was a national parish from its founding in 1881 until 1911; then it was assigned territorial limits.

Assumption Church is rectangular in plan, of buff-colored brick construction, with a 130-foot bell tower and steeple at the northwest corner of the building. The horizontal stripes of reddish brown brick on the tower are reminiscent of northern Italian church design.

Three stairways lead right up from the sidewalk. There is a shallow vestibule, and then the body of the church. The auditorium is bright and spacious and richly decorated in Italian Renaissance style.

On the south wall above the altar is a large stained glass window picturing the Assumption of Mary into heaven after the style of Titian. In the lower part of the same window is the *Dormitio Virginis*, the sleep of the Virgin, after a painting by Michelangelo. This beautiful window was installed in 1906 and came from the Munich school in Germany.

The windows in the nave of the church were done by Drehobl Brothers of Chicago in 1966. The subjects were selected by Rev. Thomas M. Ferrazzi, pastor of Assumption since 1938. Each window presents a scene from a painting by one of the old masters: Lippi, Battoni, Mantegna, Voguel, Reni, Campana, with one exception. One window shows Pope John XXIII calling the Second Vatican Council and includes pictures of cardinals Stritch, Meyer, Cody and bishops Sheil and O'Donnell.

The art work in Assumption Church is especially noteworthy. The three large paintings on the ceiling and the medallions of the twelve apostles were done by Joseph Grill in 1939. He was president of the Art Institute of Chicago. Five oval paintings in the sanctuary, all reproductions of masterpieces, were done by Louis Caracciolo in 1952. The large paintings above the two side altars of St. Peregrine and St. Anthony Pucci were executed by Joseph Tomanek. The 12-foot mosaic located above and behind the main altar is a replica of Da Vinci's *Last Supper* and was imported from Milan.

St. Francis Xavier Cabrini founded the Assumption grammar school in 1899. It was closed in 1945 as the neighborhood changed from residential to commercial. Although there are no families living within the boundaries of the parish today, the church has a full schedule of services which are attended by Catholics who work in the area. The parish has been served from its beginning by the Servite fathers and brothers.

Church of the Epiphany
1885
201 South Ashland Avenue
(1600 West)

Architects: Burling and
Whitehouse
Style: Romanesque
Seating: 750-800

**A fine example of Richardsonian
Romanesque with elegant
woodwork and beautiful mosaics.**

The Church of the Epiphany
was founded in 1868. By the
mid-1880s the congregation
had outgrown its frame
church and planned "to build
a warm, cheerful, devotional
parish church, large
enough to shelter a good
congregation, at once a place
of reverent worship and a
home for God's children."
(*Parish History and Yearbook,
1897*) The building committee
engaged Francis Whitehouse
to draw up the plans. He was
the architect son of the Rt.
Rev. Henry John Whitehouse,
second bishop of the
Episcopal diocese of Illinois.

Whitehouse designed a
Romanesque church with
high-pitched gables
reminiscent of Henry Hobson
Richardson's Trinity Church
in Boston. Epiphany Church
is constructed of rusticated
Lake Superior sandstone. The
Norman bell tower with its
fine cut stone decoration
houses three large bells. From
the three-gabled lower facade
on the Ashland side of the
church, one enters the
vestibule or narthex. A sign
on the front door welcomes
the visitor to come in to rest
and to pray.

Epiphany is a warm, friendly
church. Red carpeting leads
up the center aisle between
beautifully polished cherry
wood pews. There are no
interior pillars. The ceiling is
supported from four piers by a
marvelous system of open
wood trusses which converge
like a rosette above the center
of the church.

The sanctuary of Epiphany is
60 feet wide and almost as
deep. To facilitate their
responses to the celebrant,
the choir sits in this area
on beautiful cherry
wood benches. The 1892,
three-manual Ferrand and
Votey organ with Austin
console is also located in
the choir area.

50

Directly above the main entrance to the church are the new Schumacher Memorial fanfare trumpets turned in Germany by Giesecke and Sons. The trumpets are played from the organ console.

The first rector of this church designed the altar as a sarcophagus for himself. He was transferred to Iowa before he died, but the altar remains as a monument to him. Above the altar is a mosaic mural of the Resurrection done by M. C. Darst of New York and installed in 1912. Above that is a high relief stone carving of the Epiphany flanked by trumpeting angels. The Resurrection scene is also flanked by angels; these are done in Venetian glass mosaic and date from 1885. Beyond these angels are two more Venetian glass mosaics designed by Charles Halloway, the Mother and Child on the left, and Jesus Bearing his Cross on the right, 1896 and 1897 respectively.

The large Tiffany-style stained glass windows around the nave were all stolen on a winter night in the early 1970s. A few of the smaller windows up above were damaged and replaced, but most of them are original.

Epiphany began as an affluent Episcopal parish when an Ashland Boulevard address was as fashionable as any in Chicago. Today, under the direction of Rev. R. L. Whitehouse, a distant relative of the architect, Epiphany serves a struggling population on the Near West Side. The parish conducts St. Gregory's Private Day School for Boys. Neighborhood boys attend classes here, sing in the choir, serve mass, and go on to higher education. Next door the Episcopal Diocese sponsors a food kitchen, a day care center, and a half-way house for alcoholics.

Epiphany Church with its various social, spiritual, and educational programs is thoroughly involved in improving life on the Near West Side.

St. Gabriel Church
1887-88
4501 South Lowe Avenue
(632 West)

Architects: Burnham and Root
Style: Romanesque
Seating: 850

"[O]ne of the most characteristic designs which Root ever put forth, as personal as the clasp of his hand."

The Chicago architectural firm of Burnham and Root had just designed the Rookery Building on LaSalle Street and would soon be working on the Monadnock Building on Jackson when they designed St. Gabriel's Church in the Town of Lake.

John Root's original watercolor sketch for the design of St. Gabriel's shows a Romanesque-style building with a central bell tower modeled after Henry Hobson Richardson's Trinity Church in Boston (1872-77). This plan was rejected by the parish because of its cost and apparently by Root also because of its lack of originality.

The design of the church as it was actually built was based upon that of a church in Toulouse, France, but it retained certain elements from the sketch and from the Richardson church in Boston; namely, the Latin cross floor plan, the simple massiveness of design, and the strong round arches of the Romanesque style.

From a biography of John Root by the poet Harriet Monroe comes this description of the church at the corner of 45th Street and Lowe Avenue:

St. Gabriel's Church is treated on large simple lines, and is one of the most characteristic designs which Root ever put forth, as personal as the clasp of his hand. The material is a warm brown brick, shading from red almost to black. The broad gable over the archway of the entrance springs, at the right, from a campanile very noble in its proportions. This tower is square, with round turrets at the angles, ending in conical roofs, the one at the corner of the building being a turret larger than the others. The corbelled belfry, with its pyramidal roof, imparts to the tower a lofty grace. The facade of the transept repeats the lines of the main facade, apart from the tower, with a triple window in place of the entrance. (John Wellborn Root, Prairie School Press, 1966)

The present vestibule and portico were added to the church while Rev. Thomas Burke was pastor, sometime between 1915 and 1928. The original three-door main facade was similar in design to the transept facades—a large central arch flanked by two smaller ones.

The threefold arch theme is carried out inside the church where the main altar is located within a huge round arch and the side altars are set in smaller ones. The nave and transept ceilings are barrel-vaulted. One colonnade of Romanesque arches creates an ambulatory behind the permanent altar and additional colonnades form the side aisles of the nave.

Root chose the Romanesque style because he felt it was appropriate to "a simple home of the people." He felt St. Gabriel's was one of his finest designs and he was especially pleased with the power and impact of the tall masonry bell tower which he described as "the breaking of the day."

The richly colored stained glass windows in St. Gabriel's are the work of the Daprato Statuary Co. of Chicago and were installed around 1920. The high altar was originally lighted by frosted glass windows in the apse wall where the paintings are today.

Root designed the body of the church with low, wide proportions, but made the tower tall and forceful. The effect of breadth and solidity was accentuated by the inward slope or batter of the exterior brick walls near the foundation.

The tower was originally 160 feet tall, but due to structural deterioration it was rebuilt in 1945. It was shortened about 14 feet at that time, the corbel table was removed, and the high pyramid roof was abbreviated to a cone with a Celtic cross on top.

The legendary Father Maurice Dorney, founding pastor of St. Gabriel's, built the church, befriended the meat packers Gustavus Swift, Philip Armour, and John Sherman, engaged their financial support for the church, got jobs for his Irish immigrants in the Union Stock Yards, mediated labor disputes, and campaigned from the pulpit against saloons on residential streets in the neighborhood.

Dorney became such an institution in Chicago that when he died in 1914 thousands attended his wake, the newspapers eulogized him, and flags were flown at half staff over the Stock Yards. Additional thousands joined the cortege to Mt. Olivet Cemetery. The procession consisted of ninety-seven limousines, extra street cars, and a special train on the Grand Trunk Railroad.

The Sisters of Mercy have directed St. Gabriel's grammar school since its beginning in 1881 and a high school from 1894 until 1968.

The people of St. Gabriel's have always been working people and home owners. They were immigrant Irish originally; there is a greater ethnic mix today.

The church was cleaned and painted for the centennial of the parish in 1980.

Lake View Presbyterian Church 1887-88
3600 North Broadway
(700 West)

Architects: Burnham and Root
Style: Shingle
Seating: 400

A classic example of Shingle style architecture, designed by John Wellborn Root.

The Lake View Presbyterian Church was founded in 1884. Early services were held in the Lake View town hall. The little church we see today at the corner of Broadway and Addison was erected before the town of Lake View was annexed to the city of Chicago in 1889. There were only scattered houses and woods in the area then. But the people wanted a church, and they engaged the firm of Burnham and Root to design it.

When the church was first being planned, its construction budget was limited. So John Root, the design partner of Burnham and Root, was forced to abandon the intricate forms associated with most church buildings for a simpler, less detailed design. As constructed, the church was a handsome rustic structure surfaced with wood shingles above a rusticated limestone foundation. It was one of the classic examples of a style of architecture now called the Shingle style. The most prominent feature of the church was and still is the octagonal tower with its high conical steeple.

But the structure seen today has been altered from its original form. During the late 1890s, the congregation grew so rapidly that it became necessary to enlarge the church. An extension was built onto the north end of the building, thus changing the original east-west axis of the chapel to north-south. The current appearance of the church dates from the 1940s when siding was placed over the shingle surface. At this time also the belfry louvers were covered to prevent pigeons from roosting in the tower.

John Root carried the design of the high-pitched roof and the sharply pointed steeple to the inside. The balusters on the balcony railing and on the stairway railings have similarly pointed peaks. Another notable interior feature is the design of the stained glass windows in the sanctuary. This is ornamental glass with simple, yet very attractive floral and geometrical patterns.

In 1898, a fine Lyon & Healy pipe organ was installed to replace an old portable organ. The pipe organ was renovated around 1950 by N. Doerr Co. of Chicago.

The parish hall which adjoins the church on the west side was built in 1911. It houses the Lake View Academy, an accredited alternative Christian high school. The parish also sponsors a senior citizen nutrition site, social service counseling, a thrift shop, and a program to teach English to immigrants.

Since the late 1970s a Korean Presbyterian congregation has used the church for their services on Sunday afternoons.

Lake View Presbyterian Church has experienced many changes in its history, but it continues to creatively adapt its ministries to many different peoples in many different circumstances.

Notre Dame Church
1887-92
1336 West Flournoy Street
(700 South)

Architect: Gregory Vigeant
National Register of
Historic Places, 1979
Style: Romanesque Revival
Seating: 1,200

The historic French church, damaged by fire, but now being restored.

The words *Notre Dame de Chicago* above the door of this old brick church on the West Side recall the illustrious French history of Chicago. Jacques Marquette, the Jesuit priest-explorer, wintered near here in 1674-75 and wrote the first account of life in this area. Father Pierre Pinet, another Jesuit, lived and worked among the Miami Indians on the north branch of the river in the 1690s. Jean Baptiste Pointe du Sable was the first permanent resident of Chicago in 1778. Antoine Ouilmette and Colonel Jean Baptiste Beaubien were among the first citizens when the town was incorporated in 1833. And Father Jean Marie Irenée St. Cyr built the original St. Mary's, Chicago's first Catholic church, near the southwest corner of Lake and State streets, in 1833. The first Catholics of Chicago were nearly all French and Indians.

Although Notre Dame parish was founded in 1864, it was actually a continuation of an earlier French church known as St. Louis which was organized in 1850.

Notre Dame Church is a Romanesque Revival building, 130 by 103 feet, surmounted by a 90-foot dome and cupola. The main body of the church is almost circular in plan with a high vaulted ceiling. There are extensions to the north and south for the sanctuary and the narthex.

Thirty-three beautiful stained glass windows, all imported from Europe, decorate and illuminate the church. The two in the shallow transepts, depicting the Nativity and the Crucifixion of Jesus, measure 16 by 26 feet each.

In 1918 when most of the French-speaking residents had moved out of the neighborhood, Cardinal Mundelein gave Notre Dame parish to the Blessed Sacrament fathers from Canada who made the church into a city-wide center for devotion to the Holy Eucharist.

In October of 1925 in preparation for the Eucharistic Congress to be held in Chicago the following year, a new pipe organ was built by Casavant Freres of St. Hyacinthe, Quebec, was installed in the church. Several years later in 1929, the sanctuary was enlarged and redecorated and a new altar was put in.

During the 1930s Notre Dame flourished as a metropolitan center for perpetual adoration of the Blessed Sacrament. In the late 1950s and 1960s many homes in the neighborhood were razed to make way for the Congress (now Eisenhower) Expressway, the West Side Medical Center, and the Chicago Circle Campus of the University of Illinois. In the aftermath of urban renewal, Notre Dame has remained a viable parish. Its members today are mostly of Italian or Hispanic descent.

On the night of June 7, 1978, the gilded statue of Our Lady high atop the cupola was struck by lightning and caught fire. The blaze was difficult to extinguish and there was extensive water damage to the church. As of 1980, the interior had not yet been restored.

First Immanuel Lutheran Church 1888
1124 South Ashland Avenue (1600 West)

Architect: Frederick Ahlschlager
Style: Victorian Gothic
Seating: 400

The second oldest Lutheran congregation in Chicago; the interior is typical of nineteenth century Lutheran churches.

The Illinois limestone church with the bright red doors on Ashland Avenue just north of Roosevelt Road houses the second oldest Lutheran congregation in Chicago. (First St. Paul's on La Salle is the oldest.) First Immanuel was founded in 1854 on Twelfth Street just west of Blue Island Avenue on the site where St. Ignatius College Prep stands today. This church served German immigrants to the West Side. In 1864 the congregation moved to Taylor and Brown (Sangamon) streets and in 1888 erected the beautiful Gothic church on fashionable Ashland Avenue. In its first fifty years, Immanuel was responsible for the beginning of seven other German Lutheran congregations: Zion, Trinity, St. Matthew, Holy Cross, St. Mark, Emmaus, and Ebenezer. Immanuel reached its numerical peak in 1900 with 3,000 members. One English-language service was introduced in 1901, and all services were in English during and after World War I.

The main entrance of First Immanuel is flanked by sturdy columns and pinnacles. It is sheltered with a Gothic arch and has a stone gable above. A rose window that was originally above this entrance was destroyed in a storm sometime between 1948 and 1952. The opening was filled with construction blocks and a glass brick cross. Another change in the facade took place in 1919 when the steeple on the north tower had to be removed because of rotting timbers.

The narthex or vestibule, just inside the door, has a beautiful wooden staircase that leads up to the choir and balcony.

The auditorium of First Immanuel is bright and simple and typical of many Lutheran churches built around and before the turn of the century. The space is longitudinal in plan with a high vaulted ceiling. There is a balcony around three sides of the auditorium which is supported by pillars with Corinthian capitals. The pillars continue up through the balcony and support the Gothic vault of the ceiling. On the east end of the balcony is a fine Kimball organ installed in 1937.

The interior space of the church focuses on the altar and pulpit in front. Above the altar in the red-carpeted sanctuary is a life-size statue of Christ with arms uplifted in welcome and blessing. Behind the statue is a beautiful hand-carved wooden reredos with Gothic spires and tracery. The wooden pulpit with its quaint cupola-canopy complements the woodwork of the altar and reredos.

In over 125 years of its existence, First Immanuel has had many missions and served many people in an ethnically changing neighborhood. The Sunday school housed in the parish hall, 1952, is the principal mission agency. But there is a pre-school program now as well as an outreach to the West Side Medical Center.

Today, First Immanuel, under the care of Rev. Donald Becker, draws its members from throughout the Chicago metropolitan area.

Church of Our Saviour
1888-89
530 West Fullerton Parkway
(2400 North)

Architect: Clinton J. Warren
Style: Romanesque
Seating: 350

A lovely Victorian Romanesque church with beautiful wood carving and stained glass windows.

Not long before he designed the Congress Hotel on Michigan Avenue, the eminent Chicago architect, Clinton J. Warren, designed the Church of Our Saviour on Fullerton.

The Fullerton Avenue Presbyterian Church, a long, narrow frame building erected in 1864, had occupied this site before the construction of the Church of Our Saviour. There is reason to believe that part of the original Presbyterian church, the sacristy, altar, and organ areas, may have been incorporated into the present church.

The Church of Our Saviour is an Episcopal parish serving the Lincoln Park neighborhood on Chicago's North Side. The church and rectory are constructed of brick with a grey limestone facade on Fullerton Parkway. The parish hall is a wood frame structure attached to the rear or north end of the church.

Entrance to the church is by way of a round-arched portal at the base of the square, turreted bell tower. The interior walls of the nave are decorated with reddish brown terra cotta tiles. The wood-paneled ceiling rises four stories and is supported by open wood trusses. The ends of the pews are beautifully carved and there is handsome ornamental wood carving on each of the columns which support the balcony at the rear of the auditorium.

The interior of the Church of Our Saviour is softly yet adequately lighted by chandeliers and by stained glass windows. Most of these windows were made with light-colored glass and simple, geometrical patterns. But five windows in the nave, the ones with figures of Christ, Mary, and Moses, were created by Louis Tiffany of

New York. The window in the sanctuary behind the altar with its beveled glass and floral patterns is especially beautiful.

There are two organs in the church: a new electronic Allen organ in the balcony and a Hook and Hastings tracker-action pipe organ, now being restored, in the area just east of the altar. This organ came from a previous Church of Our Saviour and thus predates the present church.

The Church of Our Saviour has experienced the decline and the restoration of its neighborhood. The present congregation reflects the diversity of the area; it consists of about 350 members almost evenly divided between married and single, many professional people, a wide range of ages, and mostly white. Sunday services are held at eight and ten-thirty.

**Metropolitan Community
Church   1889
4100 S. Martin Luther King
Drive   (400 East)**

Architect: Solon S. Beman
Style: Romanesque
Seating: 2,000

A handsome Richardsonian
Romanesque church with elegant
interior design and woodwork.

This Romanesque church
was erected by the Forty-First
Street Presbyterian Church
in 1889. It was the home of
the First Presbyterian Church
from 1912 to 1926. In that
year it was purchased by the
Metropolitan Community
Church and they have
occupied it up to the
present time.

The rusticated red stone,
the broad gables, and the
massive tower make this
a fine example of the
Richardsonian Romanesque
style of architecture that
flourished in the 1880s. The
tower was named for Dr.
Martin Luther King in 1968.

Inside, a very handsome
paneled wood ceiling is hung
from the roof and also
supported by four piers which
stand at the four corners of the
sanctuary. On the west wall of
the church, filling almost the
whole area, is a 4,500-pipe
E. M. Skinner organ installed
in 1916. Ernest Skinner
himself came from Boston to
supervise the installation of
the instrument. The first
recital was given by M. Vierne
of Paris in 1917. The church
has had a renowned ministry
of music over the years.
The Senior Choir of the
Metropolitan Community
Church sang on radio station
WGN during the 1950s.

The choir benches are located
in front of the organ, the
pulpit in front of the choir.
The sanctuary is carpeted in
green and surrounded by
beautiful wooden pews on
three sides with a full balcony

above the pews. The
auditorium is bright and
warm, and the buff-colored
walls serve to highlight the
fine woodwork in the church.

The community house,
adjoining and immediately
behind the church, contains
the pastor's study, a chapel,
classrooms, a gym, and dining
facilities. All of the church
buildings are in excellent
physical condition.

The Metropolitan Community
Church, affiliated with the
Council of Community
Churches in Columbus, Ohio,
has been a vital and
prominent religious center
in the black community in
Chicago. Rev. Theodore
Richardson has been minister
and director of this church
since 1956.

United Church of Hyde Park
1889
1440 East 53rd Street

Architect: Gregory Vigeant
    Interior renovation,
    1923-24,
    Charles D. Faulkner
Style: Romanesque
Seating: 600

This church, built in 1889, houses the oldest Protestant congregation in Hyde Park, dating from 1860.

The rusticated limestone church at the northeast corner of 53rd Street and Blackstone Avenue houses the oldest Protestant congregation in Hyde Park. The Hyde Park Presbyterian Church was organized in 1860. They met in a small white frame chapel at 53rd and Hyde Park Boulevard until they built a stone church on the present site in 1869. The congregation grew so much during the 1880s that they needed larger quarters. Gregory Vigeant was engaged to draw up plans for the present church using material from the old building in the construction of the new one. This was done in 1889, the same year that Hyde Park was annexed to the city of Chicago.

A sturdy, square masonry tower with a pyramid roof stands at the southwest corner of the church flanked by broad gabled elevations facing Blackstone and 53rd streets respectively. The tower contains the main entrance to the church, the side elevations each contain a very large stained glass window. These windows and the upper openings in the tower are all framed in ornamental cut stone in the shape of ogee arches.

The sanctuary of Hyde Park Presbyterian was completely remodeled with a Romanesque styling by Charles D. Faulkner in 1923-24. The four-manual, 45-rank E. M. Skinner organ was installed at that time as well as the narthex and the balcony. Originally, the sanctuary went all the way to the west wall so that both large stained glass windows were fully visible. These windows with their multicolored scale-like pieces of glass are among the earliest examples of impressionist church art.

The sanctuary is crowned with a large twelve-sided glass dome, each side bearing the name of one of the apostles. In the Lecture Hall, just to the north of the sanctuary, is a large ornamental stained glass window inscribed with the word "Service" and dedicated to the memory of William H. Ray, a trustee of the church who died in 1889.

The beautiful Lily window, the only pictorial window in the sanctuary, was made by Joseph Evan MacKay and installed in memory of William Olmsted and Charles Arms in 1900.

The United Church of Hyde Park was organized in 1930 with the merger of the Hyde Park Congregational Church, founded in 1885, and the Hyde Park Presbyterian Church. The union was reconstituted in 1970 with the incorporation of the Hyde Park Methodist Church, which had been founded in 1889.

The United Church building is the oldest church structure in Hyde Park. It houses an active, multi-ethnic community of Christians who are deeply committed to ministry in the church and in the Hyde Park neighborhood.

**Antioch Missionary Baptist
Church   1889-90
6234 South Stewart Avenue
(400 West)**

Architects: Bell and Swift
Style: Romanesque
Seating: 1,300

**An impressive Romanesque
structure built with split granite
boulders.**

The fine Romanesque church on the southwest corner of Englewood and Stewart avenues was constructed by the Englewood Baptist Church and dedicated on September 14, 1890. The building is constructed of split granite boulders with Bedford stone trim. An imposing round tower with a graceful conical roof rises above the main entrance at the corner of the building. Broad gabled facades each with three large, round-headed windows face north and east. What was originally the parsonage occupies the south end of the building. It now contains church offices.

The auditorium is large and spacious, almost square in plan, with amphitheater seating focused on the pulpit and choir area at the southwest corner of the room. There is a balcony extending out from the east and north walls which is supported by columns.

The auditorium is illuminated by chandeliers and beautiful ornamental stained glass windows.

The Antioch Missionary Baptist Church, a large and active black congregation under the direction of Rev. W. N. Daniels, purchased this church complex in 1958. It is well maintained and in excellent physical condition today.

St. Mary of Perpetual Help Church   1889-92
1035 West 32nd Street

Architect: Henry Engelbert
Style: Byzantine-Romanesque
Seating: 1,100

The great dome of St. Mary's is complemented by a succession of domes, half domes, and arches inside.

Of the many steeples, spires, and domes in Bridgeport, St. Mary's dome is by far the largest and most impressive. This huge dome is entirely of wooden construction with ornamental copper covering. The apex of the dome is 113 feet above the floor of the church. The rest of the building is of brick construction with Romanesque windows and arches.

The central dome is not the only one. Inside St. Mary's there is a succession of domes and half domes, arches, columns, and pilasters, all lavishly decorated and leading up to the white marble altar in the chancel.

St. Mary's was most recently decorated by John A. Mallin in 1961. Under the traditional painting of Our Lady of Perpetual Help above the main altar stand pictures of the great saints of Poland; from left to right, St. Stanislaus Kostka, Bl. Kunegunda, St. John Cantius, St. Adalbert, St. Stanislaus, bishop and martyr, St. Casimir, St. Hedwig, and St. Andrew Bobola.

The organ in St. Mary's is a four-manual Austin organ installed in 1928 and still in use today. It contains a great organ, swell organ, choir organ, echo organ, solo organ, pedal organ, and floating string division playable on every manual. The pipes range up to 32 feet.

Originally a mission of St. Adalbert's, St. Mary's was established as a parish in 1886 for the Polish Catholics of Bridgeport. The parish grew with the immigrant population and established an elementary school and a high school, both under the direction of the Sisters of St. Joseph. St. Mary's is served by the Chicago diocesan clergy. Msgr. Edward J. Smaza has been pastor of the church since 1950. The parish plant occupies most of a city block. The parish continues strong and active with services in Polish and English.

St. Alphonsus Church
1889-97
2950 N. Southport Avenue
(1400 West)

Architects: Adam Boos and
Josef Bettinghofer of Chicago;
then Schrader and Conradi of
St. Louis
Style: Gothic
Seating: 1,300

This landmark of the Lake View community contains some of the finest rib-vaulting in the city.

The tower of St. Alphonsus
rises 260 feet above the
intersection of Lincoln,
Southport, and Wellington
avenues. It makes the church
a local landmark to the Lake
View community. The
buildings of the parish
comprising church, rectory,
theater, school, and convent
occupy a full city block.

St. Alphonsus is a Gothic
church with a great stone
porch. It has pointed arches,
large and small pinnacles,
crockets, and a long, high
nave with ribbed vaulting.
The facade of the building is
blue Bedford stone while
the body of the church is
constructed of red pressed
brick. There are eight bays
along either side of the nave.

These are surmounted by four
gables at the clerestory level.
The building is 208 feet long,
80 feet wide, and the interior
of the nave is 60 feet high.

Some might say that this is
the kind of church that would
never be rebuilt if it were
badly damaged. On October
20, 1950, as workmen put the
finishing touches on a new
roof, some sparks from a stove
fell through the roof and
ignited the rafters. A great fire
soon engulfed the ceiling,
roof, vaulting, and choir loft.
The whole roof was destroyed
but the body of the church
was saved. It has been said
that while plans were being
made to replace the Gothic

vaulted ceiling with a flat
roof, Cardinal Stritch
intervened and ordered the
ceiling rebuilt exactly as it
had been. This was done,
except that steel beams were
used where wood had been
before. St. Alphonsus has
one of the most beautiful
rib-vaulted ceilings in
the city.

This monumental Gothic
church is named for
St. Alphonsus Liguori
(1696-1787), the founder
of the Redemptorist order of
priests and brothers. The
Redemptorists serve this
parish and St. Michael's in
Old Town from which
St. Alphonsus originated.
Both were national parishes
founded by German-speaking

immigrants. Though the Lake View neighborhood is very cosmopolitan today, there is still one Mass offered in German at St. Alphonsus every Sunday.

The German baroque-style stained glass windows depicting scenes from the life of Christ, Mary, and St. Alphonsus were made by Mayer & Co. of Munich. The organ is a three-manual pipe organ built by Casavant Freres of St. Hyacinthe, Quebec, Canada and installed here in 1950 after the fire. This instrument, #2042, was acquired from another church.

The cornerstone, dated 1889, marks the beginning of the basement church which was completed in 1890 and is still in use today.

St. Alphonsus, the patron of moral theologians, was renowned for gentleness and compassion. He conducted popular missions and effected a reform in preaching from pompous oratory to simple expression that people could understand. The priests at St. Alphonsus parish carry on his traditions today. The school is directed by the School Sisters of Notre Dame.

**Pilgrim Baptist Church
1890-91
3301 South Indiana Avenue
(200 East)**

Architects: Adler and Sullivan
National Register of
Historic Places, 1973
Style: Chicago School
Seating: 1,500

Adler and Sullivan's synagogue masterpiece, designed for the oldest Jewish congregation in Chicago.

The Pilgrim Baptist Church, built originally as the K.A.M. Synagogue, is one of the few remaining structures designed by the world-famous architectural firm of Adler and Sullivan. Dankmar Adler's father had been rabbi of the K.A.M. congregation from 1861 to 1883. The architects had just completed the Auditorium Building on Michigan Avenue and the Ryerson tomb in Graceland Cemetery when they designed this building on Indiana Avenue. Elements of the synagogue bear resemblances to both the Auditorium and the Ryerson tomb.

The K.A.M./Pilgrim Baptist Church is noted for its outstanding acoustics, thanks to Adler, and its magnificent ornament done by Louis Sullivan. Both of these elements remain in excellent condition today.

Original plans for the synagogue specified that it be built entirely of ashlar masonry, both the base and the clerestory levels in stone, with a shallow hip roof leading up to the clerestory. But a shortage of funds called for a new design and the use of less expensive materials. The north and west walls were built of rusticated Bedford stone, the east and south walls of brick. The clerestory level was originally covered with pressed sheet metal and later with shingles. The shallow hip roof was never built at all. The clerestory is covered by a steeply pitched roof similar in design to the roof on the Ryerson tomb. The rough stone base and the great Romanesque arches recall the Michigan Avenue facade of the Auditorium Building.

The ground floor of the present church building is occupied by a chapel, classrooms, meeting rooms, and offices—essentially unchanged from the original construction. The spacious auditorium is upstairs. The pews are arranged in a curving fashion so that all face the pulpit and choir.

There is a balcony around three sides of the auditorium, and a tunnel-vaulted ceiling rises up in the clerestory. This vault, now painted, was once stained and varnished wood. The stained glass windows in the clerestory have been painted over.

Broad bands of gold-painted terra cotta ornament decorate the balcony, the base of the clerestory, and the half dome that contains the pulpit, organ, and choir. The ornament, in elaborate floral and geometrical designs, is an example of the Sullivan genius which would become world famous.

Kehilath Anshe Ma'ariv (Congregation of the Men of the West) was founded in 1847, the oldest Jewish congregation in Chicago. They occupied this Indiana Avenue structure, their fourth house of worship, until 1922 when they sold it to the Pilgrim Baptist Church. The Jewish community was then moving southward. Black people were coming into this neighborhood.

The Pilgrim Baptist Church was founded in 1915 and has been at this location since 1922. In the middle 1920s Rev. J. C. Austin became pastor and led the church to become one of the strongest black religious communities in the country. Membership was well into the thousands. When Rev. Austin died in the 1960s, his son was elected to succeed him. Membership is still over one thousand, but attendance is down. Many members have moved away from the neighborhood but still return to attend services here.

Our Lady of Sorrows Basilica
1890-1902
3101 West Jackson Boulevard
(300 South)

Architects: Henry Engelbert,
John F. Pope, and
William J. Brinkman
Style: Renaissance
Seating: 1,200

The interior of this magnificent
edifice is probably the finest
example of Renaissance
ornamentation in Chicago.

"Basilica" is an honorary title which the pope gives to a church because it has noteworthy architectural and artistic value and is a center of devotion within a diocese. Our Lady of Sorrows well fits this description. It was raised to the rank of a basilica by Pope Pius XII in 1956 primarily because it was in this magnificent edifice that the Sorrowful Mother Novena, a series of nine services, began in 1937 and eventually spread to two thousand other churches and chapels throughout the country and the world. At its peak in the late 1930s there were thirty-eight services every Friday in this church attended by over seventy thousand people! The Sorrowful Mother *Novena Notes* had a circulation of a million copies a week and was the largest Catholic publication in the United States.

This parish was founded in 1874 by the Servite friars for the handful of people living on the prairie west of Western Avenue between Twelfth Street and Lake Street. The parish grew with the city.

The present church was begun in September 1890 and roofed in by Christmas the same year. Then a delay. In June 1895 the transepts, sanctuary, and lower church were added; during the following year, the facade and chapels. The 200-foot towers were finished in 1900, and the interior, designed by William J. Brinkman in pure Renaissance form after the style of Bramante, was finished in December 1901. The edifice is constructed of Chicago common brick with a limestone facade.

The great coffered, barrel-vaulted ceiling rises 80 feet above the white marble floor. The nave is 65 feet wide, not including the chapels, and 180 feet long from the narthex to the main altar. More than eleven hundred separate ornate panels make up the ceiling.

four-manual Lyon & Healy organ, perhaps the oldest working pipe organ Lyon & Healy ever installed.

The gracious marble altar in the west transept is dedicated to Our Lady of Sorrows, that in the east transept represents the Blessed Virgin, resplendent in marble and Venetian mosaic, inviting the seven holy founders of the Servite order to be her "Servants." The two large murals near the altar of Our Lady of Sorrows, depicting the desolation of Mary, were also executed by Giusti in 1917, while the murals in the east transept were painted by Richard Schmid in 1956 to commemorate the designation of the church as a basilica. Also of note are the seven oil paintings of the *Via Matris* by C. Bosseron Chambers (1939), and the large mural of St. Anthony Pucci, O.S.M., painted by Michelangelo Bedini for the beatification ceremony at St. Peter's, Rome, 1952.

This magnificent basilica, the first in Illinois and one of only two in Chicago (Queen of All Saints in Sauganash is the other), is now being restored. The towers have been repaired and painted, the stained glass windows cleaned and refitted, and interior decorating is planned as funds become available.

The parish originally served the working class Irish and Italians of the West Side until the later 1950s and early 1960s when the neighborhood gradually became Spanish-speaking. Then in the 1960s increasing numbers of poorer black families, mostly Baptists, moved within the parish boundaries and the parish sought new ways of serving their spiritual, social, and educational needs.

The high altar is built entirely of white Carrara marble and is flanked on either side by gilded balconies patterned after those in the Sistine Chapel in the Vatican. The huge painting by Frank L. Giusti above the main altar depicts the Lamb of God in glory. The two paintings on either side continue the Eucharistic theme: The first mass of St. Philip Benizi, also painted by Giusti, and the Communion of St. Juliana on her deathbed, one of the early works of Henry C. Balink (1917).

On the balconies above the sanctuary stands the

Quinn Chapel A.M.E. Church
1891-94
2401 South Wabash Avenue
(50 East)

Architect: Unknown
  Chicago Landmark, 1977
  National Register of
  Historic Places, 1979
Style: Victorian Gothic
Seating: 1,500

This landmark church houses the oldest black congregation in Chicago.

The Chicago Landmark plaque near the front door of Quinn Chapel reads: "This church houses the oldest black congregation in Chicago, tracing its origins back to 1844. Members of the congregation have played a significant role in the development of the city since that time. The church is a reminder of the late nineteenth century character of the area."

Quinn Chapel is a brick and rusticated gray stone building. There are two towers on the front of the church; each contains a gabled entrance to the building. The north tower is higher containing the belfry; it is turreted and is topped by a simple metal cross. Between the towers is a gable roof; beneath that, a broad Gothic arch containing five lancet windows; and beneath that, a gabled projection with five colonnaded windows.

Much of the interior of the structure is original. The first floor houses the Sunday school and offices and a kitchen; the second floor, the bright, spacious chapel. The original wooden pews are arranged in curving fashion fanning out from the sanctuary. The sanctuary contains the pulpit, the choir seating, and a fine old William H. Delle pipe organ purchased from the German Pavilion of the 1893 Columbian Exposition. On the back wall of the sanctuary is a mural painting of the Risen Christ done in 1904 by Proctor Chisholm, a member of the congregation. A balcony with wooden pews extends around both sides and the rear of the chapel. The whole church is well maintained and in excellent physical condition.

Quinn Chapel is named for William P. Quinn, an early bishop of the African Methodist Episcopal church. He was the bishop of the midwest diocese in 1847 when this congregation officially joined that church. Quinn Chapel played an important part in the abolition movement in Chicago and served as a station on the underground railroad. Members of this congregation were instrumental in founding the Bethel A.M.E. Church, Provident Hospital, the Elam House, and the Wabash Avenue Y.M.C.A.

Other members have served in both houses of the Illinois legislature. Presidents William B. McKinley and William Howard Taft spoke in this church in 1899 and 1911 respectively. Milton Lee Olive, III, who received the Congressional Medal of Honor posthumously in 1966 and after whom Olive Park on Chicago's lakefront is named, was a member of Quinn Chapel.

Quinn Chapel continues to exert a positive, vital, religious influence on the city of Chicago.

St. John Cantius Church
1893-98
821 North Carpenter Street
(1032 West)

Architect: Adolphus Druiding
Style: Renaissance-Baroque
Seating: 2,000

This massive Renaissance church contains magnificent examples of baroque ornament and wood carving.

St. John Cantius is the first of the great Polish churches which the northbound Kennedy motorist sees to his right just after leaving the Loop or from the Ontario Street feeder ramp. The parish was founded in 1893 from St. Stanislaus Kostka and at its peak in 1918 served more than 23,000 people, had over 2,000 children in its school, and its convent housed 47 School Sisters of Notre Dame. The Resurrection fathers and brothers operate the parish.

St. John's is a huge brick church, 230 feet long and 107 feet wide, with a rusticated limestone facade. Its tower rises 129 feet above the street and houses a four-faced clock and three bells, the largest of which weighs over 5,000 pounds.

The three-portal round-arched entranceway is approached by a broad three-tiered flight of steps. Above the doors is a series of six Ionic pilasters, and above them a massive pediment carrying the Polish coat of arms. The Latin inscription on the entablature translates, "For the greater glory of God."

The interior of St. John Cantius is dominated by a great baroque altar and reredos of beautifully carved woodwork with gold ornament. Above the elaborately decorated tabernacle is a picture of St. John Cantius giving food and drink to the poor of Krakow. Above him is an oval picture of St. Ann with her daughter the Virgin Mary, and above that, on the apse ceiling, a painting of the Risen Christ in glory.

The side altar on the north side of the church enshrines a replica of the famous Black Madonna of Czestochowa.

The pulpit nearby is hand-carved richly ornamented woodwork. There are balconies in each of the transepts and a double balcony at the rear of the nave. Each of these balconies has a finely carved wooden balustrade.

The second balcony in the nave contains the console and pipes of a large four-manual Kilgen pipe organ. The stained glass windows in St. John's were made by the Gawin Co. of Milwaukee, and the interior murals were painted by Lesiewicz around 1920. Eight stone columns with Corinthian capitals support the vault of the nave.

The rectory and school buildings flanking the church were both designed by Henry J. Schlacks of Chicago.

The construction of the Kennedy Expressway and the Ontario Street feeder together with the industrialization of the neighborhood displaced most of St. John's parishioners. People who have moved away return to worship here on Sundays and special feast days of the church. Services are held in Polish and in English.

St. Martin Church
1894-95
5848 South Princeton Avenue
(300 West)

Architects: Louis A. Becker
of Mainz, Germany and
Henry J. Schlacks of Chicago
Style: German Gothic
Seating: 1,000

One of the finest examples of
German Gothic architecture in
the United States.

St. Martin's Church at 59th
and Princeton is considered to
be one of the finest examples
of German Gothic architecture
in the country. The great
steeple rises 228 feet above
the street and contains four
bronze bells ranging in weight
from 2,500 to 5,000 pounds
each. The building is
constructed of Indiana
limestone. The cut stonework
on the exterior elevations is
extraordinary. Gothic spires,
blind arcades, gargoyles,
crockets, and fine tracery
abound.

The *Chicago Inter-Ocean* for
August 31, 1894, reported
that, ''The church rests upon
a massive foundation of
concrete, steel beams, and
dimension stones. The
immense weight concentrated
under the tower, owing to its
great height, is taken care of
by a foundation which itself is
a departure in this class of
work. The tower, although
a part of the church, is not
attached to it, and has a
separate foundation of 120
oak piles.''

The original statuary group of
St. Martin and the Beggar was
made of wood and carved in
1895 by Sebastian Buscher. It
was replaced in 1939 by
a new group designed by
Hermann J. Gaul and made of
lead-coated copper on a brass
angle superstructure. This
group was covered with gold
leaf in 1949 and again in
1960. It shines so brightly in
the sun that airplane pilots
use it as a landmark when
coming into Midway Airport
or Meigs Field.

Inside the bronze doors of St. Martin's the visitor will find a wealth of wood carving and stained glass. Many of the statues, the altars, the communion rails, and the confessionals are hand-carved oak with a small forest of spires decorating each altar.

The German-speaking community of Chicago grew dramatically between 1872 and 1886 as Catholics fled Bismarck's *Kulturkampf.* Many settled in what was then the suburb of Englewood and built St. Martin's with Rev. John M. Schaefers, a recently arrived German priest.

The church contains much work of German artisans. The stained glass windows depicting the life of Christ in the apse, saints Martin and Boniface in the transepts, and other saints throughout the nave, were imported from Munich and Innsbruck. The stations of the cross, all wood carvings, were done by a Westphalian craftsman. They present the passion of Christ in quaint medieval settings. It was only in the 1930s that the figures were painted as they are seen today.

The organ of St. Martin's, one of the finest in the city, is a four-manual, 72-register, 3,000-pipe organ built by Johnson & Son in 1880. The instrument originally stood in the Central Music Hall, the predecessor of Orchestra Hall. When Marshall Field & Co. acquired the Music Hall site for its State Street store and razed the old building, Mrs. Marshall Field, Jr. donated the organ to St. Martin's. The console is a Casavant, #454, built in 1911.

The name, St. Martin, tells two stories. Originally, St. Martin of Tours (316?-397 A.D.), the Roman soldier who on a bitterly cold night met a beggar at the city gates and having nothing but his weapons and his clothes, drew his sword, cut his cloak in two, gave half to the beggar, and wrapped himself in what remained. People laughed, the famous legend goes, but that night Martin saw Christ dressed in the half of the cloak he had given away saying, "Martin, still a catechumen, has covered me with this garment."

Now the parish honors Martin de Porres (1579-1639), the saintly black Dominican brother of Lima, Peru, at whose canonization in 1962 Pope John XXIII said he forgave the bitterest injuries, lovingly comforted the sick, provided food, clothing, and medicine for the poor, and helped as best he could everyone he met.

St. Martin's is an active black parish, deeply involved in the Englewood community. It operates a large elementary school, a day care center, an athletic program, and many other community services. Special annual liturgies are celebrated in honor of St. Martin de Porres and Dr. Martin Luther King, Jr.

St. Vincent de Paul Church
1895-97
1004 West Webster Avenue
(2200 North)

Architect: James J. Egan
Style: French Romanesque
Seating: 1,100

A French Romanesque church adorned with exquisite marble work and fine stained glass windows.

When Rev. Edward Smith, a Vincentian priest from LaSalle, Illinois, walked up Webster Avenue in 1875 to begin St. Vincent's parish, he had a dream; but he could hardly have envisioned that his tiny seventy-five member parish would grow in less than a century into a thriving, populous parish with a cathedral-like church, a grade school, a high school, and a great urban university. Father Smith built the massive Bedford stone church that we see at the corner of Webster and Sheffield avenues today. Sadly, his funeral in 1896 was the first mass offered in the new church.

The high altar in St. Vincent's with its adoring angels was designed by Augustine O'Callaghan and was fashioned from the finest white Carrara marble with inlaid mother-of-pearl and Venetian mosaic. The stone carving was done in Pietrasanta, Italy. The details of the altar took almost six years to complete, from 1903 to 1909. The marble and mosaic communion rail was donated by the children of the parish in honor of Pope Pius X in 1914.

The beautiful German baroque stained glass windows in St. Vincent's were designed and executed by Mayer & Co. of Munich. The five windows in the sanctuary, dedicated in 1897, depict the Annunciation, Nativity, Crucifixion, Resurrection, and Pentecost. The large rose window in the east transept honors Christ the King, that in the west transept, St. Vincent de Paul, the seventeenth century founder of the Vincentian order.

On May 15, 1955 an electrical fire broke out in the church. The ensuing fire and heat threatened an explosion. To relieve the pressure and ventilate the church, fire fighters broke out the large St. Cecilia window on the south facade. The present rose window was created and installed by the Conrad Schmitt Studios of New Berlin, Wisconsin, in 1956. The sun of splendor at the center of this window represents God the Father from whom all blessings radiate. The eight doves stand for the eight beatitudes. Twelve angels sing the divine praises.

The organ in St. Vincent's, installed in 1901 with over 2,800 pipes, was built by Lyon & Healy of Chicago. It was rebuilt by the Teller Organ Co. of Erie, Pennsylvania, after the fire in 1955.

St. Vincent's parish originally served Catholics of Irish and German descent who lived in the West Lincoln Park neighborhood. Later, Italians joined the parish. A large number of Irish and Italians still belong, together with Spanish-speaking families who live in the area. St. Vincent's also serves De Paul University students.

Holy Angels Church
1896-97
605 East Oakwood Boulevard
(3940 South)

Architect: James J. Egan
Style: French Romanesque
Seating: 1,800

Intricate stone carving and extensive oak woodwork decorate this beautiful church.

Irish Catholics under Rev. Denis Tighe formed Holy Angels parish in 1880 and built this beautiful Bedford stone church in 1896. Black Catholics under Rev. George Clements and his predecessors Rev. Joseph G. Richards and Rev. James A. Duffin built Holy Angels into a nationally recognized model of convert instruction and elementary education.

The decorative stonework on the facade of Holy Angels is especially intricate and delicate. The stringcourse of angels over the entrance, another band of stone "foliage" above that, and the balconies on the 145-foot tower are masterpieces of stone carving.

Inside, the church is bright and spacious, recently redecorated for the centennial of the parish. The great barrel vault ceiling arches 65 feet above the floor. The ceiling is hung from huge laminated wooden beams which span the width of the building. There are no pillars inside the church.

There were oak trees on Oakwood Boulevard in 1896. The interior furnishings of Holy Angels, the pews, wainscoting, confessionals, communion rail, balconies, and pulpit are all made from sturdy quarter-sawed oak.

The Celtic crosses on the roof gable and in the sanctuary are reminders of the Irish people who built the church, worshiped in it, and whose children were taught here by the Sisters of Mercy until 1946. After a period of transition, Holy Angels has flourished as a black Catholic parish known for its pioneering convert work, its ethnic pride, and its excellent educational record.

St. Vitus Church
1896-97
1820 South Paulina Street
(1700 West)

Architects: Kallal and Molitor
Style: Romanesque
Seating: 350

The scale, proportions, and detailing of St. Vitus make it an excellent example of Romanesque architecture.

The inscription over the doorway, *Chram Bl. Vita,* is a reminder that this church in the heart of the old Pilsen neighborhood was built by the Czech immigrants who first lived here. Later, Slovaks and Poles made up most of the membership of the church. Since the 1960s, Mexicans have been in the majority.

This modest-sized Romanesque church is constructed of brown face brick with limestone trim. The brickwork, the straightforward design, and the proportions of the building are noteworthy. The main doorway is framed with double stone pilasters and has a simple pediment above. Two sturdy towers, one much higher than the other, flank the central facade which is gabled. Both towers and the area above the main door have round-arched stained glass windows. The three front doorways and all the nave windows have white keystones capping their brown brick arches.

The interior of the church has a simplicity about it that reflects the simple faith of the immigrants. There is a one-piece, hand-carved mahogany frame around the picture of Our Lady of Guadalupe enshrined at the side altar. The frame was carved by local Mexican craftsmen.

St. Vitus was served by the Benedictine priests from its founding in 1888 until 1966, and by Chicago diocesan priests from then until the present time.

**Grant Memorial A.M.E.
Church   1897
4017 South Drexel Boulevard
(900 East)**

Architect: Solon S. Beman
Style: Greek Revival
Seating: 1,500

**This building, designed by Solon
Beman, was the first of many
Greek Revival churches built by
the Christian Scientists in
Chicago and throughout the
United States.**

At the World's Columbian
Exposition in Jackson Park in
1893, Mary Baker Eddy was
fascinated by the Merchant
Tailors Building designed
by Solon Beman. This was a
Greek Revival building, as
were most of the buildings
at the fair. Beman was
subsequently engaged to
design the First Church of
Christ, Scientist, in Chicago.
He took as his model for the
church the much admired
Palace of Fine Arts at the fair,
now the Museum of Science
and Industry. This building,
in the Greek Revival style,
thus became the prototype
of many Christian Science
churches built in different
cities throughout the United
States. Beman designed five
such churches in Chicago: the
First, Second, Fourth, Fifth,
and Sixth. Beman developed
a close relationship with Mrs.
Eddy and eventually became
a Christian Scientist himself.

The church at 4017 South
Drexel Boulevard is
constructed of Bedford
limestone. The handsome
portico features two Ionic
columns with pilasters at the
sides. Above the entablature
and dentil cornice is a large
plaque with the inscription
from Revelation: "Now is
come salvation and strength,
and the kingdom of our God,
and the power of his Christ."
Above this is a broad cornice
and a pediment with three
acroteria.

The front of this church is
not wide, but the building
extends back the full length
of the lot to the alley. On
the second floor is a
large, beautifully domed
auditorium. It has sloped
seating arranged around the
reader's desk which is located
in the middle of the north

wall. The ornament on the
reader's desk as well as the
detailing on the molding
throughout the room is
inspired by classical Greek
forms. The pipes for the
four-manual Skinner organ
are housed behind a Palladian
facade at the west end of
the room.

The interior as well as the
exterior of this church is
in excellent condition. The
bright, spacious auditorium is
painted in soft yellow with
white columns and molding.
The seats are dark wood;
the carpet is red. Stairwells
from the first floor enter the
auditorium at all four corners
of the room and at two places
in the middle of the seating.
The ceiling, with its broad

hemispherical vaulting and
shallow coffers, is especially
graceful. The whole space
is truly elegant.

The Grant Memorial A.M.E.
Church was organized in 1914
and purchased this building
in 1950. It is a very active and
numerous congregation under
the direction of Rev. Roy L.
Miller. Grant Memorial has
five choirs, a Sunday school,
and an extensive program of
visiting the sick and shut-ins.

St. Paul Church
1897-99
2234 South Hoyne Avenue
(2100 West)

Architect: Henry J. Schlacks
Style: Gothic
Seating: 700

A medieval cathedral in brick adorned with brilliant mosaics.

St. Paul's is a symphony in brick, combining the finest elements of Gothic design, a unique collaboration of architect and craftsmen, simplicity of material, and brilliant mosaics. Ripley's *Believe It or Not* described St. Paul's as "the church built without a nail." It raises its spires like a French Gothic cathedral over the houses and factories of the Lower West Side. But it is like a medieval cathedral in more ways than one. Henry Schlacks worked with the pastor and his immigrant German parishioners to build their own church just as architects worked with townspeople to build the great cathedrals of Europe. This unique combination of architect and craftsmen produced a building here in Chicago that aroused intense architectural interest throughout the country. The church is distinctive for its beauty, proportions, and engineering. Of the many churches Henry Schlacks designed in Chicago, this was his favorite. He worked on it full time at the beginning and then on and off for the next thirty years.

St. Paul's parish was founded in 1876 by Rev. Emmerich Weber for German-speaking working class immigrants who lived south of 18th Street and west of the river. The people, mostly from the Rhine and Moselle valleys of Germany, worked in the lumber district east of the parish.

In 1896 Rev. George Heldmann wrecked his predecessor's 900-seat basement church and used the material to fill the site he had chosen for the present church. He then engaged the promising young architect,

Henry Schlacks, who was just completing St. Martin's Church at 59th and Princeton, and together they planned the new St. Paul's.

Schlacks, who had studied at MIT and trained in the offices of Adler and Sullivan, proposed a church that would be familiar to the people, similar to churches they had seen in the old country, and fireproof as well. Schlacks had traveled widely in Europe and was familiar with the churches of the Moselle Valley and the successful brick interiors of churches designed by Johannes Otzen of Berlin. Father Heldmann wanted a church with two very high spires, two side chapels, and two sacristies.

Schlacks then designed the first brick Gothic church in America, complete with brick vaulting, and he modeled the great towers after those of the fourteenth century Cathedral of St. Cortin in Quimper, France. Since no builder in Chicago was acquainted with the proposed method of construction or could even give an approximate estimate of the cost, Schlacks became the contractor and the parishioners supplied the labor.

The brickwork in St. Paul's, especially the brick vaulting, is extraordinary. A reddish brown fire brick was chosen that could be made into a great variety of shapes, so that it could form continuous moldings. This brick was supplied by the Webster Brick Co. of Webster, Ohio. Terra cotta was used on the window tracery, the sculptured "eyes" in the vaulting, and the capitals of colonnettes, and some exterior ornament—only where it was impossible to use brick.

The twin towers on the east elevation of the church are 32 feet square and their spires rise to 245 feet above the street. The towers, piers, and buttresses of the building all rest on bedrock which at this particular location is just 20 feet below street level.

The exterior of St. Paul's was completed in 1899. Interior furnishings came later. The main altar of Carrara marble was designed by Schlacks, executed in Italy, and installed in 1910. He also designed the communion rail, 1912. The marble floor and pulpit were installed in 1916.

The pipe organ in the choir loft is a Wiener organ. It was installed in 1900 and played regularly until 1973 when it became necessary to install an electronic organ.

In November, 1903, Archbishop Quigley removed Father Heldmann as pastor because, the *Chicago Tribune* reported, he had failed to file the annual financial reports required by the diocese. The parish was soon afterwards given over to the care of the Benedictine fathers who served there until 1966.

In 1922 Rev. Leonard Schlim, O.S.B., commissioned Henry Schlacks to select an artist for the mosaics that had been specified in the original plans. The architect engaged the Cav. Angelo Gianese Co. of Venice, Italy to create 2,500 square feet of mosaic. The individually colored pieces of glass, the largest no more than one-half inch square, were fitted together, packed, shipped to Chicago, and installed in the church by John Martin in 1930. These mosaics are regarded as outstanding examples of the art. The most notable are the images of Christ and the twelve apostles on the chancel arch.

Time and remodeling have taken their toll on St. Paul's. The original chandeliers are gone. Crockets, finials, crosses, a flèche above the crossing, and two smaller towers have been removed. The original red tile roof has been redone in asbestos, and some Gothic ornament has been removed from the two eastern towers. But this remarkable church still retains its grand silhouette and the distinction of being one of the finest churches in Chicago.

**Ebenezer Baptist Church
1898-99
4501 South Vincennes
Avenue   (500 East)**

Architect: Dankmar Adler
Style: Georgian
Seating: 1,100

Built as Temple Isaiah, this impressive building was the last major work of Dankmar Adler.

The large building on the southeast corner of 45th Street and Vincennes Avenue that now houses the Ebenezer Baptist Church was built as Temple Isaiah in 1899. It was the last major work of Dankmar Adler who died the following year. From 1880 to 1895 Adler was in partnership with Louis Sullivan and the two produced buildings that made major contributions to the art and science of architecture. The interior of this building recalls the grand auditorium spaces designed by the firm.

This imposing structure, 127 by 97 feet, is constructed of pinkish brown pressed brick with Bedford stone trim. The building has a Greek cross plan with pitched roofs over each arm of the cross. The main entrance on Vincennes has a free-standing portico with four Ionic columns, an entablature, and a balustrade. Above this is a round segmented arch which encloses a large stained glass window, now bricked over. The central facade rises three stories, is gabled, and is flanked on either side by a two-story stairwell block. These blocks have balustraded parapets and at the second level they

contain smaller round-arched windows which complement the large one on the Vincennes Avenue facade. The north and south elevations of the building each contain three tall arched windows. At the east end of the building there is a two-story annex, separate but connected, which contains church offices, classrooms, a library, social and dining facilities.

The auditorium of the church is 90 by 80 feet with the individual seating curved and sloped toward the pulpit platform on the east side of the room. A great barrel-vaulted ceiling with a north-south axis spans the auditorium. There is a balcony around three sides of the room with the organ console and pipes in the west part of the balcony.

The interior of the auditorium is lighted by seven spherical chandeliers which hang from the great vault and by six large ornamental stained glass windows, three on each side of the room.

Except for the iron gates across the main entrance and the blocked-in window on the west elevation, this church looks much the same as it did when it was a synagogue. Its acoustics are said to be nearly perfect and the ornament on the balcony railing recalls the former partnership of Adler with Sullivan.

The Ebenezer Missionary Baptist Church was founded in 1902 from the old Olivet Baptist Church on 27th and Dearborn streets. The new church first met in Arlington Hall at 31st and Indiana. The congregation grew rapidly, and in 1903 they moved to a building at 35th and Dearborn where they worshiped for the next eighteen years. In 1921 Ebenezer purchased the Isaiah Temple and has been at this location ever since. This congregation has carefully maintained the building over the years.

Ebenezer is a large and prominent black congregation under the direction of Dr. Frank K. Sims since 1959. It has several choirs, many social and spiritual organizations, youth and senior citizen divisions, and an active missionary program. The name *Ebenezer* is a biblical word which means "rock of help."

Metropolitan Missionary Baptist Church 1899
2151 W. Washington Boulevard (100 North)

Architect: Hugh M. G. Garden
Style: Greek Revival
Seating: about 1,000

This elegant church on Washington Boulevard was designed by Hugh M. G. Garden for the Third Church of Christ, Scientist.

The large, white, classical-styled church on the southeast corner of Washington and Leavitt was built for the Third Church of Christ, Scientist, in Chicago. The white, velvet-finished enameled brick on the exterior of the building was furnished by the Tiffany Enameled Brick Co. The ornamental disks on the main frieze, the window frames and architraves, together with the ornamental soffits are all made of terra cotta supplied by the American Terra Cotta & Ceramic Co. The building has a galvanized roof and numerous geometrically patterned leaded glass windows.

The church is almost square in plan, somewhat longer on the Leavitt Street side. The entrance portico on Washington Boulevard features two marble columns and three double doorways. Large plaques high on the north wall flank the entrance and proclaim "The kingdom of the world is become the kingdom of our Lord and of his Christ" and "He that overcometh shall inherit all things and I will be his God and he shall be my son." And over the entrance doors, "Who is so great a God as our God."

The interior design of this church is similar to that of other churches erected by the Christian Scientists. The auditorium on the second floor is reached by way of stairwells at the four corners of the building. The reader's stand, pulpit, and choir area are on the south side of the auditorium. The individual seating is arranged around the pulpit and the floor slopes toward the front as in a theater. There are no interior pillars in the seating area.

The Metropolitan Missionary Baptist Church, founded in 1920, is a thriving, active Christian community under the direction of Rev. Jesse Taylor. They acquired this church building in 1947. Immediately east of the church and connected with it is the Ernest F. Ledbetter Educational Center built in 1971.

St. Hedwig Church
1899-1901
2100 West Webster Avenue
(2200 North)

Architect: Adolphus Druiding
Style: Renaissance
Seating: 1,500

A masterpiece of Renaissance design and detailing, one of the great Polish churches on the Northwest Side.

The massive gray brick church of St. Hedwig with its twin cupolas is easily visible a few blocks west of the Kennedy Expressway at Webster Avenue. This is a Renaissance Revival church with an impressive classical facade. A central portico with four granite columns shelters three massive doors with large transom windows above. The entablature carries an abbreviated Latin title which announces the church to be under the care and in honor of St. Hedwig. Above the entablature is a stone balustrade. Behind this at the back of the porch are four Ionic columns with windows between them supporting a large pediment with a cross on top. The central facade is flanked by two square towers, capped with matching cupolas. The first levels of the towers are made of smooth limestone with rusticated limestone quoins. Above this, the tower walls are of brick, punctuated by classically framed windows.

St. Hedwig's has a Latin cross plan. The main altar is ornately carved wood in a classical style. The reredos is topped with a large pediment which corresponds to those on the Webster Avenue facade and on the transepts of the church.

The interior of St. Hedwig's contains paintings by the Polish artist Zukotynski. The stained glass windows depicting Polish saints were imported from Bavaria. Sixteen solid granite columns support the vault of the nave, and two choir lofts with elaborately decorated railings can be seen at the rear of the auditorium. The church has a large Kilgen pipe organ with two consoles, one on each balcony.

St. Hedwig parish was founded in 1888 from St. Stanislaus Kostka to serve the growing population of Polish Catholic immigrants on the Near Northwest Side. In the 1920s the parish numbered over 3,700 families. The expressway coming through the neighborhood made the parish smaller. Today the parish numbers about 1,400 families, Polish, Latino, and English-speaking. Members of the Congregation of the Resurrection serve this parish. The grade school is operated by the Sisters of Nazareth.

St. Hedwig (1174-1243) was a Polish woman of noble birth who married Henry, Duke of Silesia, and through the use of her power and wealth brought peace to her people and founded many hospitals, monasteries, and convents in Silesia.

Ecclesiastical Stained Glass in Chicago

by Erne R. and Florence Frueh

"Nobody takes in all the details of the windows at Chartres . . . What sinks in to the faithful is not just an empty play of lines and colors, nor is it the stories themselves, it is the emotion of the artist who dealt with these stories." (Jean Bazaine, *Le Vitrail Francais*, 1958)

It was the advent of Gothic architecture in the mid-twelfth century that made stained glass the glory of ecclesiastical art. With its ribbed vaulting, pointed arches, and flying buttresses, this revolutionary style opened up immense expanses of window space filled, like those at Chartres and Sainte Chapelle, with glowing stained glass pictures relating the stories of the Scriptures to the faithful, most of whom could neither read nor write.

The demand for stained glass continued through the 1500s, but by the seventeenth and eighteenth centuries the art had been debased by designers and glaziers who merely imitated oil painting and brushed impermanent, dulling enamels on the surface of the glass. Lacking the integrity and radiance of the medieval work, stained glass became a neglected and almost forgotten art.

The revival of stained glass in the nineteenth century was stimulated by a series of remarkable developments which together would, by the close of the century, make stained glass an important industry and again a flourishing art. Chief among these were: the first scientific analysis of light and color in the great stained glass windows of the twelfth and thirteenth centuries; the manufacture of colored glass equal and sometimes actually superior to the medieval product; the unprecedented demand for ecclesiastical stained glass resulting from the restoration of hundreds of Gothic churches and the construction of new ones; and, finally, the reforms of William Morris, the leader of the English Arts and Crafts Movement, who advocated a return to sound medieval craftsmanship.

Disheartened by the inferior workmanship and mediocre design of machine-made decorative wares, Morris, following his own precepts, set up workshops for the production of handmade crafts, including a studio for stained glass. Using the best materials, he trained his own craftsmen and hired the best contemporary painters—his close friends the Pre-Raphaelites Dante Gabriel Rossetti, Ford Madox Brown, and chiefly Edward Burne-Jones—to create designs for stained glass windows in their distinctive style. In doing so, while he adhered to medieval techniques, Morris broke away from traditional ecclesiastical stained glass styles and designs and opened the way, albeit unknowingly, for the radical changes that were to come in the twentieth century.

Morris's reforms spread rapidly to Europe and America. In Chicago his ideas exerted a strong influence upon architects, artists, designers, and glassmen, some of whom would make important contributions to stained glass art.

The revival of stained glass coincided with Chicago's building boom and population explosion that followed the Great Fire of 1871. Over the next sixty years hundreds of religious structures sprang up in the city and its suburbs generating an enormous demand for ecclesiastical stained glass.

In the decade between 1890 and 1900 Chicago had more than a dozen firms specializing in the production of stained glass. By 1915 it was a major center with more than fifty workshops. Most of these firms catered to local clients, but some did business throughout the country. Their work may still be seen in many Chicago churches. These churches also possess some fine examples by Louis Comfort Tiffany and John La Farge, considered by many to be America's foremost artists in stained glass, and, surprisingly enough, two gems designed by Burne-Jones and executed by the firm of William Morris.

But even before Tiffany became internationally known for his opalescent glass, Healy & Millet, a distinguished Chicago decorating firm specializing in stained glass, had already won the highest acclaim of French critics. At the Paris Exposition of 1889 the firm had exhibited a "remarkable collection of small panels" in the new "American glass." Several of these panels were purchased by the French Government for the *Musée des Arts Décoratifs* in Paris.

Healy & Millet worked closely with architects Adler and Sullivan, for whom they executed the splendid stained glass windows in the Auditorium Theater Building. A notable example of their ecclesiastical art can be seen at the Second Presbyterian Church on South Michigan Avenue.

An entirely original style of art glass, angular and "absolutely in the flat," was introduced by Frank Lloyd Wright at the turn of the century. Unlike the scenic or conventionalized floral windows prevalent at the time, Wright's windows are elegant geometric compositions designed to integrate with his total architectural schemes.

Typically, Wright used little stained glass, preferring instead leaded clear glass set with small pieces of colored glass arranged in deceptively simple abstract patterns to permit unobstructed nature views. As he explained, "Nothing is more annoying to me than . . . any form of realism to get mixed up with the view outside." Although Wright's windows can be appreciated in single units owned by major museums, including Chicago's Art Institute, they are best see *in situ* in such important buildings as the Robie House or Unity Temple, where they are fully integrated with his architecture.

Decidedly different from the work of Healy & Millet and Wright was that of Thomas Augustin O'Shaughnessy, an independent artist, who, after years of experimentation, developed his own formula for "pot metal" glass from exceedingly fine sand he had found near Ottawa, Illinois.

Remarkable for its clarity and satiny smooth luster, O'Shaughnessy's glass was ideally suited for capturing the luminous quality of the medieval Book of Kells, which had long been his objective. Filled with complex Celtic iconography and intricate designs adopted from the great illuminated manuscript, his celebrated windows at Old St. Patrick's Church are unique in modern ecclesiastical stained glass art.

Since stained glass is an adjunct of architecture, it has always presented special problems for the artist working in that medium. Unlike the painter who can predetermine the size of his canvas and control his colors at will, the stained glass artist must work within the architectural framework, always aware that his choice of colors, even in the best of circumstances, will be subject to the unpredictable behavior of light. Although modern tools and new materials have somewhat eased the craftsman's task, the making of stained glass windows continues to be a laborious process, little changed from that described by the German monk Theophilus in his exhaustive treatise on the arts written in the early twelfth century.

Medieval stained glass artists and craftsmen worked closely with the architect, often setting up their workshops at the site of the church under construction. There, in large crucibles, they mixed their ingredients—basically sand, potash, and lime for white or clear glass and oxides for color. Copper, for example, produced ruby; oxide of iron, green or yellow; cobalt, blue; and manganese, purple. The entire mixture was then fired far beyond the melting point to produce the colored pot metal glass similar to the commercial or handmade "antique glass" produced today.

Next the glassman gathered a glob of molten glass on a blow pipe and blew a bubble in the shape of a cylinder which he tapped off, slit, and rolled flat on a board while the glass was still cooling. After it had hardened the glass was cut into small pieces to fit over each numbered part of a cartoon (a prepared drawing of the window design) which had been sketched on a whitewashed board.

Facial features, hair, hands, feet, drapery folds, and other details too small to render with chips of glass were painted on the glass with viscous black or yellow brown oxides. Each piece was then numbered with its corresponding number on the cartoon, removed from the board, and placed in a kiln for refiring. This permanently bonded the painted portions to the glass. When cooled the pieces were reassembled according to their numbers on the board, fastened with H-shaped strips of lead called cames, and soldered at each joint. Spaces between the glass and the lead were filled with putty or cement, which weatherproofed and strengthened the window and, incidentally, also emphasized the design. Finally, after being thoroughly cleaned, the window was carried to the aperture, cemented into the wood or stone frame, and additionally secured by horizontal metal bars.

In the early fourteenth century it was found that silver nitrate or "yellow stain" painted onto the glass in different densities and fired at different temperatures produced colors ranging from the palest yellow to deep orange, and even burnt sienna. This revolutionary discovery enabled the artist to paint, for example, a head, hair, and halo in different colors and shades on the same piece of glass, thus reducing the number of leadlines in a window.

Another important innovation was "flashed glass." Glass with a thin film of color on one or both sides, usually ruby or blue, was rubbed with powdered stone. This rubbing exposed the clear or white glass beneath. In the late nineteenth century this time-consuming process was supplanted by the superior method of using hydrofluoric acid to eat or etch away unwanted portions of the glass. "Except for this late refinement," Robert Sowers pointed out in his *Stained Glass: An Architectural Art*, "all of the practicable techniques of color manipulation now known were perfected in the Middle Ages."

Medieval stained glass was imperfect at best, varying in thickness as well as texture. Often the glass was rough and uneven and craftsmen had no way to prevent air bubbles, specks, and cracks. But these defects, if they can be called that, gave additional color, sparkle, and dimension to the glass. Indeed, Tiffany and La Farge deliberately sought such imperfections for these same effects, as stained glass artists still do today.

In the twentieth century new materials and techniques—*dalle de verre*, fused glass, glass *appliqué*, slab glass, and epoxy resins—have eliminated even the need for leading. These innovations, as well as the availability of hundreds of ready-made colored glasses, have given designers and craftsmen artistic opportunities undreamt of in the Middle Ages. Even more important has been the work of such eminent contemporary artists as Matisse, Braque, Leger, Rouault, and Chagall, whose magnificent stained glass windows have brought fresh vision and renewed vitality to the age-old art.

In making a selection representative of ecclesiastical stained glass windows in Chicago, care was taken to present as many styles and techniques as possible within the framework of the preceding pages. All are splendid examples, though by no means the only ones, of what can be seen in and about the city.

St. James Chapel of Quigley Preparatory Seminary North, completed in 1918, the same year its windows were installed, is freely modeled after Sainte Chapelle in the French Gothic style. Like those at Sainte Chapelle, the long lancets in the small, jewel-like chapel contain hundreds of medallions depicting miniature religious scenes arranged in a sequence often found in medieval churches and cathedrals.

Five lancets (40 by 10 feet) on either side of the nave depict, in over two hundred panels, stories of the Old Testament and important early Christian personages and events. Five (30 by 7 feet) facing east in the chancel are devoted to the life, miracles, and parables of Christ. The west wall features a stunning rose window (16 feet in diameter), at the center of which stands the Virgin Mary encircled by sixteen radiating ruby red petals set with symbols of her many attributes.

Stained Glass

The windows were designed by Robert Giles, an artist for the John J. Kinsella Company, the Chicago firm which executed them. They are composed of thousands of particles of English antique glass in vibrant red, green, blue, and yellow with splashes of lavender and brown. Blackish brown oxide sparingly applied by the artist's wife delineates the facial features and other fine details. The St. James Chapel windows demonstrate the painstaking labor involved in assembling stained glass windows. It took 150,000 pieces of glass to complete the chancel windows and over 500,000 for those in the nave.

The **Second Presbyterian Church,** an English Neo-Gothic edifice with an Arts and Crafts interior, offers a veritable gallery of stained glass art. The church contains twenty-two windows installed bewteen 1890 and 1918—two by Burne-Jones and William Morris; one by Healy & Millet; fourteen by Tiffany; one by La Farge; and four by McCully & Miles, a large Chicago glass and decorating firm. All vary artistically, but as Henry Adams wrote about the windows at Chartres, "their charm is in variety, in individuality," and in their harmony with the interior design.

The Burne-Jones windows (6 by 2 feet) are in the vestibule as you enter. To the right, robed in rich red is St. Margaret, casually resting a delicately sandaled foot on a great green dragon. To the left, draped in velvety purple and blue is St. Cecilia, dreamily playing a small portative organ in a lush green forest. Both are typical Burne-Jones figures, ethereal and willowy. As in hundreds of windows designed in collaboration with Burne-Jones, who made only the figurative cartoons, Morris composed the bold leadlines and painted the hands, faces, drapery folds, and delicate grisaille work.

In the east wall, centered high in the balcony, is *The Ascension* (30 by 17 feet) and immediately below it the five panels of *The Scourges* (each 6 by 2 feet), Tiffany's unique conception of Christ's trials on earth. The remaining Tiffany windows and La Farge's *Angel in the Lilies* (16 by 9 feet, the size of all the nave windows) are located on either side of the balcony.

These exceptional works afford the visitor a rare opportunity to examine at close range the various techniques invented by Tiffany and La Farge to eliminate the use of paint except for facial expressions. "By chemistry," explained Tiffany, "and years of experiments, I have found means to produce figures in glass in which not even the flesh tones are superficially treated—built up of what I call 'genuine glass'."

In *The Ascension* gold and silver dust sprayed onto the glass before it cooled produced the iridescence for which Tiffany is famous. The folds of Christ's white robe and those of the awed multitude below in rich red, green, blue, and purple are shaped with varying thicknesses of opalescent glass, giving a sculptured effect. In the striking studies of *The Scourges*, prism-shaped pieces of glass in brilliant reds, blues, and greens set at sharp angles catch the constantly changing rays of light that flash about the grim figures. Air bubbles and other flaws intensify the coruscating colors.

The Jeweled Window, a mosaic, is in the form of a Greek icon divided into two medallions. Above is a jeweled cross, below are the initials IHS, the first three Greek letters in the name Jesus. Thousands of pieces of chipped, irregularly faceted glass, individually leaded, make the work glisten like a great gem in dazzling hues of amber, gold, red, green, blue, and burnt sienna.

The Peace Window, another mosaic, is made of small pieces of flat glass which, in contrast to the faceted brilliance of *The Jeweled Window*, give the work a soft, diffused glow. An intricate pattern of circles and diamonds in blue, green, red, and purple surrounds three intertwining medallions each containing an angel, the center one unfurling a scroll inscribed with the word PEACE.

An outstanding example of Tiffany's secular art in a religious setting is *The Pastoral Window*. In this study the Creator and nature are one. A profusion of purple iris in the foreground borders a running stream that leads to verdant forests and distant hazy blue mountains surmounted by a pearly pink sky. All the colors and shading come from the layered opalescent glass; no paint was used.

sancta margarita

To the glory of God
and in memory of
Franklin Darius Gray
Born May 19 1915 Died November 19 1905

sancta cecilia

To the glory of God
and in memory of
Ann Olive Phelps Gray
Born May 4 1829 Died July 10 1905

Jeweled Window
Louis C. Tiffany
Second Presbyterian Church

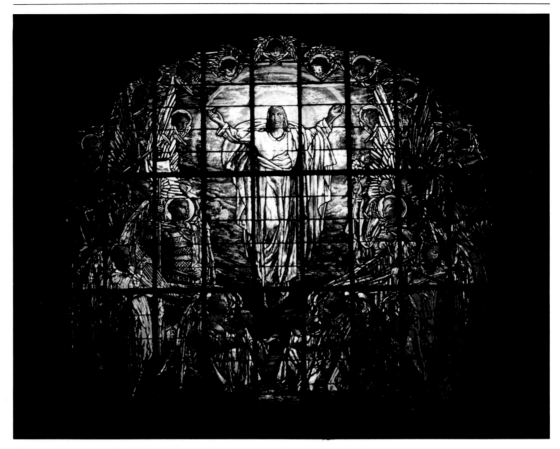

The Ascension, east facade
Louis C. Tiffany
Second Presbyterian Church

Page 85
Rose window, west facade
John J. Kinsella Company
Quigley Preparatory Seminary North

Page 87
St. Margaret and St. Cecilia, narthex windows
Sir Edwar Burne-Jones and William Morris
Second Presbyterian Church

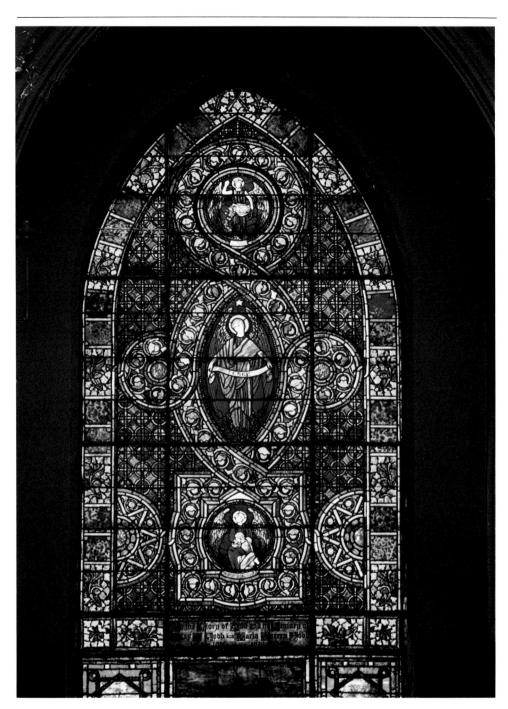

Peace Window
Louis C. Tiffany
Second Presbyterian Church

Pastoral Window
Louis C. Tiffany
Second Presbyterian Church

Tiffany's remaining windows depict such traditional biblical themes as *Christ Blessing the Little Children; The Angel at the Open Tomb; The Mount of the Holy Cross; St. Paul Preaching to the Athenians;* and *Behold the Lamb of God.* All are made of laminated opalescent glass, predominantly in shades of milky white, soft green, purple, blue, and mauve.

La Farge's *Angel in the Lilies* reflects the influence of the Pre-Raphaelites and William Morris, whom he knew. The trance-like posture of the winged angel, her ecstatic expression, and the massed field of lilies in which she stands are reminiscent of paintings by Rossetti and Burne-Jones. The undulating folds of the angel's gray robe and the milk white opalescent petals of the lilies are unusually thick, varying from one to four inches.

Detail, "Cast Thy Garment about Thee and Follow Me" Healy & Millet Second Presbyterian Church

Healy & Millet's *Cast Thy Garment About Thee and Follow Me* depicts the drama of St. Peter's release from prison by an angel. The poignant scene is made memorable by the artists' unusually sensitive portrayal of the saint still doubtful of his freedom and the angel who reassures him. Thin pieces of opalescent rippled glass in purple, blue, green, and gold were cut and leaded diagonally to shape the long, flowing folds of the robes. The same glass cut with and against the grain shapes the cypress trees and other nature forms of the background.

Beside the Still Waters and the untitled triptych beneath it were designed by an unknown artist and executed by McCully & Miles. They are in the Arts and Crafts style and present simple pastoral scenes in various shades of green. Pebbled glass causes the illusion of flickering light on the clear pools of water and the verdant foliage of the trees.

"Beside the Still Waters"
McCully & Miles
Second Presbyterian Church

Left:
"Presentation of the
Child Jesus in the Temple"
The Munich Studio, Chicago
SS. Cyril and Methodius

Right:
Faith Window
Thomas A. O'Shaughnessy
St. Patrick Church

"Let There Be Light, And There Was Light"
Abraham Rattner
Chicago Loop Synagogue

The twenty-three splendid windows at **SS. Cyril and Methodius Church,** installed in 1913, the year the church was completed, were designed by Max Guler, a German immigrant artist, and executed by the Munich Studio which he had founded in 1903. The firm, one of several Chicago establishments founded or staffed by European-trained immigrant craftsmen, specialized in ecclesiastical stained glass windows and received commissions from clergymen throughout the country.

Guler had studied painting in Munich, and, not surprisingly, his work reflects the influence of the German Baroque style in his use of elaborate ornamentation, asymmetrical figure groupings, strong contrasts of light and shadow, and much architectural detail. Most of the windows present traditional biblical themes but, since the church was built for a Bohemian congregation, some express the parishioners' religious and patriotic ties to their native country. This is apparent in the windows portraying SS. Cyril and Methodius bringing the church to the Slavic people; St. Ludmilla and her young grandson, Wenceslaus; St. Wenceslaus ruler of Bohemia; and The Baptism of Borivoj, Bohemia's first Christian duke.

A fine example of Guler's art is The Presentation of Christ in the Temple (18 by 9 feet, the size of all the nave windows). The principal figures are the Virgin Mary robed in shimmering light gold, and the slumbering Christ Child wrapped in white swaddling clothes. Contrasted and subordinate to them are Simeon, Joseph, and Anna in heavy mantles of deep brown, blue, and gray. The asymmetrical groupings—Mary and Joseph to the left, Simeon, Anna, and the children to the right—are adroitly balanced and joined by Mary's outstretched arms and the large, green palm branch, a symbol of rejoicing, held by a child.

Guler's predilection for abundant architectural and ornamental detail can be seen in the menorah deeply carved into the massive rectangular post; the egg and dart and Greek key designs on the lintel behind Mary and Joseph; the deep shadows on the variegated marble floor; and the rich ornamentation in the white marble arch enclosing the entire composition. Although the window is heavily painted with oxides, as are most Guler windows, the glass retains its luminosity because of Guler's masterful brushwork.

When Thomas Augustin O'Shaughnessy, a devout Irish Catholic, received the commission in 1911 to design and execute the stained glass windows at **Old St. Patrick's Church,** it fulfilled his long-held ambition to transmute into stained glass his profound knowledge of Celtic art and history.

All the windows are made of O'Shaughnessy's pot metal glass in delicate pastel shades of pink, yellow, blue, green, and mauve set off by an abundance of leaf green and pearly white. Even on Chicago's grayest days, the light streaming through the luminous glass is reflected in soft rainbow tints on the beige walls, venerable oak pews, and gray marble floors, giving the interior of the church an ethereal aura.

The twelve windows in the nave (18 by 7 feet) are devoted to the heroic deeds of Ireland's early scholars, teachers, and missionary saints. Each is bordered at the top and bottom with exquisite, interweaving motifs adopted from the Book of Kells. In the arched skylight, forty feet above the altar, are the four evangelists. In the balcony is the magnificent triptych of Faith, Hope, and Charity, the center panel of which is O'Shaughnessy's celebrated *Faith Window* (24 by 7 feet), the culmination of his art and a complicated study of Irish symbolism.

In the form of a huge Celtic cross, the window is constructed of thousands of tiny pieces of mosaic glass fastened with barely perceptible bronze cames. At the top of the cross is a large shamrock, in the center of which is the Eye of the Deity looking down upon his works and creatures. Below the shamrock are supplicating angels gowned in satiny white tinged with pale pink, yellow, and blue. At the center of the crossbar, standing in the aura of the sun and the moon and haloed by twelve radiating stars, is the Virgin Mary, a serene figure robed in shining white. Within the upright and transverse sections of the cross are miniature studies of Irish saints and scholars, some of whom were depicted life-size in the nave. The base of the cross in reddish orange symbolizes the fires of purgatory from which a spirit robed in pure white is being transported to heaven by angels. A complicated pattern of circles, spirals, and whorls embellishes the various themes and unifies the entire work.

Detail, clerestory window
Unity Temple
Frank Lloyd Wright, architect

The radiant light in Frank Lloyd Wright's **Unity Temple** is all the more astonishing because of the building's massive block-like exterior, which scarcely suggests the ingenious interior lighting plan so vividly described by Wright in his *Autobiography*. "The large supporting posts," he writes, "were so set in plan as to form a double tier of alcoves on four sides of the room. I flooded these alcoves with light from above to get a sense of a happy cloudless day. And with this feeling for light the ceiling . . . became skylight sifting through and between the intersecting concrete beams, filtering through amber ceiling lights. Thus managed the light would, rain or shine, have the warmth of sunlight. Artificial lighting took place there at night as well. This scheme of lighting was integral, gave diffusion and kept the room space clear."

The twenty clear leaded casement windows in the alcoves stretch in a continuous horizontal band around the four sides of the room. Each repeats a highly abstract floral design of tiny pieces of subtly tinted yellow glass. As the light changes, the walls become shimmering "ribbons of glass" through which one sees trees, sun, and sky. The yellow, orange, and light brown glass in the twenty-five deeply recessed panels of the skylight, each containing the same blocky geometric pattern, casts a warm amber glow throughout the small but "noble room." A neo-plastic design—similar to those later seen in paintings by Mondrian—in gray and white, outlined by dark zinc cames, decorates the long slotted apertures in each of the four stairwell towers. This diffuses soft light into what would otherwise be dark areas.

Wright entrusted only a few firms to execute his exacting designs. The windows at Unity Temple were executed by the Temple Art Glass Company. Two other firms chosen by Wright for their outstanding craftsmanship were Giannini & Hilgart and the Linden Glass Company.

The distinguished American artist Abraham Rattner (1895-1978) had always wanted to make a stained glass window. Indeed, when he received the commission for Chicago's **Loop Synagogue** in 1957 he had, as early as 1940, made drawings of Judeo-Christian themes with stained glass in mind.

Rattner was an intense man with a passion for perfection. Upon receiving the commission for the Loop Synagogue, he made an intensive study of Judaic liturgy and made innumerable preliminary sketches of his conception. He worked in Paris with Jean Barrilet, one of the world's leading glass fabricators, drawing cartoons, choosing and assembling the glass, and even climbing ladders to hold pieces of glass against the light to determine the placement of colors.

When the window was installed in 1960, just before the High Holy Days, it must have been an overwhelming experience for the congregation who first viewed it, as it is for worshipers and visitors today. The monumental window (40 by 30 feet), constituting the entire east wall of the small sanctuary, is composed of hundreds of pieces of antique glass predominantly in ultramarine, cobalt, and cerulean blue.

Rattner was fond of double meanings and the window, entitled *And God Said, Let There Be Light And There Was Light*, can be interpreted in more ways than one. On one level it refers to the light of God's universe; on another, to the enlightenment bestowed on those of the faith through its ancient symbols; and finally to the celebration of light as it streams through the constantly changing colors, which themselves have symbolic meaning. Green signifies youth; violet, wisdom and old age; blue, the regeneration of the spirit; gold, prophecy; red, fire and creative power; and white, eternity.

At the extreme left, the focal point of the entire composition, is a brilliant gold shield and star of David encompassed by symbols of the twelve tribes of Israel. Below, in flames of red and blue, is the burning bush. At the center is a huge tree of life topped by a jeweled menorah, the seven-branched candlestick symbolic of the light of God. Other ancient symbols are the citron and the palm, representing the bounties of harvest time; and the shofar, the ram's horn sounded to call the faithful together at the High Holy Days. At the extreme right is the sun surrounded by the seven planets, and another star of David, all hurtling through God's firmament. Running across the bottom of the entire window is a wide border of chipped red and gold slab glass proclaiming in Hebrew the sacred message: "Hear, O Israel, the Lord Our God, the Lord is One."

As tastes and architectural styles changed after World War I, stained glass windows were considered old-fashioned. Many were neglected or wantonly destroyed. But the tremendous revival of stained glass since the 1960s has made Chicagoans aware of their rich heritage in this age-old art. Now valued as major cultural assets of the city, stained glass windows are being restored and preserved in churches and synagogues as well as in public and private buildings.

There are good and bad stained glass windows in Chicago, as there are everywhere. In the end, to paraphrase Jean Bazaine, it is not only the play of lines and colors or the stories that matter, but, above all, the emotion expressed by the artist and the impact of his art upon the viewer.

Crossing of nave and transepts
St. Mary of the Angels Church
Worthmann and Steinbach, architects

St. Josaphat Church
1900-1902
2301 N. Southport Avenue
(1400 West)

Architect: William J. Brinkman
Style: Romanesque
Seating: 1,000

This fireproof church features a
gilded mahogany reredos and a
magnificent coffered ceiling.

St. Josaphat's Church is
solid, dignified, and richly
ornamented. The building is
of steel skeleton construction,
88 by 190 feet. The exterior is
white pressed face brick with
Bedford stone trim. The twin
towers are 105 feet high with
walls that are 6 feet thick
at the base. Each tower is
decorated at the top with a
quaint collection of turrets,
gables, steeple, columns, and
balconies.

The main entrance of the
church on Southport Avenue
features a richly ornamented
round arch springing from
Corinthian columns and
surmounted by a gable. This
arch is situated between two
smaller ones. Each of the
three arches shelters heavy
wooden doors.

Above the main entrance is
a series of concentric stone
arches. An arcade runs across
the lower portion; a rose
window with stone tracery
fills the upper section of the
arches. This and all the other
windows in the church are
stone mullioned, the glass
being cemented right into the
stone. In a niche above the
rose window stands a bronze
statue of St. Josaphat, bishop
and martyr, and above that,
brick corbelling under the
main gable.

The vestibule or narthex of
the church is of white Italian
marble with a maroon and
gold coffered ceiling. Inside
the auditorium, the visitor
first sees the gilded mahogany
baldachin above the
permanent altar, and then
the barrel-vaulted coffered
ceiling which spans the nave,
88 feet across.

St. Josaphat's has a ceramic
tile roof. Steel roof beams are
supported by twelve large
angle and plate steel columns.
The plaster panels of the
coffered ceiling are applied
directly to metal lath. There
is no wood in the roof and
the building is absolutely
fireproof.

It is interesting to note how the entrance arch sets the theme for the baldachino or canopy above the permanent altar as well as for the communion rail design and the ornament on the confessionals.

The seven stained glass windows in the apse of the church, depicting scenes from the life of Christ, are the work of Mayer & Co. of Munich. The brightly colored stained glass windows in the nave were done by F. X. Zettler of Munich and were installed in 1903.

The three-manual Kilgen organ with its beautiful cabinet has 54 ranks and was installed in 1924.

Construction of this church was delayed when a cyclone completely destroyed the steel framework on August 11, 1899. After parishioners cleared the rubble, the structure was dismantled and rebuilt, and the cornerstone of the present building was laid in 1900.

St. Josaphat's was founded in 1884 to serve Kashubian Catholics in the West Lake View neighborhood. These Slavic immigrants, with their own language and customs, came to Chicago from the area around Danzig in Prussia. Prior to the formation of St. Josaphat parish, the Kashubes attended either the Polish church of St. Stanislaus Kostka or the German church of St. Michael. The present parishioners are mostly Kashubian Americans and Polish Americans, together with Mexican Americans and other ethnic groups. On a weekend there is a Polish Mass, a Spanish Mass, and three English Masses.

The interior detailing of this church is especially noteworthy. Green scagliola, which is a material composed of cement or plaster that has the appearance of marble, is used in the wainscoting of the nave and apse, while Roman marble is used in the floor of the auditorium.

The wood carving throughout St. Josaphat's is elaborate. This is evident in the three hand-carved mahogany chairs used by the celebrants of the liturgy, in the winding staircase of the pulpit, and in the intricate detailing of the communion rail.

St. Boniface Church
1902-4
1348 West Chestnut Street
(860 North)

Architect: Henry J. Schlacks
Style: Romanesque
Seating: 900

Elaborate stone carving at the entrance and beautiful wood carving inside decorate St. Boniface Church.

The tall, square towers of St. Boniface are the first that the northbound motorist sees on the west side of the Kennedy Expressway as he leaves downtown Chicago. The parish complex at Chestnut and Noble faces Eckhart Park and lifts its four towers vigorously over the neighborhood that began as German in the 1860s, became predominantly Polish in the 1920s, Latino in the 1960s, and is largely Spanish-speaking today.

The three-door main entrance to St. Boniface is graced by eight stone columns, each one carved differently from the others. The capitals are all Corinthian, but like the shafts, no two are alike. The ornamental stone molding on each of the three entrance arches is different too. Above each arch is a stone gable, then a series of slender columns rising to round cut stone arches, and then a rose window outlined by an ornamental limestone arch.

A brick corbel table just under the roof line completes the central facade. The four towers carry the same theme with corresponding arrangements of columns, round arches, and corbel tables. The principal belfry contains bells that were installed in a previous church in 1883. The present edifice, completed in 1904, is constructed of brown pressed brick with Bedford stone trim.

Inside, St. Boniface is rich in woodwork and stained glass. The hand-carved oak communion rail reflects the same variety of column design seen at the entrance. The pews are all of oak with round arch decoration. Carved oak confessionals and wooden statues of the saints are located around the interior of the church. But two pieces deserve special note: the Pieta, Our Lady of Sorrows, on the west wall, and the mission cross in the sanctuary.

The stations of the cross are originals, painted on copper by a Bavarian artist named Feuerstein.

There are ten stained glass windows in the sanctuary and a large complex light in each transept: the Last Supper in the west transept, the Agony in the Garden in the east. All of the windows were done by F. X. Zettler of Munich. The rose window above the organ depicts St. Cecilia, the patroness of music. A Nativity scene, designated the Madonna of Mannheim, fills the lunette in the narthex above the main entrance.

The organ in St. Boniface is a three-manual Wangerin organ installed in 1908 with the help of a gift from Andrew Carnegie.

Holy Trinity Cathedral
1903
1121 North Leavitt Street
(2200 West)

Architect: Louis H. Sullivan
  National Register of
  Historic Places, 1976
  Chicago Landmark, 1979
Style: Russian Provincial
Capacity: about 250

Louis Sullivan's landmark
church, combining his genius for
ornament with the finest
elements of Russian-Byzantine
architecture.

Louis Sullivan wrote that it was his sincere wish and hope that Holy Trinity would be one of "the most unique and poetic buildings in the country." His wish was fulfilled, his hope has been realized.

A little community of Russian immigrants founded St. Vladimir's Russian Orthodox parish in Chicago in 1892. Some years later under the leadership of Rev. John Kochurov, they rejected a plan for an elaborate, metropolitan church and engaged the services of Louis Sullivan to design a more modest structure in a Russian Provincial style of architecture. The parishioners

were country people who had come from southern Russia near the Ukraine and the area around the Carpathian Mountains.

Although constrained by a limited budget, Sullivan nevertheless designed a church and rectory which combined his own genius for ornament with the finest elements of the Byzantine tradition, one of the oldest in Christendom.

E. E. Viollet-le-Duc, a French authority on Russian art, wrote a book in 1877 which Sullivan very likely consulted. Viollet wrote, "In reviving Slavic art it therefore will be necessary to

appreciate exactly the qualities that govern it, these are: elegance, not without boldness; the attentive study of the effect of the masses; a discreet ornamentation that is never powerful enough to destroy the principal lines and leaves a repose for the eye . . ."

These qualities are realized in Holy Trinity Cathedral. There is a consummate massing of forms, simple yet elegant; and Sullivan confined his ornament to the portal canopy, to the upper portions of the bell tower, the window frames, and the soffits of the eaves.

Holy Trinity is a small building, 47 by 98 feet, situated on an east-west axis. The main body of the church is square with extensions at ground level and with an octagonal dome above. The exterior is simple with occasional touches of Sullivanesque ornament; for instance, the fretwork over the entranceway. The walls are load-bearing brick covered with stucco, and the dome, roof, and belfry are wood with metal trim and latticework. "The tower of Holy Trinity is one of the most exciting designs ever produced by Sullivan," wrote Theodore Turak. "It combines a picturesqueness with a rich plasticity." ("A Celt Among Slavs," *The Prairie School Review*, Fourth Quarter, 1972, inside cover) It is tall and regal, a stately square tower surmounted by one octagonal belfry, then another with its angular window hoods, then a steeple, the onion-like shape, and a Slavonic cross above it all.

Inside the front door, the visitor enters the square vestibule, the rectangular narthex, and then the nave/sanctuary with its elaborate icon screen imported from Russia in 1912.

The interior of Holy Trinity is as elaborate as the exterior is simple. There are no pews. The worshipers stand and kneel together surrounded by a multitude of saints and blessed depicted in icons all around the church.

The services are sung in Old Slavonic and English. They have an air about them which is at once ethereal, mysterious, and enchanting. The candles, incense, *a cappela* choir, and celebrants create an atmosphere which is heavenly, indeed. "He [Sullivan] aimed at precisely the effect he achieved—a sense of an intimate community humbly drawn together by the structure before the exaltedness of Deity." (T. Turak, p. 14)

Holy Trinity was begun with a gift of $4,000 from Czar Nicholas II, following the Russian tradition of state-subsidized churches. The project was completed substantially as planned for around $27,000. Sullivan requested only half the commission due him for his work because of the warmth he felt toward his clients and the pride he took in this work. The church was consecrated in 1903 by Patriarch Tikhon of Moscow. It was designated a cathedral in 1923 and was placed on the National Register of Historic Places in 1976. It is the oldest Russian Orthodox church in Chicago.

Presentation Church
1903-9
750 South Springfield Avenue
(3900 West)

Architect: William F. Gubbins
Style: Spanish Renaissance
Seating: 600

This church is noteworthy for its Spanish Renaissance facade and beautiful stained glass windows.

Few churches in Chicago have such an elaborate facade as Presentation on Springfield Avenue. The cut limestone is replete with columns, arches, rusticated stone, numerous pilasters, and finials. Twin bell towers with copper-domed cupolas rise high over the North Lawndale neighborhood. The body of the church is cruciform and constructed of common brick. The interior, last decorated in 1948, has Renaissance ornament and decoration. The beautiful stained glass windows in Presentation were created by the Munich Studio of Chicago. Many of the windows are beautiful reproductions in glass of masterpieces in painting by Raphael, Murillo, and other famous artists. Max Guler, the founder of the Munich Studio in Chicago, had been a china painter in Germany. The delicacy of that art can be seen in these windows.

Because of structural deterioration, Presentation Church was recently closed and the community is now worshiping in a new church converted from existing space in another one of the parish buildings.

Presentation was founded in 1898 to serve Irish Catholics who lived south of St. Mel's. In 1923 the congregation numbered over 1,300 families with 1,100 children in the school. During the late 1950s Presentation became a black Catholic parish and continues so today. The parish operates a grade school and sponsors many community service programs.

St. Agatha Church
1904-6
3151 West Douglas Boulevard
(1330 South)

Architects: Egan & Prindeville
Style: French Romanesque and Byzantine
Seating: 650

A rusticated brownstone church in the French Romanesque style with elaborate ornamental stone carving and beautiful interior design.

The Latin words over the beautiful three-portal entrance to St. Agatha's announce that "this door is open to everyone." And indeed it is. The rusticated brownstone structure with the Celtic crosses on the high gables was built by Irish Catholics some eleven years after the parish was founded in 1893. Today St. Agatha's is a focal point of the black community in the Lawndale neighborhood.

The church is cruciform and raises two square towers, one much taller than the other, over the Douglas Boulevard parkway. The towers are noteworthy, richly decorated with colonnades, Roman arches, brackets, and gargoyles. The church has several stringcourses or bands of intricately carved stone running all around its exterior. The ornamental stonework decorating the doorways of the church is extraordinary for its intricate patterns.

St. Agatha's is cathedral-like inside, 126 feet long and 94 feet wide at the transepts. The ceiling is coffered, barrel-vaulted, and supported by marble columns which rise up within the body of the church. The pews, confessionals, and other interior woodwork are beautifully carved black oak. Fine stained glass windows by F. X. Zettler of Munich adorn the nave, transepts, and clerestory. In 1940 the church was decorated by the John C. Mallin Co. of Chicago. High winds in the fall of 1980 seriously damaged the large stained glass window in the west transept of the church.

In the early 1970s the sanctuary of the church was remodeled. Choir seating replaced the old altar, a simple free-standing altar was erected on a platform in the center of the church, and the sanctuary walls were painted

with large murals by James Hasse, S. J. The murals present the history of salvation with Adam and Eve and Jesus, Mary, and Joseph

depicted as black people.

St. Agatha's has an active congregation, a fine gospel choir, and a grade school.

**Hyde Park Union Church
1904-6
5600 South Woodlawn
Avenue   (1200 East)**

Architect: James Gamble
Rogers
Style: Romanesque
Seating: 600

This impressive Romanesque
church contains a treasure of
stained glass windows by Louis
C. Tiffany and Charles J.
Connick.

The early pages of the history of the Hyde Park Baptist Church are dotted with names of people who were prominent in the history of the University of Chicago: Burroughs, Harper, Burton, Goodspeed, Gilkey, and others. The First Baptist Church of Hyde Park, as it was known until 1904, was founded in 1874 and for many years occupied a small frame church on Dorchester Avenue near 53rd Street.

The congregation grew in numbers and prestige in the 1890s, purchased the property at the southwest corner of 56th Street and Woodlawn Avenue, and engaged James Gamble Rogers to design their new church. Rogers went on to design many famous buildings, including the Harkness Quadrangle at Yale University. Planning for the new church in Hyde Park was accelerated by a generous gift from John D. Rockefeller, Jr., in 1901.

Construction of the church began in 1904. The building is rectangular in plan, almost square. It is constructed of red sandstone with limestone trim. The blocks of sandstone are laid up in a variegated pattern which contrasts nicely with the regular patterns of the limestone. The church has a broad gabled roof.

On each side of the Woodlawn Avenue facade is a sturdy square tower with round-arched entrances to the auditorium. Between the towers is a row of five stained glass windows on the first floor, two windows above, and then, in the center of the facade, a magnificent rose window.

Upon entering the church, the visitor will first notice the huge wooden beams of the open-truss ceiling and then the brilliance of the stained glass windows. Four windows are by Louis C. Tiffany of New York, one is by F. X. Zettler of Munich, and the rest were created by the Charles J. Connick Studios of Boston.

In the center of the chancel is a large Celtic cross carved by Lang, the famous German wood carver. Above and around the cross is a beautifully carved half-circle arch. This Romanesque arch, a motif which appears about 200 times in the church, has both height and breadth. It reminds the worshiper of the God above him and the persons around him.

The organ in Hyde Park Union Church was built by E. M. Skinner in 1914 and completely rebuilt by the M. P. Möller Organ Co. in 1955. It is a three-manual, 30-rank pipe organ.

The members of Hyde Park Union Church today come from the neighboring community and from the University of Chicago, but their affiliated membership is spread across the country.

Ebenezer Lutheran Church
1904-12
1650 West Foster Avenue
(5200 North)

Architect: Andrew E. Norman
Style: Gothic
Seating: 700

This church was built as a link with the homeland and with the religious heritage of the Swedish people who settled in Andersonville.

When the Swedish immigrants were moving into the Andersonville neighborhood around the turn of the century, they wanted their church to be a link with Sweden, a reminder of where they had come from. The Ebenezer Lutheran Church was built accordingly. The high flight of steps up to the door, the hand-carved wooden altar, the beautifully carved pulpit, communion rail, and baptismal font, together with the simple Gothic lines of the church were all in the tradition of the Swedish *Kirke.*

Ebenezer is a biblical term which literally means "stone of help." It commemorates God's assistance to his people.

The south and west sides of Ebenezer are faced with rusticated limestone; the east and north sides are brick. The church is cruciform. Its silver spire on the west tower rises high above Foster Avenue. A second smaller spire on the east front of the church complements the taller one. Both of these spires were repaired at a cost of over $100,000 in 1977. The original slate shingles, which were falling off, were replaced with a lead-coated copper covering.

The main doors of the church are framed in a stone Gothic arch complete with crockets. A Gothic-arched stained glass window above the front doors lights the balcony area.

The red-carpeted interior with the carved wooden pews and altar furniture gives this church a warm, reverent feeling. Ebenezer has a fine three-manual, Möller pipe

organ with 40 ranks which was installed in 1963. It accompanies several choirs. This church has a reputation for fine sacred music.

Ebenezer Lutheran Church was founded in 1892 and held its early services in a rented store on Summerdale Avenue near Ashland. The construction of the present church was delayed and prolonged due to shortage of funds. Though the auditorium was closed in and used for services as early as 1908, the final dedication only took place in 1912.

Although Ebenezer began as a strictly Swedish-American congregation, over the years English gradually replaced Swedish in the worship and teaching programs. The membership and ministry of this church have changed with the community. Today more than twenty-five nationalities make up the congregation.

St. Bridget Church
1905-6
2940 South Archer Avenue
(1500 West)

Architects: Egan & Prindeville
Style: Romanesque-Lombard
Seating: 1,200

St. Bridget's, the first Catholic parish in Bridgeport, has a distinctive Lombard-Romanesque style of architecture.

St. Bridget's on Archer Avenue, founded in 1850 from St. Patrick's on Desplaines Street, was the first parish in Bridgeport. It was established to serve the Irish Catholics who worked on the construction of the Illinois and Michigan Canal.

The Romanesque style of the present church derives from the district of Lombardy in northern Italy. It was here that the Romanesque style originated; it later spread through southern France, Spain, and Germany.

In a booklet marking the 100th anniversary of St. Bridget's parish in 1950, the author wrote, "To our knowledge, it [St. Bridget's Church] was the first and only specimen of this architectural design on this continent. The style was originated by the Irish monks who migrated to Europe and into Italy where they built the first church of its kind in Navarro [sic] in 1170 . . ."

St. Bridget's is constructed of Chicago common brick with a light brown pressed brick facade and limestone trim. A flight of steps leads up to the three-portal entrance on Archer Avenue. Each doorway is flanked by stone columns and decorated with a broad round arch. Above the entrances is a large, round-headed stained glass window flanked by two smaller ones. The Archer Avenue facade is visually organized under a broad gable trimmed with limestone and topped with a Celtic cross. At the southwest corner of the building is a handsome square tower relieved with windows and Romanesque arcading.

The interior of St. Bridget's is rectangular. Its nave is covered with a barrel vault that reaches from the choir balcony in the rear to the communion arch in front.

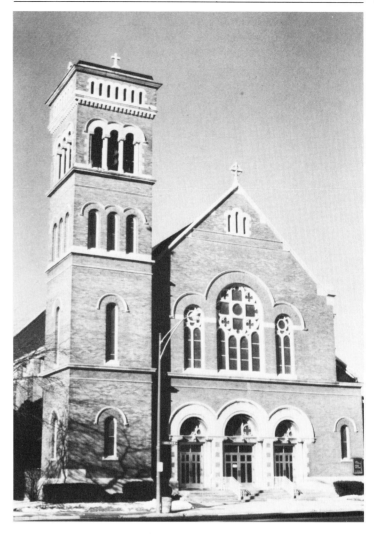

There are six stained glass windows on each side of the nave. These were made by the Munich Studio of Chicago and depict scenes from the life of Christ. The organ in St. Bridget's is a two-manual pipe organ made by Nicholas Doerr of Chicago.

Plaster ornament on the communion arch and on the borders around the inside of the church is richly detailed. The sanctuary was tastefully remodeled, the interior was redecorated, and new altars were installed by Rev. Walter Chelminski who was pastor of St. Bridget's from 1953 to 1975.

In 1963 St. Bridget's was faced with possible destruction when the construction of the Stevenson Expressway threatened to cut several feet off the church building. But the city fathers were persuaded to reroute the expressway and it now passes less than five feet north of the church.

The late mayor Richard J. Daley was married in St. Bridget's Church.

Formerly an Irish parish, St. Bridget today serves people of Polish, Irish, German, and Mexican descent who live in the northern part of Bridgeport.

Holy Trinity Church
1905-6
1120 North Noble Street
(1400 West)

Architects: Olszewski
of Washington, D.C. and
William Krieg of Chicago
Style: Renaissance and
Baroque
Seating: 1,350

**A splendid example of
Renaissance architecture with
baroque ornament.**

Just south of Division Street
on the west side of the
expressway, the Kennedy
motorist sees the imposing
facade of Holy Trinity Church.
Four Corinthian columns
support an entablature and
pediment forming the central
portico. Three pairs of huge
wooden doors with windows
above form the main entrance
to the church. These doors are
flanked by two more with
round segmented arches. All
five doorways stand at the top
of a broad flight of stone
stairs. Massive square towers
with Corinthian pilasters
stand on either side of the
portico. The windows in the
towers are richly framed with
pediments on the lower
windows and segmented
arches on those above. As
the towers rise toward the
copper-clad cupolas, the
stone ornament becomes
exuberantly baroque:
balustrades, urns, Corinthian
capitals, stone finials, and
above each cupola, a cross.
The open niche between the
towers is adorned with a
segmented arch, Corinthian
pilasters, scrolls, and
acroteria.

The interior decoration of
Holy Trinity is equally rich
and elaborate. The nave is
spacious, 200 by 125 feet, and
furnished with fine oak pews
throughout. Because the
three-part vaults of the ceiling
are iron, there are no interior
columns in the nave. The
whole ceiling is richly
decorated with paintings by
K. Markiewicz done in 1926.
The stained glass windows
were commissioned in 1940
and installed in 1955. Most
were designed by the Polish
artist, Irena Lorentowicz.

Holy Trinity parish was
founded in 1873 by the
St. Joseph Society of St.
Stanislaus Kostka Church and
it was originally staffed by the
Resurrection fathers. Disputes
and misunderstandings
caused the church to be
closed and reopened several
times until in 1893 Francis
Satolli, the Apostolic Delegate
to the United States, requested
the Holy Cross fathers of
Notre Dame, Indiana, to
appoint one of their Polish
priests as pastor of Holy
Trinity. Rev. Casimir
Sztuczko, C.S.C., came and
continued as pastor until his
death in 1949. Under his
leadership, the parish
established a grade school and
a high school.

Care of the parish returned to
the Resurrection fathers in
1975. The elementary school
closed in 1974. The high
school remains under the
direction of the Holy Cross
brothers. Over the years Holy
Trinity Church has been the
center of many Polish-
American activities.

Services at Holy Trinity are
held in Polish and English.
There is a lower church as
well as the upper church.
Though there is a diminishing
number of local parishioners,
people come back to Holy
Trinity from all over the
Chicago area.

St. John Berchmans Church
1906-7
2519 West Logan Boulevard
(2600 North)

Architect: J. G. Steinbach
Style: Spanish Romanesque
Seating: 700

Built to serve Belgian Catholics in Chicago, this church and parish plant present an impressive facade along Logan Boulevard.

The southbound motorist on the Kennedy Expressway sees the impressive yellow brick complex of St. John Berchmans parish just off to the west at Logan Boulevard.

St. John Berchmans was a seventeenth century Belgian Jesuit. This parish was founded in 1905 to serve Belgian Catholics in Chicago. The first pastor was a Belgian Jesuit priest from St. Ignatius College on Twelfth Street. Dedication services for the church were held in Flemish, French, and English.

The sturdy, yellow brick church at the corner of Logan and Maplewood has a rusticated limestone base and cut limestone trim. It measured 116 by 56 feet originally, but an addition was built onto the south end in 1949 to increase the seating capacity.

A broad flight of steps leads up to the three double doors of the main entrance. Round cut stone arches decorate all of the doorways and window openings of the church. A large rose window is centered on the Logan Boulevard facade and the roof line is decorated with brick corbelling and copper flashing.

St. John's has a cruciform plan, but the transepts are very shallow. The nave has a simple barrel vault.

But the outstanding feature of St. John's are the opalescent stained glass windows installed in 1921 by the Kinsella Co. of Chicago. Each window is a mosaic tableau of biblical figures and Christian saints. The Deluge in the east transept and the Blessed Sacrament window in the west transept are especially fine. The scenes are staged in lovely landscapes and

brilliant sky perspectives. There is a minimum of paint on these windows. All the delicate hues and shades were obtained by mixing opal with the sand and other materials in making the glass. John Kinsella selected the window themes in 1914. He died a few years later and the east transept window was donated in his memory. The work on the windows was completed under the direction of Robert Giles.

By the late 1920s, St. John Berchmans had ceased to be a Belgian parish. Polish Americans joined the parish and remained in the majority until the 1960s. Today the parish and the neighborhood are predominantly Spanish-speaking. St. John Berchmans has a full schedule of weekend masses, operates a grade school, and sponsors many community service organizations.

St. Michael Church
1907-9
83rd Street and South Shore Drive   (3100 East)

Architect: William J. Brinkman
Style: Gothic
Seating: 1,500

This noble Gothic edifice stands as a witness to the faith and pride of the Polish Catholics who built it.

St. Michael's is the largest parish in the South Chicago community and its great Gothic church raises its steeple 250 feet above steel mills, parks, and residential neighborhoods. The parish was founded in 1892 as a national parish to serve Polish Catholics who lived in the "Bush." One of its early pastors, Rev. Paul Rhode, who built the church, was made the first Polish bishop in the United States in 1908. The parish is staffed by Chicago diocesan priests.

St. Michael's Church is a masonry building constructed of brown brick with limestone trim. Cornices, corbel tables, and other ornamental features are done in beige brick. The building is cruciform in plan with very large Gothic-arched stained glass windows in the transepts and above the entrance on the south facade. These windows and others throughout the church were designed and executed by F. X. Zettler of Munich, Germany. The east transept window showing Mary with the apostles in the upper room at Pentecost is especially fine.

The wood carving of the communion rail and the reredos behind the altar is exceptional, as well as that on the shrine of Our Lady of Czestochowa. St. Michael's has a three-manual, 37-rank Möller pipe organ which has been renovated several times since its installation in 1908.

The ethnic composition of this parish has expanded in the past fifteen years to include Spanish-speaking families. More than 250 Mexican families reside in the parish; and the school, conducted by the Sisters of Nazareth, is about 60 percent Mexican. St. Michael's sponsors a Polish language school as well as English classes for the Spanish speaking.

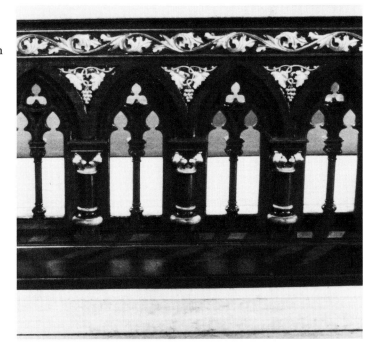

115

Unity Temple
The Unitarian Universalist
Church in Oak Park   1906-9
875 Lake Street at Kenilworth

Architect: Frank Lloyd Wright
　　National Register of
　　Historic Places, 1970
Style: Prairie
Seating: 400

Frank Lloyd Wright's landmark church, a "noble room," combining the architect's genius for design with the first use of reinforced concrete for a public building.

A church with no tower, no steeple, no nave? "Let us abolish in the art and craft of architecture," wrote Frank Lloyd Wright," . . . any symbolic form whatsoever." Wright had been a member of Unity Church for twelve years. He was one of eight architects considered for this commission. He explained in his autobiography, "I told the [building] committee a story. Did they not know the tale of the holy man who, yearning to see God, climbed up and up the highest mountain — climbed to the highest relic of a tree there was on the mountain? There, ragged and worn, he lifted up his eager perspiring face to heaven and called upon God. He heard a voice bidding him get down . . . go back . . . go down there

in the valley below where his people were — there only could *he* look upon God's countenance. . . .

"Why not, then, build a temple, not to God in that way . . . but build a temple to man, appropriate to his uses as a meeting-place, in which to study man himself for God's sake? . . .

"The first idea was to keep a noble room for worship in mind, and let that sense of the great room shape the whole edifice." (*An Autobiography*, Horizon Press, 1977, p. 178)

In a way, form follows theology.

The "noble room" is a cube at the north end of a narrow site. Its interior plan has the congregation sitting at three different levels on three sides of the speaker. The pulpit is set well into the middle of the space so that no worshiper is more than 45 feet from the pulpit. The room is lighted from above. High windows on four sides and skylights in the ceiling feature some of Wright's finest abstract glass designs. The interior rectilinear design is accentuated by dark strips of hardwood molding. The plaster surfaces are painted with warm, earth-tone colors, reddish browns, soft greens, and yellows. The acoustics of the space are excellent and have been praised by speakers and musicians alike.

in the concrete. In recent years the exterior of the temple has been almost completely resurfaced. The surface had broken away in many places as reinforcing rods, not set deeply enough in the concrete, had rusted.

The design of Unity Temple is a masterpiece of complexly interlocking rectilinear solids. The ornamental concrete work in the exterior piers is repeated on each of six facades. The same wooden molds were reused for each series of piers. The ornament on the piers was designed to coordinate the huge concrete masses with the delicate window treatment.

In 1907, before the church was completed an Oak Park newspaper, the *Oak Leaves*, predicted that, "Unity Church will in the future be regarded as a pioneer in the creation of an American order of architecture whose governing motive shall be not what forms have been used in the past but what ones are suited to present conditions." (Cited by Thomas A. Chulak, *A People Moving Thru Time*, published by The Unitarian Universalist Church in Oak Park, 1979, p. 27)

The doors to the "noble room" flank the pulpit on each side so that the congregation, when they get up to leave, will move toward the minister on their way out.

Unity Temple is actually two spaces, the church and the parish house. They are connected by a low link that serves as the entranceway to both. The building is a monolithic reinforced concrete structure, the first public building in the United States built with poured concrete. The exterior of the building was softened and given a sort of stucco appearance by being scrubbed down after the wooden forms were removed. The scrubbing exposed the pebble aggregate

Unity Temple has been designated by the American Institute of Architects as one of seventeen buildings designed by Frank Lloyd Wright to be retained as an example of his architectural contribution to American culture. The Unitarian Universalist congregation has made great efforts in recent years to restore the church to the excellent condition it is in today.

Greater Holy Temple,
Church of God in Christ
1908-9
5701 West Midway Park
(500 North)

Architect: William E.
Drummond
  Chicago Landmark, 1961
  National Register of
  Historic Places, 1977
Style: Prairie
Seating: 350

**This landmark church, built for
the First Congregational Church
of Austin, is an excellent example
of Prairie School architecture.**

William E. Drummond served
as Frank Lloyd Wright's head
draftsman from 1899 to 1909.
His design of this church is
clearly related to Wright's
Unity Temple, but it is
original and in itself an
excellent example of Prairie
School architecture.

This church is rectangular
in plan. In fact, the genius
of the design is in the simple
composition of rectangular
forms. It is rectilinear
throughout. A strong vertical
emphasis comes from the
window piers, the stairwell
pylons, and the height of
the nave. The horizontal
emphasis comes from the
stone courses, the Roman
brick, and the lower side
aisles. The vertical and

horizontal themes are
interlocked.

The building is constructed
of buff-colored Roman
brick with stone trim. It is
two stories high with the
sanctuary above and a
meeting room below.

The entrance to the church is
recessed at street level and
flanked by two massive brick
piers topped by large planters.
Inside to right and left,
stairwells with skylights
ascend to the sanctuary area
which again features crisp,
clean rectilinear design. The
walls are buff-colored; and the
nave, like Unity Temple, is
lighted by a large leaded glass
skylight. There are windows
along the side aisles too.

The skylight is dramatically
framed by a dark-stained
oak trim which measures
8½-by-8½ inches. All the
windows in the narthex and
sanctuary are multi-colored,
geometrically designed,
leaded glass units. There is an
openness and cleanness
about this church which is
very attractive.

Drummond designed this
building for the First
Congregational Church of
Austin. It was sold in 1926 to
the Seventh Day Adventists;
in 1958 to the Eastern Rite
Catholics who called it Our
Lady of Lebanon Church; and
in 1973 it was sold to the
Greater Holy Temple,
Church of God in Christ.

**The Annunciation Cathedral
1910
1017 North LaSalle Drive
(150 West)**

Architect: N. Dokas
Style: Renaissance-Byzantine
Seating: 350

Similar in design to the cathedral
in Athens, Greece, this church
was built by the original Greek
Orthodox congregation in
Chicago.

Annunciation Cathedral was built by the original Greek Orthodox congregation in Chicago. The community was organized in 1892 by people who had come from Sparta in Greece. They met for about a year in a rented hall at Randolph and Union, in the market area where most of the Greeks were employed. Their first priest was named Phiambolis and their first liturgy was held on March 19, 1893. Subsequently the community rented a Masonic temple at Clark and Kinzie streets for five years. But internal rivalry caused the congregation to disband a few years later. It reorganized some time later, however, and erected in 1910 the church we see today on LaSalle Drive.

The Annunciation, modeled after the cathedral church in Athens, Greece, is constructed of common brick with a yellow face brick facade and limestone trim. The building has a rectangular plan with a high dome rising over the middle of the auditorium. Square brick towers flank the broad steps which lead up to the front doors of the church. Above the main entrance on the central facade is a large stained glass window, illuminated at night, which portrays the Annunciation to Mary by the angel Gabriel that she would be the mother of Christ.

In 1930 this building was lifted off its foundations and moved back on the lot for the widening of LaSalle Street.

The interior of Annunciation Cathedral is like a basilica in plan. Two rows of columns with richly gilded Corinthian capitals divide the area into three aisles. There is a half dome apse housing the altar and sanctuary at the east end of the auditorium; there is a narthex at the west end. The center aisle is spanned by a barrel vault; the side aisles by smaller round arches and vaulting. A beautiful wooden *iconostasis* with Renaissance detailing divides the sanctuary from the auditorium.

Daylight filters into the cathedral through opalescent stained glass windows which were installed in 1938. Many of the windows picture saints of the Eastern church. The dome of Annunciation Cathedral has recently been decorated with authentic Byzantine iconography by Stathis Trahanatzis.

St. Basil Greek Orthodox Church 1910
733 South Ashland Avenue (1600 West)

Architect: Alexander L. Levy
Style: Greek Revival
Seating: 1,500

The beautiful Greek Revival building at the corner of Polk and Ashland was the Anshe Sholom synagogue from 1910 to 1927.

A faint outline of Hebrew characters can still be seen on the entablature under the central pediment. Inside, metal nameplates on the beautiful wooden pews carry such names as Cohen, Bernstin, and Rabinowitz. And the pew ends themselves are decorated with carved replicas of the tablets of the law. These are the reminders that the monumental building on the northeast corner of Polk and Ashland was once a synagogue. It was Anshe Sholom and from the time it was built until 1927 it housed the intelligentsia of West Side Orthodox Jewry. In 1927 a division of the Holy Trinity Greek Orthodox community on Peoria Street purchased the building and has worshiped there ever since.

This building is of masonry construction on a steel frame with limestone facing on the south and west elevations. A broad flight of steps leads up from Ashland Avenue through the magnificent four-columned portico to the three doorways of the main entrance. The three windows above these doors contain the only remaining stained glass windows from the synagogue. The rest were sold in 1972. The central facade is crowned with a pediment and flanked by windows with smaller pediments at the main floor level. Pilasters with Corinthian capitals stand at the corners of the building. A dentil cornice adds to the decoration of this fine classical structure.

But the most prominent architectural feature of this church is the hemispherical dome over the center of the building which is supported

by an octagonal drum with open arches and fine Ionic columns.

Inside the church, the dome is decorated with a painting of the *Pantocrator*, God the Creator of all things. A large balcony with a beautiful gilded railing runs around the north, south, and west sides of the auditorium. The life-size figures on the icon screen at the front of the sanctuary have a distinctly Western appearance because the painter, Philemon Savatis, came from the Western-influenced island of Korfu. The smaller icons, however, painted by the Ioasophaion Brothers from Mount Oros in Greece in 1930 have an Eastern appearance.

A small area behind the icon screen was damaged by a fire in 1979 and was later repaired.

The people of the St. Basil Greek Orthodox congregation come from all over the Chicagoland area to worship here with the Rev. Spyridon Kavvadias, the pastor. The building is maintained in good condition.

Mt. Pisgah Missionary Baptist Church   1910-12
4600 S. Martin Luther King Drive   (400 East)

Architect: Alfred S. Alschuler
Style: Italian Renaissance
Seating: 2,500

The Italian Renaissance design of this former Sinai Temple set the trend for synagogue architecture for more than a decade.

Alfred Alschuler, a young Jewish architect, had graduated from Armour Institute in 1899, worked for a year in the office of Dankmar Adler, entered a partnership with Samuel Treat for four years, and in 1904 began his own practice. In 1909 he entered a competition for the design of the new Sinai Temple. He won the competition and received the commission. He then completed the design for the classically inspired temple on 46th and Grand Boulevard which would have a profound influence on synagogue design for the next decade or more, until the trend turned toward the Byzantine style in the 1920s.

The building itself is a large edifice faced with Bedford stone. The "free and simple" outlines of the structure expressed the "broad religious views of the [Jewish] congregation," wrote the architect. The building is rectangular in plan with a classical portico on the King Drive facade. The overall plan of this church is

unusual. Because of the shallowness of the lot, the primary east-west axis of the building is also the shorter axis. Amphitheater seating in the auditorium has individual seats which all face the pulpit platform on the west side of the room. A balcony runs around the north, east, and south sides of the auditorium. A skylight in the ceiling once allowed daylight into the sanctuary. But this is covered over now.

The Chicago Sinai Congregation, Chicago's first reform synagogue, was organized in 1861. After several locations in the downtown area and on the Near South Side, Sinai moved to 46th and Grand Boulevard in 1912. Within a decade, however, this neighborhood began to undergo racial change; the Jews moved away, and in 1944 the temple was sold.

Corpus Christi parish, three blocks south on Grand Boulevard, purchased the Sinai Temple and its adjoining community center and

opened Corpus Christi High School there in 1945. The school continued in operation until 1962 when Hales Franciscan High School opened at 49th and Cottage Grove Avenue.

Mt. Pisgah Missionary Baptist Church, organized in 1929 by the late Rev. G. W. Alexander, purchased the auditorium and the community center in 1962. This church, under the direction of Rev. Joseph Wells since 1941, has a large, active congregation. Between 1,500 and 2,000 persons attend services every Sunday. Outreach programs in the community center serve many more people in the neighborhood.

Since 1950 the Chicago Sinai Congregation has worshiped in a fine new temple at 54th Street and South Shore Drive. This temple, somewhat in the International style, was designed by the firm of Friedman, Alschuler (Alfred Jr.) and Sincere.

**Anshe Emet Synagogue
1910-11
3760 N. Pine Grove Avenue
(700 West)**

Architect: Alfred S. Alschuler
Style: Georgian
Seating: 1,169

This Georgian style synagogue designed by Alfred Alschuler contains brilliant stained glass windows portraying ancient and modern Jewish themes.

The handsome Georgian style synagogue on the southwest corner of Grace Street and Pine Grove Avenue was erected by the North Chicago Hebrew Congregation, the legal name for Temple Sholom, in 1910-11. Alfred Alschuler's design for this synagogue was a refinement and modification of his design for the Sinai Temple on South Grand Boulevard which he had just completed. (See page 124.) Compare the massing of forms in these two structures. The advanced, colonnaded, unpedimented portico is distinctive of Alschuler's design.

Anshe Emet was founded on Chicago's West Side in 1873. Their first house of worship, designed by Frederick Ahlschlager, was built in 1893 at 1363 North Sedgwick. From 1922 to 1928 the congregation occupied a new synagogue at 627-33 Gary Place, now Patterson Avenue, near Broadway. In 1928 they purchased the synagogue at Grace and Pine Grove when Temple Sholom moved to their new temple on Lake Shore Drive.

The Anshe Emet synagogue is rectangular in plan, is faced with red brick, and has stone trim. The three main doors on Pine Grove are sheltered by a four-column portico with an inscribed entablature and a balustrade above. Set back from this is a large stained glass window, a star of David on a stone disk, and then the gable of the roof.

The interior of the main sanctuary has amphitheater seating which faces the bema at the west end of the room. The ark is situated in the center of a beautiful wooden reredos with a broken pediment and a star of David at the top. The auditorium has a balcony at the east end.

The auditorium is lighted by seven large stained glass windows designed by Todras Geller and A. Raymond Katz. These windows portray great moments in Jewish history as well as the goals for which American Jews are striving. The windows were executed by Drehobl Brothers of Chicago and installed in 1935.

In the Hall of Memories adjoining the auditorium are twelve brilliant stained glass windows, each 5 feet by 8 feet, representing the Twelve Tribes of Israel. They were designed by Archie Rand and dedicated on April 12, 1981.

Anshe Emet, which means "Men of Truth," is a large, prominent Conservative Jewish congregation under the direction of Rabbi Seymour J. Cohen since 1961. Anshe Emet operates a day school, a large Hebrew school, and an extensive program of social, religious, and educational activities. They have built a modern and efficient complex of buildings to serve their many community activities.

St. Mel—Holy Ghost Church
1910-11
4301 West Washington
Boulevard   (100 North)

Architect: Charles L. Wallace
Style: Romanesque
Seating: about 1,000

Once one of the great Irish parishes of the city, St. Mel's today serves the black community on the West Side.

The monumental Indiana limestone edifice on the southwest corner of Kildare and Washington once housed one of the largest Irish Catholic congregations in the city. On a Sunday morning through the 1930s, 1940s, and early 1950s, there would be six masses in the upper church, six in the large basement chapel, and another six in the Holy Ghost chapel several blocks away. Holy Ghost, originally a German parish founded in 1896, was incorporated into St. Mel's in 1941. St. Mel's was founded in 1878.

The auditorium of the church is broad and spacious; there are no interior pillars, and the floor slopes, as in a theater, toward the sanctuary in front. The church is cruciform in plan. The apse contains a large Carrara marble altar and reredos and five baroque-style stained glass windows. These windows present scenes of sacrifice from the Old and New Testaments.

There are large rose windows above the choir and in each of the transepts. Smaller windows in the transepts picture the twelve apostles. The nave windows portray scenes from the life of Christ. All the beautiful windows in the church are in the German baroque style and were made by F. X. Zettler of Munich.

St. Mel's Church has a three-manual Kilgen pipe organ which is now being renovated. The acoustics in the church are excellent.

At the clerestory level there are large pictures painted with oil on canvas and fixed to the walls. These present the Doctors of the Church—Basil, Gregory, Augustine, Albert, Aquinas, Alphonsus, and Francis de Sales. These pictures epitomize the teaching function of the parish which once supported two grade schools and a high school. St. Mel-Holy Ghost is now a black parish and it operates an excellent grade school for the children of the neighborhood.

Holy Innocents Church
1911-12
735 North Armour Street
(1500 West)

Architects: Worthmann and
Steinbach
   Restoration, 1962-63,
   George S. Smith
Style: Spanish Romanesque
with Byzantine elements
Seating: 1,200

Behind the Spanish Renaissance facade, a spacious sanctuary with a splendid dome above the crossing of the nave and transepts.

It is the large green tile dome of Holy Innocents with six smaller domes around it that the northwest-bound motorist sees straight ahead from the Ontario feeder ramp to the Kennedy Expressway. Holy Innocents is a large brown brick building with limestone trim. It is 183 feet long and 70 feet wide at the entrance. The church is cruciform in plan and has many large art glass windows imported from Austria.

This parish was founded in 1905 to serve the growing number of Polish Catholic families who were settling in the area around Armour and Superior Streets. The parish complex includes the church, two school buildings, a rectory, and a convent.

A fire in May, 1962, caused extensive damage to the interior of the church. It took almost a year to restore and improve the building. Mural paintings were replaced, a new Byzantine-style marble altar with mosaic ornament was installed, and not long afterwards a large, 10-by-13-foot mosaic of Our Lady of Czestochowa was put up in the north transept shrine.

Holy Innocents was founded as a national parish, but it became a territorial parish in 1975 when nearby St. Columbkille was closed. Today the neighborhood is predominantly Latino. While the parish serves everyone, its membership is still mostly Polish. Some Polish people have remained, many former parishioners return to worship here every week, and there are recent Polish immigrants too. Services are held in English Polish, and Spanish. Holy Innocents is staffed by the Chicago diocesan clergy and the Felician Sisters operate the school. The parish has many organizations and is actively involved in neighborhood development.

St. Andrew Church
1912-13
3550 North Paulina Street
(1700 West)

Architects: Egan & Prindeville
    Renovation, 1931-32,
    Joe W. McCarthy
Style: North Italian
Renaissance
Seating: 1,100

Erected in the North Italian Renaissance style, this church was almost doubled in length in the early 1930s.

St. Andrew's was for many years, 1935 to 1966, the parish of Bishop Bernard J. Sheil, founder of the CYO, the Catholic Youth Organization.

The large, reddish brown brick church with stone trim on the southwest corner of Addison and Paulina was erected in 1912-13. But the parish grew so dramatically in the 1920s that the pastor commissioned Joe W. McCarthy to enlarge the church. It was extended westward, almost doubled in length, and a new main altar and marble reredos were installed. The crucifix is amber marble. The huge altar edifice was imported from Italy. The church as its stands today is 150 feet long, longitudinal in plan, with the apse at the west end. The interior of the church is bright and well illuminated by large stained glass windows on both sides of the nave. The interior walls are painted with light, pastel colors.

St. Andrew's faces Paulina Street. Its two-portal entranceway is flanked by heroic stone statues of saints Peter, Andrew, and Paul. Each is on a pedestal and sheltered by a stone canopy. Above the doors is a large rose window, and the central facade is flanked by twin towers with ornamental stone balconies and Italianate brackets under the eaves at the top.

The whole complex, church, school, gym, rectory, and convent are in excellent physical condition.

Though the parish was begun in 1894 to serve English-speaking Catholics who did not wish to attend the German-speaking St. Alphonsus Church, St. Andrew's today consists of an ethnically mixed congregation of Irish, German, Filipino, Italian, and Spanish-speaking people.

SS. Cyril and Methodius Church   1912-13
5001 S. Hermitage Avenue
(1734 West)

Architect: Joseph Molitor
Style: Renaissance
Seating: 600

Built by Bohemian Catholics in the Back of the Yards neighborhood, this church possesses a treasure of stained glass windows.

Max Guler was trained as a china painter in Munich, Germany, before coming to the United States in 1896. With Dennis Shanahan and L. Holzchuh he founded the Munich Studio in Chicago in 1903 and produced European-style stained glass windows of very high quality. Fifteen of these windows are in SS. Cyril and Methodius Church in an old Bohemian section of the Back of the Yards neighborhood. Guler used antique or hand-blown colored glass imported from France and Germany. Facial expressions, patterns on garments, floral designs, and other ornamental details were painted on the glass with iron oxide or yellow stain. The glass was then fired again and finally assembled.

The windows in SS. Cyril and Methodius are German-baroque in style. There is a lavish richness of ornament: scrolls, columns, capitals, and foliage. There is an infinite attention to detail evident in the windows and a brilliance of color. The eight windows in the nave are each 8 by 18 feet with a lunette featuring a praying angel above each. The subjects of these large windows are biblical and Bohemian.

SS. Cyril and Methodius were brothers who came from Macedonia and brought the Christian faith to the Slavic people in the ninth century. They are pictured doing this in a window above the altar on the east wall of the apse. The faith is symbolized by the model church which the brothers are carrying.

The Greek columns on the facade of the church are also a tribute to and a remembrance of the origins of Cyril and Methodius. The beige face brick on the outside of the church is very nicely articulated with the limestone trim. The tile roof of the church and the copper gutters and downspouts date from the original construction in 1913. The tall, free-standing campanile with its balconies, Palladian windows, and steeply rising roof is a masterpiece of Italian Renaissance design.

In response to the liturgical reforms of the Second Vatican Council, the interior of SS. Cyril and Methodius was renovated and simplified between 1965 and 1971. Much of the work was done by the parishioners themselves. The neutral tan walls and the absence of multiple altars and statues serve to focus attention on the new altar and the figure of the Risen Christ above it. The simplicity of the interior also serves to highlight the beauty of the stained glass windows.

The original parishioners of SS. Cyril and Methodius were Bohemian immigrants who worked for the most part in the Union Stock Yards to the east of the parish. The neighborhood of small, single-family houses dominated by the graceful bell tower of the church looks much the same today as it did when the parish was founded in 1891. There are still a few Bohemian families in the neighborhood and more who return here for church. But most of the area is now inhabited by Spanish-speaking people.

St. Adalbert Church
1912-14
1656 West 17th Street

Architect: Henry J. Schlacks
Style: Roman Basilica
Seating: 1,900

This magnificent, basilica-style church was modeled after St. Paul's Outside the Walls in Rome.

The twin 185-foot towers of St. Adalbert's dominate the skyline of the Lower West Side. Here in the old Pilsen neighborhood is a church built in the basilica style, the earliest style of Christian architecture.

The word *basilica*, as an architectural term, derives from the Greek word *basileus*, meaning king or ruler. It was in a building like this that ancient rulers held court. In Roman times the basilica served as a court of law with the judge presiding from the apse. The building is typically longitudinal in plan with a narthex at one end, an apse at the other. Columns run the length of the nave on both sides supporting a clerestory with windows. The ceiling of a basilica is flat; it was originally constructed of wood. In later times the ceiling panels came to be beautifully decorated as they are in St. Adalbert's.

The design of St. Adalbert's is similar to that of St. Paul Outside the Walls, one of the four major basilicas in Rome.

St. Paul's was built by Emperor Theodosius in 380 A.D. and restored in 1821. St. Adalbert's, however, is larger being 195 feet long, 113 feet wide, and 110 feet high.

St. Adalbert's is constructed of buff-colored face brick with terra cotta trim and tracery. Between the bell towers on the front of the church stands a magnificent granite-columned portico, and above it is a beautiful rose window.

The mural paintings on the north wall of the church show great events in the faith history of Poland: on the west side, the wedding of Queen Jadwiga of Poland and Prince Jagiello of Lithuania and on the east side, the victory of Our Lady of Częstochowa. The stained glass windows by F. X. Zettler of the Royal Bavarian Art Institute, Munich, show St. Adalbert, bishop and martyr, in the transepts and the patron saints of Poland around the nave. The church has a four-manual, 40-rank Austin organ.

St. Adalbert's, founded in 1874 and staffed by diocesan priests, is the third oldest Polish Catholic parish in Chicago and the mother church of the Polish parishes on the West and South sides of the city. Its school was once attended by 2,700 children. Numerous Polish organizations originated in St. Adalbert's.

The Pilsen neighborhood, though originally Bohemian, is mostly Latin now. It is home to thousands of Mexican and Mexican Americans. In St. Adalbert's, Our Lady of Guadalupe is enshrined just opposite Our Lady of Częstochowa. Services are held in Spanish, English, and Polish.

Inside St. Adalbert's is some of the finest ecclesiastical marble work in Chicago. The high altar was fashioned from 35 tons of Carrara marble and has a marble dome or baldachino supported by ten spiral-fluted columns. The marble pulpit on the west side of the church contains figures of the four evangelists and six prophets of the Old Testament. In the shallow east transept stands a full-size replica of Michelangelo's *Pieta*.

Fourth Presbyterian Church
1912-14
876 North Michigan Avenue
(100 East)

Architect: Ralph Adams Cram
National Register of
Historic Places, 1975
Style: Gothic Revival
Seating: 1,400

A splendid example of English Perpendicular Gothic, designed by Ralph Adams Cram, a leader of the Gothic Revival in America.

Ralph Adams Cram was one of the leaders of the Gothic Revival of Church architecture in America. He believed that Gothic church design never died, and he demonstrated his belief in the design of the Fourth Presbyterian Church on North Michigan Avenue. The Bedford limestone building is stately, dignified, and reverent. It is also the center of a whole complex of religious, social, educational, and community services.

"The John Hancock Building is across the street from us" is how Fourth Church people describe their location; and the Gothic spire stands for human and divine values over against the skyscrapers all around it. Beneath the spire, the arches, the tracery, and the pinnacles, just beneath the beautifully carved tympanum over the front doors, are the words, "The Master is here and calleth for thee." The church is usually open; the welcome is genuine. Fourth Church attracts the affluent and the needy, the young and the old, singles, couples, and families.

Inside, the nave extends 130 feet, east to west, is 50 feet wide, and rises 77 feet to the roof ridge. The sanctuary appears high and narrow, in accord with the Gothic ideal, and is dominated by the great chancel arch. This arch frames three stained glass windows by Connick of Boston, the central window showing the Resurrected Christ with arms outstretched and the inscription, "And I, if I be lifted up, will draw all men to me."

On the left side of the chancel is a beautifully carved organ case with gleaming pipes. For 56 years the case enclosed a four-manual, 59-rank E. M. Skinner organ. This was replaced for the church's centennial year in 1971 with a 125-rank, 6,574-pipe Aeolian-Skinner organ. The solid state, four-manual console controls seven divisions of the organ, five in the chancel and two above the east window. Fourth Church has a national reputation for sacred music.

The windows in Fourth Presbyterian Church were designed and executed by Charles J. Connick of Boston. The handsome timbered ceiling, the polychrome ceiling designs, and the wooden statuary were designed by Frederic C. Bartlett of Chicago.

Just to the south of the sanctuary in the west wing of the complex is the Blair Chapel, designed in the thirteenth century Gothic style by J. J. Sherer of Milwaukee and dedicated in 1971. The stained glass in the chapel, except for Connick's on the west wall, is by Erhardt Stoettner of the T. C. Esser Co. of Milwaukee. The paneling, beams, and furniture are hand-carved native white oak. This chapel seats 150 people and is frequently used for worship and ceremonial occasions.

Fourth Presbyterian has a series of buildings surrounding a garth. Ralph Adams Cram designed the church itself, but Howard Van Doren Shaw designed the cloister (1914), manse, parish house (1925), and the Blair

Chapel building. Shaw also created and donated the fountain which stands in the middle of the garth. Shaw's work is more in the English Romantic style providing a less formal atmosphere for the buildings used for the everyday activities of the congregation.

Our Lady of Mt. Carmel Church 1913-14
700 West Belmont Avenue (3200 North)

Architects: Egan & Prindeville
Style: English Gothic
Seating: 900

A stately example of English Gothic architecture, the mother church of Catholic parishes on the North Shore.

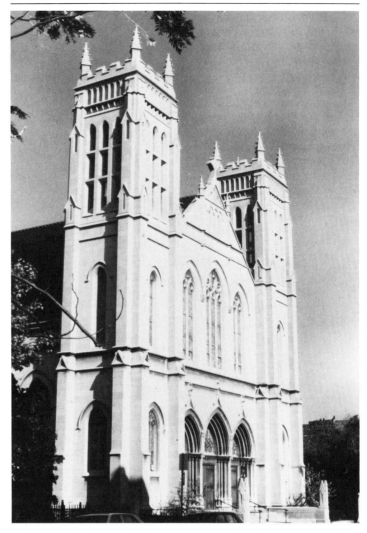

When Rev. Patrick O'Brien founded Our Lady of Mount Carmel parish in 1886, Lake View was hardly more than a wilderness. But an English-speaking parish was needed between St. Vincent's on Webster Avenue and Evanston. A modest-sized frame and stucco church was erected on Wellington Avenue at Wilton in 1886. This was Our Lady of Mount Carmel which, in Catholic circles, has been called the mother church of the North Shore.

The parish grew and flourished so that in 1912 it was divided and the territory west of Clark Street with the original church became St. Sebastian's. The territory east of Clark Street was designated for Mount Carmel parish.

At the same time, Rev. Patrick Gill, the second pastor of Our Lady of Mount Carmel, purchased property on the north side of Belmont at State Court (now Orchard Street) and there built the beautiful Indiana limestone church we see today. Inside the three huge oak doors, the church is spacious but warm and prayerful. It has a fine ribbed-vault ceiling and handsome dark ornamental woodwork. Five bays on each side of the nave contain large opalescent glass windows imported from Munich. The saints featured in the windows represent several nationalities; the founding members of this parish were mostly of Irish and German descent.

In the reredos behind the white marble altar are statues of the four evangelists; from left to right, Luke, Matthew, John, and Mark; and in the niches on the sides of the altar, saints Peter and Paul.

But looking up toward the back of the church, one sees the splendid window of St. Cecilia flanked by the lofty pipes of the 46-rank E. M. Skinner organ. This three-manual and pedal organ, with its 3,000 pipes, is a monumental work. Ernest Skinner himself came from Boston in 1929 to install it.

Our Lady of Mount Carmel is a church with quiet dignity, a reverent atmosphere, and a very active parish program. The Sisters of Mercy have conducted the school since 1888. The priests' house was built in 1923 and features a beautiful garden just to the east of the church.

Holy Cross Church
1913-15
1736 West 46th Street

Architect: Joseph Molitor
Style: Renaissance
Seating: 1,400

Rich in Lithuanian art and heritage, this massive church has over 2,000 small light bulbs decorating the structural outlines of the interior.

Approaching the Back of the Yards neighborhood on the Damen Avenue Overpass, the southbound motorist sees clearly off to the east the majestic twin towers of Holy Cross Lithuanian Church. (Only two blocks south and facing Holy Cross are the equally majestic towers of St. Joseph's Polish Church.)

Founded in 1904, this national parish was established to serve Lithuanian Catholic immigrants, most of whom worked in the Union Stock Yards nearby. The church is constructed of brown and beige face brick with limestone trim on a steel frame.

The Renaissance/Baroque facade of the church features a portico with eight tall Corinthian columns supporting a frieze and pediment. The frieze carries the Latin inscription which translates, "In the holy cross is the life of the world." The graffito art in the pediment shows the crucified Christ in the midst of traditional Lithuanian religious symbols. This art as well as decoration in the narthex, four large oil paintings inside, and the general interior decor of the church were done by the Lithuanian artist Adolph Valeska in the early 1950s.

Above the pediment on the facade of the church are three niches bearing figures of the worrying Christ, St. Isidore the farmer, and St. George — all prominent figures in the devotional life of Lithuanian Catholics. The two great towers are rich in balustrades, arches, finials, pilasters, ornamental copperwork, and cupolas.

The vast interior of Holy Cross is furnished with solid oak pews, artistic paintings, and a great number of statues. The stained glass windows, installed in 1943-44 by the Chicago firm of Arthur Michaudel, are especially bright and rich in color. There are large rose windows in each transept above the smaller windows featuring the twelve apostles and men and women saints of the church. Nave windows portray scenes from the life of Christ while windows below these feature additional saints.

The permanent altar, done in wood, is rich in ornament, gilding, and decoration. There are two choir lofts in Holy Cross and a huge pipe organ. The mosaic-like rubber tile flooring in the aisles was designed according to traditional Lithuanian patterns by the artist B. Jameikis.

Traveling up the ribs of the dome and sanctuary and running all around the interior of the church are electric light bulbs, 2,000 of them, one in every rosette.

In recent years the neighborhood around Holy Cross has become 80 to 90 percent Spanish-speaking. Some Lithuanians have remained, while others have moved away but return to celebrate the major feasts of the church year. Most of the services are conducted in English, some in Lithuanian.

**All Saints—St. Anthony
Church   1913-15
2849 South Wallace Street
(600 West)**

Architect: Henry J. Schlacks
Style: Romanesque
Seating: 800

**Built by German Catholics in
Bridgeport, this monumental
Romanesque church features
beautiful stained glass windows.**

This parish in the Bridgeport community is the result of a consolidation of two parishes, All Saints, an Irish parish which was located at 25th Place and Wallace, and St. Anthony of Padua, a German parish founded in 1873 and originally located at 24th Place and Canal. In 1913 the Western Indiana Railroad needed the property at 24th and Canal for its right-of-way and agreed, in exchange for the property, to build a new church, rectory, school, and convent for the parish at 28th Place and Wallace. All the buildings were designed by Henry Schlacks. St. Anthony's has the distinction of being one of the few Catholic churches in Chicago whose parish plant was entirely paid for from the beginning. No costs were spared in the construction. The best materials were used to build the solid brick and stone complex.

The church is basically Romanesque in design, cruciform in plan, and has two massive bell towers flanking the entrance. The bricks are laid with horizontal patterns giving the church a sturdy appearance. Corbel tables in stone decorate the gables of the nave and transepts. Round arches decorate the doors, windows, and the bell towers.

All Saints—St. Anthony has especially large and fine stained glass windows which were designed, executed, and installed by F. X. Zettler of Munich. This same firm

created the mosaic of the vision of St. Anthony of Padua which stands just above the entrance on Wallace Street.

Three large cast iron bells sound from the twin towers of the church and are heard all over the northern part of Bridgeport.

The organ in All Saints—St. Anthony is a Kilgen pipe organ built in 1914 and rebuilt in 1972. The parish has a long tradition of good choral music and congregational participation.

All Saints—St. Anthony has been under the direction of the Chicago diocesan clergy and both parishes have been the source of many vocations to the clergy and religious life. For more than one hundred years, the School Sisters of Notre Dame have staffed St. Anthony School.

**St. Nicholas Ukrainian
Catholic Cathedral   1913-15
2238 West Rice Street
(824 North)**

Architects: Worthmann and
Steinbach
  Renovation, 1974-77, Zenon
  Mazurkevich
Style: Neo-Byzantine
Seating: 1,200

**Modeled after the famous
cathedral of Kiev, St. Nicholas
was recently decorated with
brilliant frescoes and mosaics.**

St. Nicholas Cathedral in the midst of Chicago's Ukrainian Village is modeled after the multi-domed, eleventh century Cathedral of St. Sophia in Kiev. Two views of the Kiev cathedral can be seen in the fresco above the main altar in St. Nicholas. Kiev is the capital of the Ukraine and its cathedral is one of the finest examples of early Russo-Byzantine architecture. It is renowned for its magnificent frescos and mosaics. St. Nicholas is a worthy imitation of St. Sophia.

Ukrainian Catholics are Eastern Rite Christians who follow the Byzantine-Slavonic usage and acknowledge the Pope as their spiritual leader. St. Nicholas parish was founded in 1905 by a small group of Ukrainian laborers. They acquired their first church at Bishop and Superior streets from a Danish Protestant congregation in 1906. As their numbers grew, the Ukrainian Catholics purchased property at Rice and Oakley and built the church that we see there today.

The beige brick church is raised up and set back from the sidewalk on a grassy site. The building is 155 feet long, 85 feet wide, and raises its 13 domes, one each for Christ and the twelve apostles, 112 feet into the sky. Above the entrance on Oakley is a treasured mosaic of Our Lady of Pochaiv and above that an ikon of St. Nicholas the Wonder-worker.

It was made in Greece and is reputed to be the largest of its kind in this country.

The interior of the cathedral was renovated over a three year period from 1974 to 1977. The artist for the renovation was Boris Makarenko, an expert in Ukrainian Byzantine painting. All the paintings and ikons date from this renovation except the one on the rear wall of the sanctuary depicting Christ and the apostles with Mary. This one was retained from the 1928 decoration of the church. All of the paintings are patterned after the eleventh century mosaics in St. Sophia in Kiev.

The mosaics above the side altars and the mosaic stations of the cross were also designed by Makarenko and executed in Italy. The stained glass windows, retained from the original construction, were created by the Munich Studio of Chicago.

Large numbers of Ukrainian immigrants came to Chicago after World War II and settled in this neighborhood. The parish school, begun in 1936 and expanded in 1954, offers classes in Ukrainian language, literature, history, and geography. St. Nicholas was designated a cathedral in 1961 and became the seat of the St. Nicholas Ukrainian Catholic Diocese.

On a Sunday morning with the cathedral full of people and the *a cappella* choir singing, the religious experience is truly beautiful and otherworldly.

Inside the recently decorated cathedral one sees a heaven-like panorama of light blue and gold colors, pictures of Christ and his Mother, and a multitude of saints in fresco and mosaic.

From the highest dome in the center of the church hangs a brilliant nine-tiered golden chandelier having 480 lights.

Our Lady of Lourdes Church
1913-16
1601 West Leland Avenue
(4700 North)

Architects: Worthmann and
Steinbach
  Interior renovation, 1929,
  Joe W. McCarthy
Style: Spanish Romanesque
Seating: 1,000

**This beautiful Spanish
Romanesque church is known
throughout Chicago as the
church that was moved across
the street.**

Our Lady of Lourdes is known
throughout the Chicago area
as the church that was moved
across the street. This buff-
colored brick edifice with
limestone trim and red tile
roof was originally constructed on the southeast corner of
Ashland and Leland, facing
Ashland Avenue.

During the 1920s, Ravens-
wood changed from a community of single-family homes to
a neighborhood of apartment
buildings. Attendance in the
church grew rapidly. At the
same time plans were
announced for the widening
of Ashland Avenue. In
response to these developments, Rev. James Scanlon,
then pastor of Our Lady of
Lourdes, purchased property
on the west side of the street,
engaged the Crowe Brothers
Moving Co. to move the
10,000-ton masonry structure
across the street, turn it 90
degrees to face Leland, and
lengthen the nave from four to
six bays.

Crowe Brothers worked with
the Math Rauen Company, the
original construction firm. By
November 1928 they had
completed the foundation at
the new location. In early
1929 the church was raised off
its old foundation and by
March it was started on its
way across the street on cross
ties and rails. People would
stop every day to check the
progress. The project drew
the attention of engineers
throughout the United States
and Europe. Concern was
expressed that the great dome
would collapse. But because
the building was so solidly
built and so expertly moved,
it was safely transported
across the street and turned
around to face north.

Once located on its new
foundation, the dome, transepts, and sanctuary were cut
apart from the nave and
facade, separated 30 feet, and
the opening was closed with
brick and tile in a design that
perfectly matched the original.
Soon afterwards, the interior
was renovated according

to plans drawn by Joe W.
McCarthy, architect.

Our Lady of Lourdes has a
cruciform plan with a large
masonry dome above the
crossing of the nave and
transepts. There are now six
bays in the nave with large
stained glass windows at
ground level and pairs of
smaller windows in the
clerestory.

The Leland Avenue elevation
has a broad Spanish-style
entranceway embellished by
a beautiful ornamental iron
screen. The entrance is
flanked by square brick towers
with cupolas and red tile
domes.

Our Lady of Lourdes parish
was founded in 1892 to serve
the Catholic people in Ravenswood. Today the parish
consists of more than 1,500
families of nearly twenty
different ethnic backgrounds.
There are Spanish as well as
English services. The church
operates a fine elementary
school under the direction of
the Sisters of Charity, B.V.M.

St. Mary of the Lake Church
1913-17
4200 North Sheridan Road
(1000 West)

Architect: Henry J. Schlacks
Style: Roman Basilica
Seating: 800

Inside and outside, St. Mary of the Lake is a splendid model of a Roman basilica, one of the finest churches in Chicago.

In the Monthly Bulletin of the Illinois Society of Architects, Henry Schlacks wrote, "On the site of the house of Senator Pudens in Rome now stands the tower of the Church of St. Pudentiana, an ancient, picturesque campanile. While in Rome I was struck with the thought of incorporating this design in the tower for the Church of St. Mary of the Lake in Chicago." The campanile of St. Mary of the Lake is a replica of the beautiful St. Pudentiana.

This church is a splendid model of a Roman basilica. The paneled ceiling, trimmed in gold leaf and featuring paintings by the Chicago artist, Thomas, is like that of St. Mary Major in Rome. The east facade of the church and the rows of Corinthian columns inside are reminiscent of the Basilica of St. Paul Outside the Walls. The original high altar was carved from white Carrara marble and is enshrined under a carved stone baldachino. The pulpit is also of Carrara marble and has scenes from the life of St. Francis of Assisi carved in it.

The stained glass windows in the church are by F. X. Zettler of the Royal Bavarian Art Institute in Munich. The clerestory windows illuminate the interior of the church with a warm, golden light.

St. Mary of the Lake parish was founded in the Buena Park neighborhood in 1901. It was named in honor of St. Mary of the Lake University, the first institution of higher learning in Chicago, as well as for its proximity to Lake Michigan. The parish began with sixty families in a wealthy neighborhood and has grown to nearly two thousand families of greatly diverse ethnic and social backgrounds. Alongside the Irish, Germans, and Slavs, the area contains people from India, Korea, Indonesia, Australia, Latin America, Haiti, and the Philippine Islands. There are white Appalachians, blacks, and American Indians, Spanish-speaking people from Mexico, Puerto Rico, South America, and Cuba. This Uptown neighborhood also has one of the largest senior citizen populations in Chicago.

The statue of Mary on the front lawn of the church was placed there by the parishioners in memory of Rev. John J. Dennison who was the founder of the parish and pastor from 1901 until his death in 1955.

Corpus Christi Church
1914-16
4900 S. Martin Luther King Drive   (400 East)

Architect: Joe W. McCarthy
   Renovation, 1976,
   Paul Straka
Style: Italian Renaissance
Seating: 500, formerly 1,200

With its coffered ceiling, rich marble work, and Renaissance ornament, Corpus Christi was worthy of its location on Grand Boulevard and is one of Chicago's outstanding churches today.

Corpus Christi, Latin words for the Body of Christ, refer to the sacred bread which Jesus gave to his followers at the Last Supper. Accordingly, the art work throughout this Bedford stone church portrays scenes related to the history of this sacrament. The Last Supper above the main altar is a mosaic replica of Leonardo da Vinci's painting in Milan.

The stained glass windows on the north wall of the church show Jesus feeding the multitudes. The large windows on the east facade portray Pope Pius X carrying the Blessed Sacrament in procession accompanied by Rev. Thomas O'Gara, the pastor who built Corpus Christi Church, the Sisters of Mercy who taught in the school, and prominent Irish Catholic parishioners from the early days of the parish. The stained glass windows in this church were executed by the F. X. Zettler Studio of Munich, Germany.

Corpus Christi is cruciform in plan with a semicircular apse containing a white marble altar. The church has a magnificent coffered ceiling with 650 octagonal plaster panels decorated in white and gold.

The worship space in this church is bright and open, no pillars, and since a renovation in the middle 1970s, it focuses on a new free-standing altar located on a carpeted platform near the center of the church.

In June of 1975 one of the plaster panels fell from the coffered ceiling. The whole ceiling was found to be in danger of falling because the sisel which held the panels up was rotting. So the church was declared unsafe and was closed. But the people of the parish wanted their church to open again. Under the

direction of architect Paul Straka, each of the 650 plaster coffers was rehung with wire, the church was renovated, and eventually reopened for the 75th anniversary of the parish.

Corpus Christi was founded in 1901 and the present church was built by a relatively affluent Irish Catholic community between 1914 and 1916. Shortly after the church was completed, the Grand Boulevard neighborhood began experiencing racial change. By the fall of 1928 there were only 100 white persons at Sunday masses and 21 children registered for school. So the pastor resigned and the parish was closed.

Cardinal Mundelein subsequently turned the parish buildings over to the Franciscan fathers and brothers for a city retreat house. This failed.

In 1932 the Franciscans reopened the church for the black people who lived in the community and the parish began to flourish once again. It continues to do so today.

Newspapers at the time of its dedication in 1916 described Corpus Christi as Chicago's most beautiful church. It certainly ranks among the most beautiful today.

St. Jerome Church
1914-16
1701 West Lunt Avenue
(7000 North)

Architect: Charles Prindeville
  Expansion and renovation,
  1934, Joe W. McCarthy
Style: North Italian
  Renaissance
Seating: 1,700

The interior of St. Jerome's contains a dazzling display of marble, mosaic, and Renaissance ornament.

The present pastor describes St. Jerome's Church as having "probably the longest aisle in the Chicago Archdiocese." The church was completed and dedicated on October 15, 1916. During the 1920s, the Rogers Park neighborhood grew so swiftly with the construction of apartments and apartment hotels that the church needed to be extended. It was doubled in length in 1934.

The size of the church is equalled by the elaborate detail of its Renaissance/Baroque ornament. Black and gold are the dominant colors. The altars are marble and the two columns flanking the main altar are 23 feet high, each hewed from a solid block of black marble and inlaid with silver mosaic. With the entablature and pediment, this construction rises 40 feet and is surmounted by a golden cross. Between the columns is a crucifix of black Belgian marble. The figure of Christ on the cross was cut from a single piece of Portuguese onyx.

David Lowe has described St. Jerome's as "one of the city's truly superb sanctuaries in the [classical] style. . . . With its dazzling display of marbles, its walls of gold mosaic, its heroic paintings, and its carved gold leaf ceiling, St. Jerome's would not be out of place in Rome." (*Chicago Interiors*, Contemporary Books, Inc., 1979, p. 122)

Since its founding in 1895, St. Jerome's has been a very active parish in the East Rogers Park neighborhood. East Rogers Park is now a multi-ethnic community and this is reflected in the parish. The student body of St. Jerome school has children from thirty-eight different ethnic and racial backgrounds.

The parish has many activities and organizations, all coordinated by the Parish Council which was established in 1958. St. Jerome's is served by Chicago diocesan priests.

St. Mary of the Angels Church 1914-20
1850 N. Hermitage Ave. (1734 West)

Architects: Worthmann and
Steinbach
Style: Renaissance
Seating: 1,800

This monumental Renaissance
church with its great dome and
blue guiding light has been called
the Polish basilica of Chicago.

Just west of the Kennedy
Expressway, one block south
of Armitage, a motorist will
see St. Mary of the Angels
with its impressive dome, its
blue "guiding" light in the
cupola, and 32 nine-foot
angels standing guard around
the parapet.

St. Mary's has been called
the finest example of Roman
Renaissance architecture in
the country. It has also been
called the Polish basilica of

Chicago. The tile and terra
cotta dome was built to
resemble Michelangelo's
dome on St. Peter's in Rome.
The church itself is massive,
230 feet long, and 125 feet
wide at the transepts. It is
constructed of reddish brown
face brick with terra cotta
trim. The parish buildings
occupy a full city block.

The Hermitage Avenue facade
of St. Mary's is highlighted by
a large portico with eight
Corinthian columns, a
balustrade, and in the center
of this, the coat of arms of

Pope Benedict XV, during
whose pontificate the church
was built. A rose window is
situated above the portico.
The facade is completed by
several corbiesteps and finials
rising to a cross at the top.
Two square towers of equal
height flank the central
facade. An interesting detail
of the building is that the
angel motif seen on the
parapet is carried out inside
the church as well.

stained glass window in the clerestory. The nave is flanked by broad side aisles, then side altars featuring the stations of the cross done in stained glass. At the intersection of the nave and the transepts is the dome of St. Mary's, rising 135 feet above the floor. The inscription on the base of the dome reads, "Glory to God in the Highest and Peace on Earth to Men." The twelve stained glass windows in the dome picture the twelve apostles.

Above the main altar is a picture of St. Francis of Assisi's vision of the Blessed Virgin Mary with Christ the King in heaven. In the half dome of the apse is a huge six-piece canvas mural painted by John A. Mallin. It depicts Mary in glory surrounded by angels.

The organ in St. Mary's is a four-manual Kimball organ with 57 ranks.

St. Mary of the Angels was built by Polish immigrants under the leadership of Rev. Francis Gordon, C.R., the first pastor of the parish. The parish was begun in 1899 for Polish people living between St. Stanislaus Kostka and St. Hedwig's. It experienced its peak years from 1920 to 1950 with some twenty-eight parish organizations and two building and loan associations. Old parishioners, about 70 percent Polish, are becoming less active, and the congregation now includes Latinos, Orientals, and blacks. The Resurrection priests and sisters continue to serve the parish and the neighborhood.

Inside the massive wooden doors is a great space, majestic arches, elaborate renaissance ornament, and bright pastel colors. The church was decorated in 1948 by John A. Mallin. The high barrel-vaulted nave has four bays on each side. Each bay consists of a round arch, spandrel, frieze, cornice, and

St. Ignatius Church
1916-17
6555 N. Glenwood Avenue
(1400 West)

Architect: Henry J. Schlacks
Style: Roman Renaissance
Seating: 1,200

This beautifully detailed Renaissance church contains design elements adapted from the Gesù, the mother church of the Jesuit order in Rome.

Dedicating St. Ignatius Church on September 16, 1917, Archbishop Mundelein said, "The churches of the Jesuits have always been noted as repositories of the finest works of art. We see [here] the faithful observance of one of the traditions of the Society. In every great city you will find the richest, the most ornate, the most beautiful of the churches is the Jesuit church, while their residence is of the poorest. You will find in the Jesuit churches the choicest paintings of the masters, the finest compositions in music, the most eloquent of preachers in the pulpit, and the most crowded congregations in the pews. So today

we welcome St. Ignatius among the best architecturally of our Chicago churches, a monumental basilica church that will grow even more beautiful with the years." The church has lived up to the dedicatory remarks.

St. Ignatius Church is named after the soldier-saint, the sixteenth century founder of the Society of Jesus. Henry Schlacks patterned the church after the Gesù, the mother church of the Jesuit order in Rome. The Gesù, constructed in the latter part of the sixteenth century, became the archetype of many churches built in the baroque period throughout Europe and was the source of the so-called Jesuit style of architecture.

This church is 200 feet long and 150 feet wide. It is constructed of Bedford stone throughout and has a salmon-colored Spanish tile roof. At the southeast corner of the building is a free-standing six-story Roman campanile.

Six columns, 30 feet high and weighing 13 tons apiece, each carved from a single block of stone, create a stately portico on the front of the church.

A continuity of design is carried inside where classical columns support the canopy of the baldachino, are engaged in the walls around the church, are found in the communion railing, on the organ front, and in the exposition dome above the altar.

The golden canopy of the baldachino is modeled after Bernini's canopy in St. Peter's Basilica in Rome.

Above each of the side altars stands a three-quarter life-size painting by the young St. Louis artist Charles Bosseron Chambers, *The Madonna of the Sacred Coat* above the north altar and *The Light of the World and St. Joseph* above the south. The image of the Christ Child with St. Joseph in this latter painting has been called the most popular religious painting in the world. Chambers also painted the fourteen stations of the cross around the church. In 1917 his work was just beginning to be recognized.

Four large Munich-styled stained glass windows on each side of the nave and two huge ones in the transepts help illuminate the body of the church. They were executed by the Emil Frei Art Glass Co. of St. Louis. St. Ignatius is honored in a series of ten oil paintings by the Chicago artist Augustine Pall. These paintings are affixed to the ceiling above each of the stained glass windows.

Many senior citizens who are members of the parish today are the children of the people who founded and built St. Ignatius Church. The parish is now comprised of a multi-ethnic mix of people. Services in the church are conducted in English and Spanish.

St. James Lutheran Church
1916-17
2048 North Fremont Street
(900 West)

Architects: Worthmann and
Steinbach
Style: Neo-Gothic
Seating: 900

St. James, one of the early German Lutheran parishes on the North Side, founded five schools and has exceptionally fine stained glass windows.

Rev. A. C. Dahms, a former pastor of St. James, told the story about Archbishop Mundelein visiting St. James with his building committee while the church was under construction. The new archbishop reportedly upbraided his committee for not placing this quality of stained glass in the Catholic churches being built in the city. The quality of glass in St. James Church is exceptional. It was designed and installed by the John J. Kinsella Co. of Chicago. Mundelein soon afterwards commissioned the Kinsella Co. to do the windows in the St. James Chapel of Quigley Seminary on Rush and Pearson streets.

The three large memorial windows in the transepts and on the east facade of St. James picture the Nativity (north), Gethsemane (east), and the Resurrection (south). The Gethsemane scene is flanked by windows picturing the four evangelists. A characteristic of this glass is that the panels are sometimes two and three panes thick to produce just the right hue and texture. This is especially true of the deep reds and blues. The memorial panels at the bottom of each window, in German, are a reminder that this parish, founded in 1869, was for many years a German-speaking congregation. German was last used in services here in 1931.

St. James is a sturdy, solid church. It is cruciform in plan and is constructed of brown brick with limestone trim. There are two towers on the front of the church; the one to the north, much taller than the other, contains three bells and has very fine ornamental stonework. Henry Worthmann, the architect, is said to have described this tower as "a finger pointing to God for all of Chicago to see."

The interior of St. James is lofty and spacious. A Gothic arch motif is used throughout the church. The seating slopes gently toward the narrow chancel at the front. The pipes of the two-manual Wangerin organ flank the beautiful hand-carved wooden altar and reredos.

The neo-Gothic style of St. James is carried out in plaster and wood instead of stone. This gives warmth and economy and yet retains the artistic features of Medieval Gothic.

St. James is an active parish under the direction of Rev. Robert J. Degner. It has a full calendar of worship, choral, and community programs together with a grade school.

St. Benedict Church
1917-18
2201 West Irving Park Road
(4000 North)

Architect: Hermann J. Gaul
Style: Romanesque
Seating: 800

This monumental church on Irving Park Road was built by German Catholics and contains beautiful art glass windows.

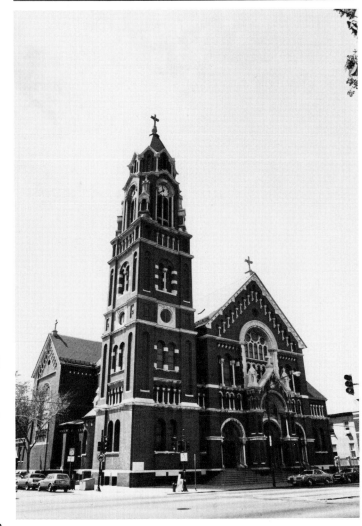

The lofty bell tower of St. Benedict's can be seen from all over the North Center neighborhood. The church is constructed of brown face brick with elaborate stone trim. The main body of the church is cruciform in plan. The front of the church is flanked by a baptistry extending to the west and the bell tower to the east. A broad flight of steps leads up to the three-portal entrance. Above the round arch of the center doorway is a bas-relief stone tympanum, another round arch, a gable with a cross, a large stained glass window above that, and then the roof gable.

An ornamental column, serving as a corbel, provides a distinctive motif that is used extensively on the outside and throughout the interior of the church.

The stained glass windows in St. Benedict's, done in the German baroque style, are especially beautiful. They were created by F. X. Zettler of Munich and installed in 1922. The large transept windows portray the Nativity on one side and Mary with the apostles on Pentecost on the other. The nave windows present scenes from the life of Christ.

During a renovation in 1967, the interior of the church was painted cream and light brown. This simplified the decoration and accentuated the beauty of the art glass windows. A modern white marble altar and sanctuary furnishings with square marble columns were also installed at this time.

St. Benedict's was founded in 1902 by German Catholics moving northwest in the city. The parish flourished and over the years has built a grade school, a high school, two convents, a rectory, a gymnasium, a religious education center, and a chapel. This complex occupies nearly a full city block. The parish continues strong and active with over 3,000 families of many different ethnic backgrounds.

St. Clement Church
1917-18
646 West Deming Place
(2534 North)

Architect: George D. Barnett
Style: Romanesque-Byzantine
Seating: 850

The exterior of St. Clement's is similar to the St. Louis cathedral; the interior decoration is a reproduction of that found in the ancient church of San Clemente in Rome.

During the reign of Emperor Justinian, during the years 532 to 537 A.D., the architects Anthemius of Tralles and Isidorus of Miletus designed and built the great church of *Hagia Sophia* in Constantinople. They elevated a huge dome, spanning 103 feet, to an unprecedented height, 163 feet at the apex, and invented for its support the first large-scale use of pendentive vaults. (See Glossary.) This dome and its supporting system were the principal elements of the Byzantine architectural style which then spread throughout Eastern Europe and flourished for a thousand years. This type of dome, in a scale-down version, graces the church of St. Clement on Deming Place.

St. Clement's also draws extensively on the Romanesque tradition of architecture which reached its high point in the eleventh and twelfth centuries in Europe. The round arch together with interlocking circles and semicircles creates a unified decorative pattern. It is seen throughout the church—over each window and doorway, on the pews, in the vaulting, on the marble communion rail, over the mosaics, and around the altars. St. Clement's is a masterpiece of Romanesque decoration.

This beautiful limestone church is also a smaller version of the St. Louis cathedral. Both churches were designed by the same architect, George D. Barnett.

St. Clement I, pope and martyr, guided the Christian church in the last decade of the first century. He was arrested and sent to the Crimea by the Roman Emperor Trajan. There he was thrown into the sea with an anchor tied to his neck. The anchor motif seen in St. Clement's Church is the symbol of this early pope and martyr.

The whole sanctuary area, the circular design in the altar railing, the ambulatory, and the Tree of Life painting on the ceiling of the apse are all reproductions of the decoration in the church of San Clemente in Rome.

The interior painting of St. Clement's was done in 1930 by a Russian priest, Gleb E. Werchovsky, who had graduated from the Fine Arts Academy in St. Petersburg, Russia, before studying for the ministry. He worked with Rev. Francis Rempe, the pastor, in selecting the subject matter for the art.

St. Clement's is especially rich in stained glass and mosaic art. The three rose windows are in honor of the three persons of the Blessed Trinity. The seven windows in the sanctuary show angels bearing symbols of the seven sacraments. The six windows in the transepts have angels holding globes representing the six days of creation. These angels follow the style of the English Pre-Raphaelite artist Sir Edward Burne-Jones.

This church, intimate in its proportions and rich in its symbolism, realizes the ancient ideal of a church: a place where God dwells among men, with a domelike heaven above, and the company of the saints all around.

St. Clement's today is a flourishing parish in a cosmopolitan neighborhood. It has an excellent grade school, and many young people come here to church. The parish, founded in 1905, celebrated its seventy-fifth anniversary in 1980.

Mosaics, which alternate with the stained glass windows in the sanctuary, picture the early Fathers of the Church. The mosaics on the large piers supporting the dome picture women saints: Agnes, Barbara, Theresa, Rose of Lima, Catherine of Siena, Clara, Mary Magdalen, and Elizabeth. Panels in the barrel-vaulted nave proclaim titles of the Blessed Virgin Mary.

**St. James Chapel   1917-20
Quigley Preparatory
Seminary North
831 North Rush Street
(75 East)**
Architects: Gustave Steinback
of New York and Zachary
Davis of Chicago
Style: Early French Gothic
Seating: 450

**The Quigley chapel was modeled
after the thirteenth century
Sainte Chapelle in Paris,
generally regarded as the
quintessence of Gothic
architecture.**

La Sainte Chapelle was built
by King Louis IX in Paris in
1243-48 to house a relic of the
"True Crown of Thorns of Our
Blessed Savior." It is a small
building widely considered to
be the quintessence of Gothic
architecture. The stonework
in the walls is reduced to a
minimum, scarcely more than
the piers, and large expanses
of stained glass make up the
walls of the chapel.

Almost immediately after his
installation as archbishop of
Chicago in 1916, George
Mundelein announced his
intention to build a
preparatory seminary and
name it in honor of his
predecessor, Archbishop
James Quigley. The seminary
would be designed in the
French Gothic style, the
school modeled after the
Palais du Justice in Rouen
and the chapel after *La Sainte
Chapelle* in Paris.

The St. James Chapel is
constructed of pearl-gray
limestone. The building is 130
feet long, 45 feet wide, and
the walls rise 110 feet above
the street. It is a three-level
structure with the chapel
above, an auditorium below,
and a student cafeteria in the
basement.

The building is ribbed
with twenty-two buttresses.
The vertical quality of the
structure was previously
accentuated by a tall spire or
flèche on the roof which was
damaged by a windstorm in
1941 and had to be removed.

The graceful porch on the
Rush Street facade lifts
upward to a cross, and above
that is the delicate tracery of a
great rose window. Standing
in niches flanking the
window are statues of St.
Gregory the Great, St. Jerome,
and St. Augustine. Above
them, from left to right, are
statues of St. Thomas
Aquinas, St. Patrick, St.
James, St. George, and St.
Francis of Assisi. All eight
statues were sculptured by an
elderly Belgian immigrant.

But the greatest treasures
of the Quigley chapel, as of
La Sainte Chapelle, are the
stained glass windows. The
brilliance, detail, and expanse
of this medieval-style glass is
unequalled in Chicago. The
windows were designed by
Robert Giles and installed
by the John Kinsella Co. of
Chicago. They were made
from small pieces of antique
English glass. The details of
hands and faces were painted
by the artist's wife.

The chapel has a simple rectangular plan, no transepts. There are seven bays of windows around the altar portraying scenes from the life of Christ. Five bays of windows on the south wall present the principal events and characters of the Old Testament. And three bays of windows on the north wall show the saints of the Christian era. Each of these bays is 10 feet wide and 40 feet high and is divided into twenty-two panels or medallions of various shapes. At the top of each bay is a cinquefoil medallion, then three vertical columns of seven panels each. There are approximately 225,000 pieces of glass in the five windows on the south wall.

The great rose window above the choir is truly the high point of the chapel. It is 28 feet in diameter, is dedicated to Mary, and is red violet and gold in color. (See illustration, p. 85.)

The altar in St. James Chapel is 16 feet long, of Italian Caen stone, carved in France, and its spire rises 50 feet above and behind the tabernacle. A statue of St. James the Greater stands in the central niche above the altar. He is flanked by six angels each bearing symbols of the Lord's passion.

The organ in the Quigley chapel is a three-manual Wangerin pipe organ. Besides the pipes which are visible in the choir, there is an additional chamber of pipes in the sanctuary providing an echo organ.

St. James Chapel is principally used by the students of Quigley Preparatory Seminary. It is not open to the public.

St. Hyacinth Church
1917-21
3635 West George Street
(2900 North)

Architects: Worthmann and
Steinbach
Style: Renaissance
Seating: 2,000

**Massive in proportions and
beautifully decorated within,
St. Hyacinth is another of the
great Polish Catholic churches on
the Northwest Side.**

The three cupolas on the
towers of St. Hyacinth rise
high above the Avondale
neighborhood on Chicago's
Northwest Side. This church
is a witness to the faith of the
Polish Catholics who built it,
and St. Hyacinth continues to
be a thriving parish today.

St. Hyacinth was founded by
Rev. Vincent Barzynski, C.R.,
from St. Stanislaus Kostka
parish in 1894. At that time
there were less than twenty
Catholic families in Avondale,
which then had few paved
streets, few sidewalks, and
little lighting. But waves of
immigrants made the parish
grow dramatically so that by
1917, when the present
church was begun, it
numbered more than two
thousand families.

The church is cruciform in
plan, built of brown brick
with elaborate stone trim and
Renaissance ornament. At the
intersection of the nave and
transepts is a great dome with
a large stained glass window
at its apex.

John A. Mallin and Co. of
Chicago did the interior
decoration of St. Hyacinth in
the 1930s. The mural in the
dome is painted on canvas,
is 200 feet in circumference,
and shows the Risen Christ
crowning Mary as queen of
heaven surrounded by a
multitude of saints. The
decoration is all Renaissance
in style and very rich. The
stained glass windows were
created by F. X. Zettler of
Munich.

The interior of the church is
huge, but at the principal
masses on Sunday all the
seats are occupied, the two
balconies are full, there is
standing room only in the
aisles, and some worshipers
must be satisfied to look in
through the doors from the
sidewalk. These masses are
offered in Polish. Almost half
of the parishioners have come
to the United States from
Poland within the last twenty
years.

St. Hyacinth parish is under
the care of the Resurrection
fathers. The school is operated
by the Sisters of the Holy
Family of Nazareth. The
parish plant consisting of
church, rectory, school, hall,
and convent, occupies a good
part of a city block.

The Organ

by Frank Pellegrini

Most churches and synagogues of architectural significance have organs. And most organists believe that the instrument thus referred to should be nothing less than a pipe organ. While there have been some fine electronic instruments built in recent years, there is no substitute for a pipe organ.

Like religious art and architecture, the musical instrument used in churches and synagogues evolved in response to human needs. What kind of instrument could best express people's religious feelings? The most immediate instrument, of course, is the human voice. When people use their voices to express their faith together, they reinforce their own commitment and they also get support from the faith expression of their friends and neighbors. Congregational singing even heightens these effects. People sing when their emotions are high and they feel enthusiastic about something. Singing demonstrates a public commitment to religious belief.

Many centuries ago a musical instrument began evolving which closely resembled some aspects of the human voice. That instrument is the organ. It extends the range of sound beyond the human voice, however, and enables people to hear music that would be too complex to sing. This music can inspire faith and enhance worship. Most churches and many synagogues in Chicago have organs.

Historical Sketch

The oldest extant pipe organ in the world is commonly believed to be a 4-rank, thirteen-note instrument built by the Romans in the ancient city of Aquincum near present day Budapest. The year was 228 A.D. This ancient organ and others like it were called *hydra*, an abbreviation for *hydraulis*. These terms are derived from the fact that these organs used a water chest to maintain a constant level of air pressure in the instrument.

Although the Aquincum organ and other hydraulic organs have been reconstructed, there is speculation as to how the original instruments actually sounded. But historians are certain that these instruments were used for secular purposes. In fact, the early Church Fathers forbade the use of musical instruments in the sacred liturgy. The *hydraulis* was explicitly banned because of its pagan ritual uses. It is interesting to note that Eastern Christians as well as Orthodox Jews still do not use organs or any other musical instruments to accompany priests, cantors, choirs, or congregations.

The development of the organ during the Middle Ages is obscure, but by the eighth or ninth century organs were being used in Christian churches in Western Europe. The chromatic keyboard began to be used in the late twelfth and thirteenth centuries. The pedalboard, used to activate the longer pipes, has been in use since the fourteenth century. Swell boxes, in which certain pipes are enclosed in a box with shutters, have been in use since the 1700s. The organ was acclaimed the "king of instruments" during the seventeenth and early eighteenth centuries.

But with the increasing interest in orchestral music and opera in the later eighteenth century, the organ became less popular as a medium of artistic expression. This trend was reversed in the middle of the nineteenth century, however, when new inventions expanded the potential of the organ and made it capable of producing a very wide range of sounds which rivaled the tonal range of an entire orchestra.

Elements of the Organ

The chromatic scale used in Western music is a series of twelve tones each one-half step apart; for example, "ti" to "do." The major scale, "do-re-mi" and so on, is a patterned arrangement of whole and half steps based on all the tones available. Long ago it was discovered that a series of pipes could be arranged to sound these tones, one pipe for each tone or pitch. The pitch of each note was determined by the length of the pipe. The longer pipes sounded the deeper tones; the shorter pipes the higher tones. And the sounding or voicing of the pipes could be controlled from a keyboard. This is how the instrument was originally conceived.

Pipes

Once the first set or rank of pipes was in operation, additional sets were added to produce pitches covering over nine complete octaves of the keyboard. The largest pipe was about 32 feet long, vibrating at sixteen cycles per second, and the shortest pipe was about an inch, vibrating at over 8,000 cycles per second.

There are basically two types of organ pipe, the flue pipe and the reed pipe. The flue pipe consists of a metal cylinder, called the body, which surrounds a column of air. A tapered cone, called the foot, is added to the bottom of the cylinder. Where the foot joins the body, a rectangular opening called the mouth is cut. Air escaping from the mouth vibrates the air inside the cylinder and produces the sound. The pitch is determined by the length of the pipe as noted above.

In the reed pipe the metal cylinder is called a resonator, and the column of air is vibrated by a brass tongue which rolls down over a long opening in the side of a tube called a shallot. The shallot and tongue are located inside the foot of the pipe.

Air Pressure

Early organ builders had to devise a way to pressurize the air which would voice the pipes. A bellows, like that used for blowing air into a fireplace, served the purpose.

Early organs used people to work the bellows. It took six men to operate the bellows in Holy Family Jesuit Church for an ordinary mass in the 1870s and 1880s, eight men for a solemn service. Later developments at Holy Family used city water pressure to operate the bellows. Modern organs use electric motors and air compressors. The pressurized air is then stored in a wind chest located directly beneath a series or rank of pipes.

The Action

The mechanism which links the keyboard to the pipes and controls the release of air into the individual pipes is called the action. A pipe is voiced by opening a valve in the wind chest on which the pipe stands. The earliest actions consisted of wire strung from the back of the keyboard to the valve located directly beneath the pipe. This purely mechanical linkage is called tracker action. Tracker-action organs can still be found in Chicago churches. This type of mechanism is highly prized for the direct and sensitive control it allows the organist to have over the release of air into the pipes. One can find tracker-action organs in St. Matthew Lutheran Church, 21st and Hoyne; St. James Church on South Wabash Avenue; The Greenstone Church at 112th and St. Lawrence, the Church of Our Saviour at 530 West Fullerton Parkway, and a new instrument in Bond Chapel at the University of Chicago. Only the instruments in the Greenstone Church, St. Matthew, and Bond Chapel are in good operating condition.

Modern technology produced electropneumatic action for organs in the 1890s. When the organist depresses a key on the console, an electrical connection is made with a magnet attached to the valve on the foot of a pipe. This kind of action allows the organ to have many more pipes and more tone colors. It also allows more freedom in the arrangement of pipes and in the location of pipes and console.

The Organ

The Stops

As organ builders placed more and more rows of pipes on a wind chest, organists wished to be more selective about the different tone colors they had available. A wooden board with holes drilled into it was placed below the feet of a row of pipes. The board could slide back and forth thus allowing air into the pipes or "stopping" it from flowing into them. Hence the mechanism is known as a stop. One can recognize stops as knobs on the sides of an organ console or as keys or tablets above the players' hands.

The use of stops as described above began in Italy during the fifteenth century. The earliest surviving organ with stops, built in 1470, is in the Church of St. Pretronico in Bologna.

Keyboards or Manuals

Organs may have two, three, four, or sometimes five keyboards. Italian organs always had more than one keyboard and later added a pedalboard which also allowed a player to use his or her feet to depress keys. Each keyboard or manual controls a separate wind chest or division of the organ. Multiple keyboards allow for the crossing of hands in polyphonic works that could not easily be played on one keyboard.

Divisions of the Organ

Organs built at different times responded to different needs and different tastes. The type of organ used in J. S. Bach's lifetime (1685-1750) is called a Baroque organ. It uses the two types of pipe described above, the flue and the reed. Ranks of these pipes are grouped together in two basic divisions: the great organ, which is the large main division, and the *positiv* organ, a smaller division often located behind the player's back.

In more recent organs another set of pipes is placed in a wooden box with shutters like vertical venetian blinds that open and close, thus modifying the loudness of the sound. This division is called the swell organ.

Small portable organs, used to accompany choirs, were often placed near the choir loft railing. The organist could play the great organ and then could turn around and play the portable choir organ. It was not long before these two were connected. Multiple keyboards then allowed the player to command multiple divisions of the same organ, the great, swell, and choir divisions.

Modern instruments with two keyboards usually have great and swell divisions. Three manual instruments usually have a great, swell, and a choir division. Larger organs can have keyboards designated great, swell, choir, bombard, echo, and *positiv* (on Baroque organs).

Romantic Organs

During the nineteenth century French and German builders began to make organs with ranks of pipes which sounded like orchestral instruments. These organs came to be known as Romantic organs. Along with the characteristic diapason sound which the basic flue pipe gives, it was not uncommon for a large instrument to have many types of flute, string, and horn sounds. The largest of these instruments are still in use today in the major churches of Paris: St. Ambroise, St. Elisabeth, St. Eugene, and St. Sulpice. The organ in St. Sulpice is monumental. It has five keyboards and a pedalboard, over 100 stops. The dynamics of the ranks range from the softest whisper to the rumble of an earthquake. The Romantic movement culminated in the early twentieth century with the construction of huge theater and church organs.

Examples of fine Romantic organs in Chicago include those in First Baptist Congregational Church on Ashland Avenue, Our Lady of Sorrows Basilica on Jackson Boulevard, Second Presbyterian Church on South Michigan Avenue, Temple Sholom on North Lake Shore Drive, and St. Mary of Perpetual Help on West 32nd Street.

Baroque Revival

In 1906 Albert Schweitzer wrote a booklet which detailed the inadequacies of the nineteenth century Romantic organ for playing the music of Bach and his contemporaries. Something was wrong; not with the music but with the organs. Most of the very old organs in Europe had been altered to suit romantic ideals. People had increased the wind pressure and enlarged the mouths of pipes to make them louder. They had thrown out mixture and mutation stops and put in stops of a more "reverent" character. This upset the unity and balance which had been the ideal of the Baroque organ builder. Schweitzer's booklet initiated a trend back to the simplicity and purity of the Baroque organ which has continued to the present time.

The kind of organ music one hears in churches and synagogues today corresponds to what the congregation wants to hear or thinks is proper for a religious service. More and more this is not the sound of the Romantic organ with its orchestral potential, but the simpler, purer sound of the Baroque organ. It seems, however, a constant fact that over the centuries the sound of the organ has responded to the worship needs of many people.

Interior, south nave
St. Adalbert Church
Henry J. Schlacks, architect

North Shore Congregation Israel
Minoru Yamasaki, architect

Baha'i House of Worship
1920-53
100 Linden Avenue,
Wilmette, Illinois

Architect: Louis J. Bourgeois
  National Register of
  Historic Places, 1978
Styles: Arabic, Byzantine,
Egyptian, Gothic, Greek,
Romanesque
Seating: 1,200

Concrete, steel, and glass
fashioned into delicate patterns
characterize this national
landmark house of worship.

Planning for the first Baha'i House of Worship in the Western world was begun in 1903 by a small group of Baha'is in Chicago. Many architects submitted designs, but the most appropriate and promising was submitted by Louis Bourgeois, a French Canadian. He worked on his design from 1909 to 1917 and then modeled it in plaster after that. Construction began in 1920.

One of the most difficult tasks was finding a sturdy, economical material for the lacy patterns of the temple's ornamentation. John Earley, an architectural sculptor from Washington, D.C., proposed a special concrete consisting of quartz and white cement. He fabricated the panels in Washington and shipped the finished sections to Wilmette by train. The panels were then hung in place on the steel superstructure which had been completed in 1931. The interior of the dome alone required 387 sections.

The House of Worship was finally completed and dedicated in 1953. It rises 191 feet from the base to the top of the dome ribs. The outside diameter of the base is 202 feet. From the floor to the auditorium to the inside apex of the dome is 138 feet. The dome is 72 feet across on the inside. The main story pylons on the perimeter of the building are each 45 feet high. Caissons were sunk about 130 feet to bedrock to support the building. The temple weighs approximately 6,750 tons and the auditorium contains 19,000 square feet of glass.

Bourgeois attested that the inspiration for the design of the temple came from on high. The convergence of lines and ribs expresses the Baha'i belief in the unity of all creation. "Into this new design, then, of the Temple," Bourgeois wrote, "is woven, in symbolic form, the great Baha'i teaching of unity—the unity of all religions and all mankind."

The House of Worship has nine sides. Nine is the largest one-digit number; it symbolizes comprehensiveness and unity. In the apex of the dome is an Arabic inscription which translates "O Glory of the All-Glorious." The dome is a symbol of man's efforts to praise his Creator.

The Baha'i faith is the latest of the world religions begun in Persia, now Iran, by Baha 'u' llah (1817-92), a "Messenger of God." The faith has since spread around the world. Devotional services are held every Sunday at 3 P.M. The service is for prayer and meditation. Scriptures are read from various religions and song is provided by an *a cappella* choir. There are no clergy, no sermons, and no rituals in this faith.

Each of the pylons on the outside of the temple carries the symbols of world religions; from the bottom, the swastika used by Hindus, Buddhists, and American Indians, the star of David for the Jews, the Christian cross, the star and crescent of Islam, the gate of Babi, and the Baha'i nine closed circles.

Greater Mt. Vernon Baptist Church 1922-23
6430 South Harvard Avenue (332 West)

Architects: Worthmann and Steinbach
Style: English Gothic
Seating: 1,000

This noble English Gothic edifice in Englewood contains a brilliant panoply of art glass windows.

Just west of the Dan Ryan Expressway at 64th Street, the motorist sees the magnificent English Gothic facade of Greater Mt. Vernon Baptist Church. This imposing edifice was built by Our Redeemer Lutheran Church in 1922. The Lutheran congregation worshiped here until 1974.

The building is of brick construction with a Bedford stone facade. The three main doors are sheltered by a series of ribbed arches which also enclose a carved stone tympanum. Above this is a plaque with the inscription, "Our Redeemer Lutheran Church," and then a large, traceried, five-lancet stained glass window. A niche at the top of the facade contains a statue of Christ. This is flanked by an open arcade and then the tops of two stone towers. The buttress work on the facade and along the nave gives the church vigorous, symmetrical lines.

Upon entering the nave of the church, the visitor first notices the height and spaciousness of the auditorium, the huge wooden beams of the open-truss ceiling, and the brilliant stained glass windows.

There are five bays along each side of the nave, each containing a large, traceried stained glass window. Even larger medallion-style windows adorn the two transepts, the chancel, and the east wall over the balcony. The lack of all other mural decoration highlights the beauty of these windows. Eight delicate chandeliers help light the sanctuary. Handsome wooden railings front shallow balconies in each transept and a larger balcony at the rear of the nave.

In the south transept balcony is the console of a three-manual Wicks pipe organ.

This instrument is in need of repair now, but the choirs of the congregation are accompanied by an electronic organ and a grand piano, both located in the sanctuary area.

The pulpit and choir platform at the front of the church is of recent construction and is decorated with red upholstery which complements the cushions on the pews and the pale pink of the walls. The lower part of the chancel walls are surfaced with carved wood paneling.

This beautiful church stood vacant for three years before it was occupied by the Greater Mt. Vernon Baptist Church in 1977. During that time children threw rocks through the stained glass windows on the south side of the nave. These windows are protected with plastic now, and repair work is under way to restore them to their original splendor.

The Greater Mt. Vernon Baptist Church was founded in 1920 in a private home on the Near South Side. The congregation grew and moved to several different locations, farther south each time. This church, under the direction of Rev. Charles W. Alexander, Jr. since 1960, has a large, active membership, several choirs, many social and educational programs, and religious services on Sunday mornings and Wednesday evenings. Visitors are warmly welcomed at the services.

The Chicago Temple
First United Methodist
Church   (1922-24)
77 West Washington Street
(100 North)

Architects; Holabird and
Roche
Style: French Gothic
Seating: 1,400

A unique combination of church and office building housing the oldest religious congregation in Chicago.

The Westminster chimes heard throughout the central Loop area sound from the tower of the Chicago Temple building at the southeast corner of Clark and Washington streets. The site, the building, and the church are unique in many respects.

The First United Methodist Church, founded in 1831, is the oldest religious congregation in Chicago and actually predates the incorporation of the city. Five different buildings for this congregation have occupied this site since 1838. The present building was erected to house the church plus eighteen floors of commercial rental space, mostly offices of lawyers, accountants, and church organizations. The spire, topped with a cross 568 feet above street level, is listed in *The Book of Records* as "The world's tallest spire," and this Temple building itself, with its unique combination of functions, is the tallest church structure in the world.

The main sanctuary, located on the first and second floors of the building, features a handsome timbered ceiling, is paneled with fumed oak on all sides, and is adorned with seven large stained glass windows.

The decoration of the sanctuary as well as the tower and spire are French Gothic in style, while the rest of the building is modern office space with marble-paneled corridors. The Gothic pinnacles, arches, and buttresses of the tower stand in marked contrast to the straight lines of the Brunswick Building next door. Stylistically, the Temple building can be compared with the Tribune Tower; they were both built at about the same time, 1922-24 and 1925 respectively.

The jewel-like stained glass windows of the sanctuary were installed beginning in 1948 and were done by the Chicago firm of Giannini and Hilgart. They are illuminated by fluorescent lights from the rear.

The ten outside stained glass windows on the east side of the building tell the story of The Chicago Temple and its involvement in the history of the city. These windows were also created by Giannini and Hilgart and were dedicated in 1965.

The wood carving in the base of the altar by Alois Lang of Grand Rapids, Michigan, shows Jesus looking over the city of Jerusalem. It is titled *Christ and the City* and it illustrates the text, "If thou hadst known . . ." Lk. 19:42. A companion piece in the Sky Chapel, begun by Lang but completed by J. Wolters, portrays Christ overlooking the city of Chicago as it appeared from the top of the Temple building in 1952.

The Sky Chapel is located in the tower of the building at the 400-foot level. It was planned in 1952 and furnished in memory of Charles R. Walgreen.

The First Methodist Church rightly claims to be the "Mother of Methodism" in Chicago. Early members of the church were founders of Northwestern University, Garrett Theological Seminary, Wesley Memorial Hospital, the Methodist Old Peoples Home, and the Lake Bluff Children's Home. Rent from the office space in the building has helped found and support many other Methodist churches in the Chicago area.

The Chicago Temple today has a full calendar of worship services which are attended on Sundays and weekdays by members, friends, and visitors from all over the country and the world.

St. Thomas the Apostle Church 1922-24
5476 South Kimbark Avenue (1300 East)

Architect: Francis Barry Byrne
   National Register of
   Historic Places, 1978
Style: Modern
Seating: 1,200

This national landmark, designed by Barry Byrne, was the first modern-style Catholic church in America.

Someone has called St. Thomas the Apostle "a Spanish fortress on an island meadow." It is radically different from every other church built up to its time and it is recognized as the first modern-style Catholic church in America. Barry Byrne, a former employee and disciple of Frank Lloyd Wright, broke away from contemporary and revival styles of architecture and created a church that used warm, natural earth colors, was sensitively attuned to its site, and was, liturgically speaking, forty years ahead of its time.

From a large enclosed garden, indeed from a grassy meadow planted with fruit trees and flower beds, rises an expanse of russet brick with cream-colored terra cotta ornament. The wall surface on each side of the church is interrupted by four pairs of deep-slit lancet windows. The bricks at the truncated corners of the nave and narthex are laid in a herringbone pattern. The sculptured terra cotta cornice and decoration around the windows and doors are among the church's most distinctive features. They reflect the influence of Alphonso Iannelli, a sculptor whom Byrne and other Prairie School architects often engaged to embellish their designs. An unknown artist did the main entrance portal. Walking from the garden to the church, the visitor is greeted by Girolami's statue of St. Thomas the Apostle.

Inside, it was Byrne's intention to design a hall that would put the members of the congregation in close contact with the celebrant of the Mass. The altar is not set back in the apse but is brought forward into the nave, and the pews run up to and actually begin to encircle the sanctuary. This innovation anticipated the liturgical decrees of the Second Vatican Council by forty years.

The simplified interior of St. Thomas is designed to focus attention on the altar. The spaciousness of the nave was achieved by Byrne's design for what was claimed to be, at the time of its construction, the largest roof structure in the world unsupported by pillars or arches. The auditorium measures 95 by 193 feet and has no columns to obstruct the view of the altar.

The stained glass windows from the D'Ogier Studios of New Hope, Connecticut, portray the Greek and Latin Fathers of the early church. Some of their faces were derived from photographs of contemporary people and portraits of historical figures: Msgr. T. V. Shannon who was the pastor when the church was built (St. Gregory the Great), Cardinal Mundelein (St. Augustine), President Coolidge (St. Bede), George Washington (St. John Chrysostom), and Thomas Jefferson (St. Bernard).

St. Thomas the Apostle parish was founded in 1869. In its early years it was predominantly Irish. Today the church serves all nationalities and all races in the Hyde Park–University of Chicago community.

The stations of the cross by the Florentine-born American sculptor Alfeo Faggi have gained international recognition. The scenes of Christ's passion stand out boldly in bas-relief from the bronze metal. There are few details, but a strong communication of feeling. In a recess near the front of the church on the left side stands a unique bronze *Pieta*. Faggi described this sculpture as Mary's attempt "to reabsorb her son into her own being."

K.A.M.—Isaiah Israel Temple
1923-24
5045 South Greenwood Avenue (1100 East)

Architect: Alfred S. Alschuler
  Chicago Landmark, 1977
Style: Byzantine
Seating: 1,325

This Byzantine style synagogue, a Chicago landmark, houses the oldest Jewish congregation in Chicago.

Kehilath Anshe Ma'ariv, the oldest Jewish congregation in Chicago, founded in 1847, has moved south with the Jewish community from Lake Street near State in 1847, to Clark between Adams and Jackson (1851-55), to Adams and Wells (1855-71), to 26th and Indiana (1875-91), to 33rd and Indiana (1891-1922), to 50th and Drexel (1922-71). They now worship with the Isaiah Israel congregation in the temple at Greenwood Avenue and Hyde Park Boulevard.

The design of this building, constructed by the Isaiah Israel congregation, derives from early Byzantine architecture and suggests the Eastern origins of the Jewish people. The whole temple conveys the Jewish concept of the beauty of holiness. The main body of the building is octagonal in plan. The exterior and interior were developed together, each modifying the design of the other. A combination of brick and limestone is used on the exterior walls. The brick was made in varying sizes and tones of color and laid up in a random bond. This produced the soft appearance of old, hand-made, sun-baked bricks. The smoke stack on the east side of the building is built to look like a minaret. The large dome is covered with flat reddish brown tiles which harmonize with the brick below.

A series of steps on the Greenwood facade leads up to the three arched doorways of the main entrance. The doors are of solid oak; they are hung on heavy bronze hinges and studded with bronze rosettes. Above the doorways are three different bas-reliefs of a menorah, the shield of David, and a scroll bearing the Hebrew word "Truth." Crowning the entrance facade are two tablets of stone with the Ten Commandments.

The main auditorium is surmounted by a lofty dome rising 80 feet above the floor. The dome springs from eight free-standing pillars inside. A balcony surrounds most of the auditorium and seven of the eight side walls are adorned with stained glass windows by the Emil Frei Art Glass Co. of St. Louis.

The arches and dome of the auditorium are built in Guastavino construction, a masonry construction based upon Byzantine engineering principles. Much of the ornament on the exterior and interior of the temple was inspired by fragments of a second century synagogue that was discovered in Tiberias in Palestine while the design for this temple was being developed.

The focal point of the whole temple is the ark which has been crafted from Italian travertine marble and brilliantly colored mosaics. The inlaid Hebrew inscription reads, "Know before Whom thou standest." The two tablets of stone against a background of colored mosaic are encircled by the inscription, "Hear, O Israel, the Lord, our God, the Lord is One."

Above the ark and concealed by grilles is the choir loft and the four-manual Möller organ installed in 1924. It has 4,055 pipes and includes harp, chimes, and echo organ. The pipes are grouped in chambers flanking the choir balcony.

A warm, intimate chapel addition with natural overhead lighting and undulating plaster walls was designed by John Alschuler, son of the original architect, and constructed in 1973. It can be found just to the north of the main sanctuary.

167

St. Thomas Aquinas Church
1923-25
5120 West Washington
Boulevard   (100 North)

Architect: Karl M. Vitzthum
Style: Tudor Gothic
Seating: 900

This English Gothic masterpiece in Austin contains magnificent stained glass windows.

The twelve-story tower of St. Thomas Aquinas is the tallest structure in the whole Austin neighborhood. It has an array of picturesque elements including pinnacles, flying buttresses, gargoyles, English Gothic windows, and surmounting the uppermost octagonal tower, a Celtic cross. This cross is a reminder of the predominantly Irish West Side Catholic community which built this massive church in the 1920s.

Above the three portals of the main entrance on Washington Boulevard is a huge stained glass window with delicate tracery. It is called the Immaculate Conception window, featuring the Virgin Mary in the midst of angels. Seen from the inside, it is a brilliant mosaic composed of thousands of pieces of glass imported from Munich, Germany, and executed in the style of early English and French cathedral windows. The church, which is cruciform in plan, has similar large mosaic windows in the east and west transepts.

the side aisles are also decorated with gold mosaics as is the area behind each of the side altars in the front of the church.

The high altar is of terra cotta construction and was installed in 1929. Rising above the altar is a unique Eucharistic tower made from two tons of cast bronze. The tower rises about 35 feet and contains twenty bronze figures. Behind the altar is a hand-carved walnut reredos with individual figures of the twelve apostles across the top. Above and behind this is a giant mural, a copy of *The Apotheosis* [glorification] *of St. Thomas Aquinas* by the Spanish Renaissance master, Zurbaran.

Along the side aisles are stations of the cross done in ceramic tile mosaic by M. Louverse of Deserves in northern France.

The three-manual Kilgen pipe organ was purchased from the Swiss Pavilion of the 1933 Century of Progress.

All of the ceiling decoration and the paintings around the church as well as the gold mosaics were done in the early 1950s by the John A. Mallin Co. of Chicago.

The tower of St. Thomas Aquinas, once a symbol of the faith of a largely Catholic community, is now a symbol of service and welcome to a largely non-Catholic community. The priests and people of the parish have been leaders in community organization and quality education in the Austin neighborhood for many years.

The upper clerestory windows, five on each side of the nave, change to the grisaille style of glass and admit an abundance of light which gives the whole church a bright, open atmosphere. Immediately beneath these windows are spandrels containing medallions of the saints set in backgrounds of gold mosaic. The vaults over

Operation PUSH
1923-24
4945 South Drexel Boulevard
(900 East)

Architects: Newhouse and
Bernham
Style: Greek Revival
Seating: over 2,000

The impressive Greek Revival
structure at 50th and Drexel
housed the K.A.M. synagogue
from 1924 to 1971.

The impressive Greek temple building on the northeast corner of 50th Street and Drexel Boulevard was built by Kehilath Anshe Ma'ariv when they moved to this neighborhood from their synagogue at 33rd and Indiana in 1923. (See Pilgrim Baptist Church, p. 64.) This building has a free-standing colonnaded portico consisting of eight Ionic columns. The inscription on the entablature read, "Hear, O Israel, the Lord our God, the Lord is One." Today this inscription is covered with a sign announcing the present occupants of the building, Operation PUSH. The temple was sold to Operation PUSH, the black civil rights organization, when K.A.M. merged with Temple Isaiah at 5045 South Greenwood Avenue in 1971. (See K.A.M. —Isaiah Israel, pp. 166-67).

The interior of this building is as impressive as its Bedford stone exterior. Five double doorways lead into the vestibule or narthex. Four doors then lead into the huge auditorium which has a basilica plan with massive Corinthian columns down each side and an apse at the east end. Pilasters with gilded Corinthian capitals adorn all sides of the auditorium. The interior color scheme is white and gold. Beautiful wooden pews with individual seats are curved and sloped toward the pulpit platform in the apse. An inscription on the frieze above the speaker's platform reads, "Know before Whom thou standest." The interior of the auditorium is lighted by three large rectangular stained glass windows on each side.

On either side of the pulpit area are round-arched openings which once held the pipes of a fine Skinner organ. The openings are draped now since the pipes were removed to rebuild the organ in the K.A.M.—Isaiah Israel Temple on Greenwood Avenue.

Operation PUSH holds services and meetings here on Saturday mornings and has done a good job of maintaining this building.

St. Clara—St. Cyril Church
1923-27
6401 S. Woodlawn Avenue (1200 East)

Architect: Henry J. Schlacks
Restoration, 1977-80,
Paul Straka
Style: Italian Renaissance
Seating: 400, originally 800

Having survived a fire and declining population, this beautifully renovated church is an expression of confidence in a new Woodlawn.

The Indiana limestone church at the southeast corner of 64th and Woodlawn has "all the features of the Roman [Renaissance] Church," wrote Henry Schlacks, the architect. St. Clara's is 150 feet long and 113 feet wide at the transepts. It has a cruciform plan. The central facade rises 60 feet and the graceful campanile twice that height. Four majestic columns adorn the front of the church, and above each is a statue of a protector of the Carmelite order: St. Joachim, St. Ann, St. Joseph, and St. Gabriel.

St. Clara's was founded as a national parish in 1894 to serve German Catholics living east of State Street. The Carmelites were given charge of the parish in 1908. After 1910 St. Clara took on territorial limits and became predominantly English-speaking.

The original interior of the church strongly reflected the spirit of the Carmelite order. Their colors, brown and white, were used throughout the church. The altar, reredos, and communion railing were of white Sienna marble, while all the interior walls were paneled with dark brown Circassian walnut. This treatment of the walls in wood, wrote Schlacks, was intended to offset the great expense of repeated decoration. The pews were also of walnut.

In 1925 St. Therese, the Little Flower, was canonized, and in that same year St. Clara's Church became the National Shrine of the Little Flower. In subsequent years tens of thousands of people from all over the country visited the shrine.

The large stained glass windows in St. Clara's are especially beautiful. They depict great events in the history of the Carmelite order.

Two transept windows, each 10 by 20 feet, and six nave windows, each 8 by 16 feet, were created by F. X. Zettler of Munich. The brown and white color scheme is repeated in the windows.

By the mid-1920s St. Clara's was a flourishing parish. Later the population of the area became transient. In the 1950s the process of abandonment began, buildings were burned, and youth gangs frightened many families away. As a result of declining population, nearby St. Cyril parish was merged with St. Clara in 1969.

In August of 1976, an arsonist set fire to the church. The entire sanctuary area, the ceiling, and the north transept window were lost. The parish dedicated itself to rebuilding the church, and in the following year Cardinal Cody approved the plans for the work. Parishioners did much of the clean-up. Rev. Nelson Belizario, O. Carm., and architect Paul Straka planned a bright new interior. St. Clara—St. Cyril was joyfully rededicated on October 5, 1980. The rehabilitation of this church was a vote of confidence in the renewal of Woodlawn. In recent years new housing has been built in the northeast end of the neighborhood. This is a black Catholic parish which has survived abandonment and looks forward in faith to resurrection.

The Moody Memorial Church
1924-25
1630 North Clark Street
(100 West)

Architect: John R. Fugard
Style: Romanesque
Seating: 4,000

A massive Romanesque structure in brick, one of the largest Protestant church buildings in America.

Dwight L. Moody, a shoe salesman from Boston with a religious calling, arrived in Chicago in 1856 and two years later opened his own Sunday school in an old saloon building on the North Side. The school soon became so crowded that the mayor of Chicago offered him the North Market Hall for a meeting place. Moody's personal ministry, beginning with a few ragged children from Chicago's alleys, grew to be one of the largest Sunday schools in the country, developed into a great church, and eventually extended around the world.

The Moody Church is an independent, interdenominational, fundamental church devoted to a ministry of evangelism and Bible teaching.

The present home of the Moody Memorial Church was dedicated November 8, 1925. The vast structure, 140 by 225 feet, has the form of a rectangle with a semi-circular end facing Clark Street. It is constructed of brick with terra cotta trim. The windows and arches are Romanesque; a corbel table encircles the roof. There is intricate ornamental brickwork around the entrance and around the windows on the Clark Street side of the building.

The auditorium measures 120 by 184 feet and rises 68 feet from the floor to the top of the vaulted ceiling. It seats 1,700 people in the cantilevered balcony and 2,300 on the main floor. Because there are no interior columns, everyone has an unobstructed view of the pulpit and choir. Seating 4,000 people, the Moody Church is one of the largest Protestant church buildings in America.

The vault of this church, its supporting piers, and the half dome on the Clark Street side

were suggested by the design of the ancient church of St. Sophia in Istanbul. The simplicity of design and the sparing use of ornament were inspired by certain Romanesque churches built in Lombardy, Italy, in the twelfth century.

The four-manual Reuter organ with approximately 4,400 pipes, is divided into 73 ranks and has a speaking range from the lowest 32-foot bass to the highest 2-inch treble. It was entirely reconditioned in 1953.

The interior of the Moody Church is lighted by stained glass windows given in memory of various pastors and laymen and seven chandeliers, each 7 feet in diameter and 16 feet high.

The Moody Church today stands for Biblical Christianity and has a full program of evangelism, education, Bible study, broadcasting, and missionary work.

St. Gregory the Great Church
1924-26
5533 North Paulina Street
(1700 West)

Architects: Comes, Perry, and McMullen

Style: Norman Gothic
Seating: 800

The Norman Gothic style of St. Gregory's is unique in Chicago, as is the beauty of its flamboyant wood carving.

Cardinal Mundelein called it "a medieval gem in a modern setting." On the fiftieth anniversary of the parish in 1954, Cardinal Stritch spoke of St. Gregory's as a church that was not done "after the style of any other church in the New World."

Massive stone columns and arches lead the visitor's eye toward the sanctuary. But two other elements capture attention immediately, the elaborately polychromed wood truss ceiling and the jeweled art glass windows. This is, indeed, a very special church.

At the east end of the nave near the ceiling stands the Holy Rood, a large wood-carved crucifix, the suffering Christ, flanked by statues of Mary and St. John. The rood is a traditional element of English Gothic churches.

But treasures of wood carving are to be found in every corner of this medieval-styled church. The pulpit features wooden statues of the four evangelists surrounded by filigree carving, and below them, statues of saints Athanasius, Bernard, Gregory, and Augustine. The lectern and candlesticks are beautifully carved oak.

The side altar shrines are dedicated to the Blessed Virgin and St. Joseph. Each has an elaborate triptych reredos carved by Lieftuchter and painted by a Spanish artist. These triptych altars won distinction when on exhibit at The Art Institute of Chicago. All the devotional shrines around the church are decorated with flamboyant and filigree wood carving, polychrome painting, and rich biblical imagery; one more beautiful than another.

The six large stained glass windows in St. Gregory's took six years to complete. They are jewel windows fabricated from English glass. The themes in these windows represent the seven sacraments. The large window in the organ gallery shows the church's patron, the sixth century pope, St. Gregory the Great, who sent missionaries to England and all over Europe and after whom Gregorian chant was named.

The organ is a three-manual Möller pipe organ built and installed in 1926. The organ chambers are decorated with richly flamboyant wood carved screens.

The bells of St. Gregory's, ranging from 450 to 2,800 pounds, hang in the massive bell tower. The church is of masonry construction, brown brick with limestone trim. It is 161 feet long, 90 feet wide at the transepts, and 52 feet from the floor to the timbered ceiling.

Although St. Gregory's began as a German-speaking parish, it now serves the thoroughly American Summerdale neighborhood of one and two family dwellings and walk-up apartments. The parish sponsors a grade school, a high school, and many community service organizations.

St. Ita Church
1924-27
5500 North Broadway
(1200 West)

Architect: Henry J. Schlacks
Style: French Gothic
Seating: 500

A French Gothic masterpiece with art glass windows in the style of Chartres.

St. Ita was a sixth century Irish abbess who founded a convent and school in Killeedy, County Limerick, not far from the boyhood home of Rev. John Crowe who built this church and named it in her honor. This is the only church in America dedicated to St. Ita. A black stone from the ruins of the old monastic school in Killeedy is imbedded in the cornerstone of the church, a symbolic link between the ancient monastery in Ireland and this modern Christian community in Chicago.

In 1923 Father Crowe proposed the new church to Cardinal Mundelein who approved the plan and suggested the French Gothic style of architecture. The Cardinal took a great interest in the building. A large "M" appears in the carved stone parapet all around the church.

Although the plan of St. Ita's was influenced by some features of the famous cathedrals of Chartres and of Brou in France, it was, for the most part, the original creation of the architect, Henry J. Schlacks.

The church took three years to build. It is 186 feet long, 70 feet wide, and 95 feet from the sidewalk to the top of the gable. The walls are four feet thick, and 3,500 tons of Bedford stone were quarried for the church and shipped from Indiana. The open, airy tower with its delicate tracery, Gothic arches, finials, and gargoyles, rises to 120 feet and contains 1,800 tons of stone.

The wood carving on the wainscoting around the interior of the church is as intricate and delicate as the stone carving on the outside. The stations of the cross are oil paintings by Max Lenniger of Munich based upon the famous stations of the Bavarian artist Feuerstein.

The stained glass windows in St. Ita's are patterned after the medallion-type windows in the thirteenth century cathedral of Chartres. There are six large windows on each side of the nave, three large windows in the apse, and a delicate traceried rose window above the choir. Father Crowe selected the subjects, Schlacks worked out the designs, and the windows were executed by Maumejean Freres of France. The windows are composed of over 200,000 separate pieces of glass. St. Ita appears in the first window near the apse on the south side of the church; St. Patrick in the first window on the north side.

The rose window on the east facade of the church is framed by the pipes, 4,500 in all, of the four-manual Wicks organ which was installed in 1951.

St. Ita's parish was founded in 1900 in the sparsely settled Edgewater district of the city and has grown into the active church, school, community-service complex that it is today. The parish now has a large Spanish population and masses are offered both in English and Spanish.

St. Basil Church
1925-26
1840 West Garfield Boulevard
(5500 South)

Architect: Joe W. McCarthy
Style: Byzantine
Seating: 1,200

Its dome, its arches, and iconography make St. Basil's a splendid example of Byzantine architecture.

St. Basil Church is named after the great teacher and founder of Eastern monasticism and modeled after the church of *Hagia Sophia* in Constantinople, begun in 532 A.D. This beautiful church on Garfield Boulevard was erected by Irish and German Catholics, and, except that it is in the form of a Latin cross, it exemplifies many of the elements of Byzantine architecture.

Facing Garfield Boulevard at the corner of Honore Street, St. Basil's has several hundred feet of parkway in front of it, with lawn, trees, and shrubs enhancing the setting.

On the front portico, throughout the interior, and especially around the altar of the church stand columns with beautifully carved capitals. The columns on the portico are granite monoliths resting on granite steps. The Latin invitation over the front doors translates, "The Master is here, He is calling for you."

The interior of St. Basil's is dominated by a great dome 61 feet across and 100 feet high. It rests on massive pendentive arches, each one bearing the image of an angel, Gabriel, Michael, Uriel, and Raphael. Unlike the Gothic arch which points up to heaven, the Byzantine dome is a symbol of heaven itself with its blue firmament and the images of the saints standing close to the faithful on earth.

The communion arch is a richly decorated fresco with images of Christ and the twelve apostles. The half dome of the apse pictures Christ the *Pantocrator* with saints Peter, Paul, James, and John. The interior decoration of the church was done by the John A. Mallin Co. of Chicago. It is all in the Byzantine style. Red, blue, and gold colors predominate.

The main altar and communion rail of St. Basil's are made of Italian marble with inlaid Venetian mosaic. The stations of the cross are all Venetian mosaics. The stained glass windows are made from imported antique glass in medallion style.

St. Basil's parish was founded in 1904 for Irish and German Catholics, many of whom worked in the Union Stock Yards. As early as 1905 the parish opened a school staffed by the Dominican Sisters of Sinsinawa, Wisconsin. The parish grew and prospered. The debt on the new church was paid off within five years of its completion and the rectory was built in 1933. During the 1930s, Poles became a large part of the parish population together with Italians, Croatians, Slovaks, Lithuanians, and others. The newest members of the parish are Latinos and blacks.

177

Bond Chapel
1925-26
1050 East 59th Street

Architects: Coolidge and
Hodgdon
Style: English Gothic
Seating: 300

Small in proportion, yet rich in
decoration, Bond Chapel is
authentic English Gothic
architecture.

Nestled amidst the buildings
of the University of Chicago
and connected to the Divinity
School by a beautiful stone
cloister is the Joseph Bond
Chapel, given by Mary Olney
Bond in memory of her hus-
band, a former trustee of the
Baptist Theological Union.
The chapel is a gem of Gothic
Revival architecture. The
limestone building is small in
its proportions, but extremely
rich in its ornamentation and
stained glass.

The eastern facade of the
chapel is almost filled with
the leaded glass and tracery of
a large Gothic window. Above
this window and leading all
the way around the building
is a stone cornice decorated
with a curious collection of
allegorical figures. An array of
evil creatures including
demons, dragons, imps, and
griffins, can be found on the
sides and back of the chapel.
Benevolent creatures, like
angels and birds, are on the
front. The use of symbolism
continues inside the chapel

where the wood carvings and
art glass portray actions and
persons proper to the
kingdom of God.

Within the wood-paneled
chapel, the dominant visual
image one receives is that
of being surrounded by a
treasure of stained glass or of
being in a jewel box. The
windows were done by
Charles J. Connick of Boston
and donated by Edgar Goodspeed in memory of his wife,
Elfleda Bond Goodspeed.
They beautifully express the
mysteries of the Christian
faith. A band on the south
windows reads: "Enter into
His gates with thanksgiving
and into His courts with
praise—Be thankful unto Him
and bless His name." And on
the north windows: "And the
peace of God which passeth
all understanding shall keep
your hearts and minds
through Jesus Christ."

The most intense concentra-
tion of symbolism in the
chapel is on the chancel
window directly above the
altar. This is a comprehensive
spectacle of the whole New
Testament beginning with the
activities of Jesus and his
disciples, the spread of the
faith, and its culmination in
the visions of the Apocalypse.

The balcony of the chapel
contains a small Schlicker
organ. On the open-beamed
roof are polychrome angels
playing musical instruments;
carved wooden angels hold
up the suspended lights of
the chapel.

Bond Chapel serves the Divinity School of the University of
Chicago; its purpose is to
provide a sanctuary for
student worship. It is used for
weddings, funerals, daily
vespers, Episcopalian services
on Sunday, and performances
by small musical groups from
time to time.

St. Chrysostom's Church
1925-26
1424 N. Dearborn Parkway
(50 West)

Architect: Chester H. Walcott
Style: English Gothic
Seating: 590

This beautiful English Gothic church contains elegant art glass windows by Charles Connick of Boston.

On Sundays around midday the 43-bell carillon of St. Chrysostom's sounds over the Near North Side. This carillon, made in Croydon, England, was installed in 1927. The bells range from 9 to 5,600 pounds, with a total weight of over six tons.

The Episcopal parish of St. Chrysostom was incorporated in March of 1894, at which time a frame church was constructed on North Dearborn Street. In 1925 the present limestone edifice was erected over the frame building even while services were being held in it. The reconstructed building received a gold medal from the American Institute of Architects in 1926. It is considered one of the most beautiful churches in the Chicago area.

Entering the church through the cloisters at the west end of the garden, the visitor will see on his left the mosaic of St. John (c. 345-407 A.D.), the Patriarch of Constantinople whose holy life and eloquent preaching merited him the title of *chrysostom*, the Greek word for "golden mouthed." This mosaic is an exact replica of a tenth century mosaic in the church of St. Sophia in Constantinople, now Istanbul.

The main altar in St. Chrysostom's Church is of hand-carved oak and the triptych which surmounts it is of carved limewood. The panels in the triptych portray the Nativity, Crucifixion, and Ascension of Christ. The design of the altar and sanctuary in this church was the last commission of Chicago architect David Adler.

Within the chancel are choir seats on the left, and on the right, the console and many pipes of the four-manual, 90-rank Möller organ installed in 1979. More pipes are located at the rear of the nave.

Between the banks of organ pipes on the east wall of the church is the great *Te Deum Laudamus* window showing Christ, the King of Glory, surrounded by men and women of the Old and New Testaments who praise His name. This window and the others in the church were created by Charles J. Connick of Boston. The north nave windows feature great women of the gospels: Mary, Elizabeth, and Martha and Mary of Bethany; while the south nave windows feature the evangelists and St. John the Baptist.

The large Ascension panel in the north transept is a remarkable painting on thin slabs of wood. It is also by Connick and was dedicated in 1937.

Throughout the church are *fleur-de-lis*, symbolizing the Holy Trinity, and beehives, symbolizing St. John Chrysostom whose words flowed like honey.

This beautiful church on Dearborn Parkway is the center of many religious, social, and educational activities.

St. Sabina Church
1925-33
7821 South Throop Street
(1300 West)

Architect: Joe W. McCarthy
Style: English Gothic
Seating: 1,000

Beautiful oak paneling and elaborate wood carving decorate the interior of this English Gothic edifice.

The Tudor Gothic tower of St. Sabina Church rises above the treetops and rooftops, a prominent landmark of faith and community service on the South Side. The parish buildings—church, rectory, school, convent, and community center—occupy an entire city block. The social and athletic programs of St. Sabina's have been known throughout the city for decades.

The lower church at the northeast corner of 78th Place and Throop was erected in 1925-26. The construction of the magnificent upper church was begun, amazingly, in 1931 and completed two years later in the midst of the Depression. The church is cruciform in plan, is faced with Indiana limestone, and is decorated inside and out with elaborate wood and stone carving.

Broad flights of granite steps lead up to the three-portal, arched entrances on Throop Street. Delicate stone tracery fills the tympanum above each double door. More stone tracery, blind arcades, and Gothic spires decorate the central facade above the doors and beneath the great rose window with its flamboyant tracery. Above the rose window and beneath the cross which crowns the central gable is the coat of arms of Cardinal Mundelein, who dedicated this church in 1933.

The narthex of St. Sabina has a magnificently ornamented gold and white ceiling. Inside the auditorium, the visitor will find the lower walls covered with dark oak paneling above marble wainscoting. Fourteen stations of the cross, each carved from a single piece of oak, appear around the nave and transepts. Above

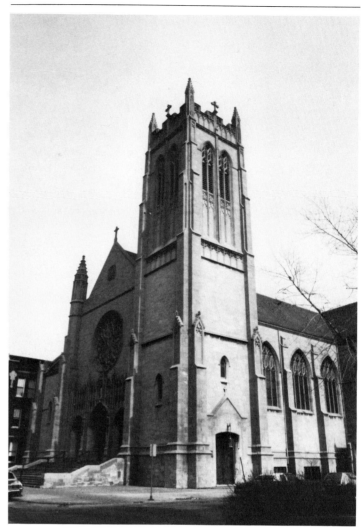

the stations are brilliant medallion-style stained glass windows made with imported European glass. The ceiling of the church has graceful ribbed vaulting, and from the ceiling hang beautiful glass and bronze chandeliers.

The delicate wood carving which adorns the pulpit, the side altar shrines, and the reredos above the high altar is the finest in the church. In accord with the liturgical norms of Vatican II, a free-standing altar has been built on a platform at the crossing in the body of the church. A large picture of the Black Risen Christ painted by Cedric E. Jenkins hangs in the middle of the reredos above the high altar.

St. Sabina Church has an illustrious history, first serving Irish Catholic families and now serving black Catholic families and many others in the Auburn Highlands neighborhood. The parish conducts a grade school under the direction of the Sinsinawa Dominican sisters, has several fine choirs, and has a full schedule of religious and social programs. St. Sabina's is one of the leading black parishes on the South Side of Chicago.

St. Philip Neri Church
1926-28
2126 East 72nd Street

Architect: Joe W. McCarthy
Style: Tudor Gothic
Seating: 1,700

This massive Gothic church in Plymouth granite has beautiful walnut paneling and delicate wood carving inside.

St. Philip Neri in the South Shore neighborhood is one of the largest churches in Chicago. It is a sturdy masonry building constructed of Plymouth granite with Bedford stone trim and a slate roof. The ornamental stone carving around the entrance-way and the tracery in the rose windows is especially fine. The main entrance to the church is adorned with a pair of beautiful iron gates, and a copper spire or flèche, 164 feet high, towers above the crossing of the nave and transepts. The church is set back on a beautifully landscaped site.

The narthex of St. Philip's has a coffered ceiling, polished stone floor, dark wooden doors, and elegant sconces and chandeliers. Beyond the narthex is the great space of the nave which is dominated by the soft yellow marble of the permanent altar and reredos. The twin towers of the reredos with intricate tracery between them are flanked by organ pipes, set like swallows' nests on the north wall. A beautiful rose window high on the north wall completes the design of the sanctuary.

The church is cruciform in plan and is reputed to have the longest communion rail in the Chicago area. Wainscoting around the interior of the auditorium is done in walnut, rises about 12 feet on the walls, and is topped with small hand-carved Gothic spires.

The stained glass windows by John Terrence O'Duggan are large, numerous, and very beautiful. Especially handsome are the rose windows in the transepts, above the altar, and above the entrance. The stations of the cross were done in mosaic by P. Dachiardi of Rome in 1930.

St. Philip Neri parish was founded in 1912 to serve a predominantly Irish-American population in South Shore. Today, the community is predominantly black, but the congregation is integrated. The parish conducts a grade school, social programs for youth and senior citizens, and is involved with several community development organizations in the South Shore area.

Architect: Bertram G. Goodhue
Style: Neo-Gothic
Seating: 1,900

Rockefeller Chapel with its lofty tower and stately nave is the most impressive structure on the campus of the University of Chicago.

"As the spirit of religion should penetrate and control the university, so that building which represents religion ought to be the central and dominant feature of the university group . . ." These words of John D. Rockefeller, founder of the University of Chicago, are inscribed on a dedication plaque in the narthex of the chapel.

This chapel was originally known as the University of Chicago Chapel. Its name was changed in the summer of 1937 after the death of its donor, John D. Rockefeller. The chapel is, visually, the most impressive structure on the campus. It is 265 feet long, 120 feet wide at the transepts, and its massive tower rises 207 feet, higher than any other building of the university.

Rockefeller Chapel is of masonry construction, brick with an Indiana limestone face. The only reinforced concrete is in the great arch which supports the west wall of the tower. The masonry walls at the base of the tower are eight feet thick. Steel beams carry the concrete slabs of the roof; but the rest of the building is brick and stone.

The south facade of the chapel rises majestically. Above the arched doorway and the massive traceried window is a procession of life-size sculptures of religious figures. They wind around the turrets and fill the slant of the gable. They are, from left to right, Abraham, Moses, Elijah, Isaiah, Zoroaster, Plato, John the Baptist, Christ, at the peak, Peter, Paul, Athanasius, Augustine, St. Francis, Luther, and Calvin. The stone sculptures of the chapel are the work of Lee Lawrie and Ulric Ellerhusen of New York.

Entering the chapel through the main doors and the narthex, the visitor is immediately struck by the great height of the walls and the length of the building. It is 79 feet from the floor to the vaulted ceiling. Massive stone piers and Gothic arches support the 800-ton ceiling.

Three huge clerestory windows, almost 43 feet high, adorn each side of the nave. These are leaded glass windows formed in intricate geometrical designs.

The chapel has an irregular cruciform plan with the east transept, the base of the tower, somewhat larger than the west. The chancel is deep and spacious and has been treated as a chapter house with rows of carved oak choir seats facing each other on either side of the sanctuary. Behind the communion table at the rear of the chancel is a lofty, delicately carved stone reredos.

The interior of Rockefeller Chapel presents a rather uniform gray appearance with two notable exceptions: the brilliant red, blue, and gold cinquefoil glass at the top of the north chancel window and the sixteen liturgical banners which decorate the nave and the east transept. The cinquefoil was designed by Harold Haydon in memory of Professor James Weber Linn and dedicated on May 19, 1979. The 15-by-5-foot banners designed by Norman Laliberte are part of a series of 44 banners created by the Canadian-American artist for display at the Vatican Pavilion of the 1964-65 World's Fair in New York City. In scores of brilliant colors, the banners depict scenes from the life of Christ, the saints, and highlights in the church calendar. They were presented to the University of Chicago in 1966 by Earle Ludgin as a memorial to his wife, Mary MacDonald Ludgin. During the Autumn Quarter of each year, the sixteen banners are replaced with another series of sixteen.

Dominating the east wall of the chancel are the mag-

nificent pipes and wood carving of the organ case. The organ, a 103-stop E. M. Skinner, is one of the finest organs in the country. The console, on the west side of the chancel, has four manuals and pedal. There is an antiphonal organ with an additional 23 stops in the choir gallery. The music performed on this organ together with the 72-bell carillon in the tower and the Rockefeller Chapel Choir is a worthy complement to the architecture of the building.

Religious services are held each Sunday in Rockefeller Chapel with sermons by the Dean of the Chapel and clergymen of various faiths, races, and nationalities.

First Presbyterian Church
1927-28
6400 South Kimbark Avenue
(1300 East)

Architects: Tallmadge and
Watson
Style: English Gothic
Seating: 1,200

**Designed by the distinguished
architectural firm of Tallmadge
and Watson, this church is
authentic English Gothic.**

The First Presbyterian Church
of Chicago was founded in
Fort Dearborn on June 26,
1833. Twelve men and four
women made up the congre-
gation with Rev. Jeremiah
Porter as pastor. After three
locations in the central part of
the city and one at 21st and
Indiana, First Church merged
with the Forty-First Street
Presbyterian Church in 1913.
Together they occupied the
church building at 41st Street
and Grand Boulevard, now
King Drive, until 1926. (See p.
58.) In that year First Church
merged with the Woodlawn
Park Presbyterian Church and
built the beautiful edifice seen
today at the corner of 64th
Street and Kimbark Avenue.

The following is an excerpt
from the 1928 dedication
booklet: "The new home of
the First Presbyterian Church
is Gothic. This is evidenced
from without by its great
tower, its traceried windows,
its pointed arches and its
leaded glass. Within, the
carved oak and 'the long
drawn fretted aisle' speak no
less eloquently of the glory of
the Gothic . . ."

In the same booklet Thomas
Tallmadge wrote, "The building in its entirety is dominated by a great tower, one
hundred and twenty-five feet
in height. . . . The material is
all of variegated Indiana
limestone. The massiveness
and plainness of the walls is
broken up by buttresses,
heavy and powerful on the
church and light and graceful
on the parish house; by
pointed windows, some open,
some elaborately traceried by
canopied niches, by carving
such as the flowered capitals
of the cloister, the heads of
the children in the north
portal or the stony figures
of the archangels crowning
the tower."

The auditorium of First
Church is 95 feet long, 62 feet

wide, and 49 feet high from
the floor to the open-truss
ceiling. Above the altar and
communion table rises a great
stone reredos, 40 feet high,
designed by Elizabeth Eberele.
It contains three stained glass
windows which portray the
Lord in Glory with Mary and
St. John. They were produced
by the Willett Studio of Philadelphia. The nave windows
are by R. Toland Wright of
Cleveland and present subjects from the life of Christ.

The organ in First Church is a
four-manual Möller organ
with 70 stops and 3,300 pipes,
including chimes and harp.

In the cloister and garth of
the First Presbyterian is a
collection of historic stones
from four former churches of
this congregation and from
other famous churches and
historic sites around the
world. A beam from the old
Fort Dearborn was installed in
the ceiling of the cloister.

First Presbyterian has a rich
history and tradition. Its surrounding neighborhood has
undergone racial change and
has declined in recent years,
but is showing signs of redevelopment now. The church
supports many social service
programs including a day care
center, a food pantry, housing
rehabilitation, and a solar
greenhouse. First Presbyterian
is a very active congregation
with a membership that is 75
percent black and 25 percent
white.

St. Viator Church
1927-29
4160 West Addison Street
(3600 North)

Architect: Charles L. Wallace
Style: Tudor Gothic
Seating: 1,200

This English Gothic church on the Northwest Side possesses a treasure of medieval style art glass windows.

St. Viator's, founded in 1888 in what was then the town of Jefferson, is one of the oldest Catholic parishes on the Northwest Side. More than twenty-five parishes have been founded from its original boundaries.

The limestone Tudor Gothic Church is set on a landscaped site facing Addison Street. It is flanked by the rectory on the west and the convent on the east. The three buildings form an attractive ensemble. The church is cruciform in plan and has a broad nave with no interior pillars.

The stained glass windows in St. Viator's, done by the Emil Frei Art Glass Co. of St. Louis, are especially noteworthy. They are designed in the thirteenth century medallion style with deep reds and blues in imitation of the windows in the cathedral at Chartres. The windows in the apse present Eucharistic themes and pictures of saints associated with the Eucharist. The nave windows on the east side all portray scenes from the New Testament, while those on the west illustrate events from the Old Testament. The east transept windows show the release of souls from purgatory; the west transept honors the Virgin Mary. The south window illustrates an inscription on the cornerstone of the church, Jesus' words, "Let the little children come unto Me."

St. Viator's parish is served by the Viatorian fathers. It has a large elementary school directed by the Sisters of St. Joseph of Carondelet, and there is an active community center on the north end of the property. The parish has a large Polish membership together with a growing Spanish-speaking population.

Architects: Loebl, Schlossman
and Demuth with Coolidge
and Hodgdon
Style: Byzantine
Seating: 1,350

**Byzantine forms, indicative of
the Middle Eastern origins of
the Jewish people, decorate this
impressive synagogue on Lake
Shore Drive.**

In 1921 three young graduate students in the School of Architecture at Armour Institute, later to become IIT, were given a project to design a synagogue. Gerald Loebl, Norman J. Schlossman, and John Demuth completed the project which not many years later would become Temple Sholom on Lake Shore Drive.

The plan for the temple is octagonal, resembling early Byzantine churches. An aisle with many memorial plaques and a beautiful terrazzo floor proceeds around seven sides of the sanctuary at ground level. The sanctuary itself is 90 by 90 feet with theater seating sloping toward the ark on the west side of the room.

The sanctuary is covered with an octagonal dome, 90 feet high, which has at its center a unique silver-tinted inverted teardrop cone which is illuminated by ten hidden lamps. The cone in turn reflects light throughout the sanctuary. The illumination of the room is very special; it is all indirect.

A special feature of the walnut-paneled sanctuary is the west wall which carries the ark, pulpit, and platform. The whole wall and platform are mounted on wheels and can be moved back into the community center to increase the seating capacity of the sanctuary from 1,350 to 2,500 for the High Holy Day

services. The choir loft and organ are located on the east wall of the sanctuary above the vestibule.

The exterior of the temple is faced with Wisconsin Lannon stone, is trimmed with Indiana limestone, and has an elaborate ornamentation in Byzantine decorative motifs. The ornament includes stone columns with richly carved and varied capitals, as well as carved stone portals, dentils, and arcades. The exterior decorative motifs are brought inside and can also be found on the wood carving in the sanctuary.

Temple Sholom has one of the largest theater organs installed in Chicago, a four-manual, 30-rank Wurlitzer pipe organ. The stained glass windows on the north and south faces of the building were brought from the congregation's previous home, now the Anshe Emet Synagogue on Pine Grove Avenue and Grace Street.

The Frankenstein Memorial Community Center is linked to the sanctuary on the west side, but is separate from it. It contains space for meetings and social events and has two floors of classrooms for religious education.

**First Unitarian Church of Chicago   1929-31
5650 South Woodlawn Avenue   (1200 East)**

Architect: Denison B. Hull
Style: English Gothic
Seating: about 400

A fine example of English Perpendicular Gothic, First Unitarian was the last stone-on-stone church built in Chicago.

The First Unitarian Church of Chicago is a pure example of English Perpendicular Gothic architecture. It is the last stone-on-stone church built in Chicago. No steel was used in the construction of the church or tower, only in the steeple. In fact, Denison Hull designed the church with no spire; but the pastor, Rev. Von Ogden Vogt, insisted that there be one. So Hull changed the design to include the slender spire with the weather vane on top which rises a total of 200 feet above the Hyde Park —University of Chicago neighborhood.

The exterior of the building is made of split-faced Indiana limestone and the interior is of sawed stone. The vaults of the ceiling are stone too. The long, narrow nave of this church conforms perfectly with the Gothic ideal. The high vaulted aisles of First Unitarian are said to lead the worshiper to a certain communion with the infinite. High above the altar is a bright rose window done by Charles J. Connick of Boston. The nave of the church is somewhat somber until it is lighted by a double row of chandeliers.

The warmest and brightest and also the oldest space in this church is the Hull Memorial Chapel, or south transept, designed by William Augustus Otis. It was built in 1896 and dedicated in 1897. The great Gothic church was actually built around Hull Chapel which features light brown Roman brick walls, magnificent traceried woodwork, a wooden hammer-beam, open-trussed ceiling, large amber-colored stained glass windows, and a two-manual Schlicker organ.

The main church has a three-manual, 34-rank, Ernest M. Skinner organ with 2,220 pipes designed especially for this church and installed in 1931. Its console is hidden from sight on the south side of the chancel.

Beneath the nave of First Unitarian is a marble burial crypt containing cinerary urns, the first such crypt in a Chicago church. The Italian marble baptismal font, designed by August H. Burley in 1867, dates from an earlier church building on Wabash Avenue, downtown.

The present church on Woodlawn Avenue, completed in 1931 at a cost of one million dollars, is the pride of the First Unitarian Society of Chicago. First Unitarian sponsors a Sunday school, the Chicago Children's Choir, the Depot— a family counseling center, a preschool, a day care center, and numerous other activities. Services are held on Sunday mornings at 10:30.

St. Gertrude Church
1930-31
6204 N. Glenwood Avenue
(1400 West)

Architect: James Burns
Style: English Gothic
Seating: 1,200

This graceful English Gothic church in North Edgewater has a brilliant array of stained glass windows.

Late in 1911 the Catholic residents of North Edgewater asked Archbishop Quigley to establish a new parish under the patronage of St. Gertrude. He did so, appointing Rev. Peter Shewbridge the first pastor. Rev. Bernard C. Heeney succeeded him in 1918 and with the parishioners built the beautiful English Gothic limestone church that stands on the corner of Granville and Glenwood avenues. St. Gertrude's was one of the few Catholic churches in Chicago constructed during the Great Depression.

The church has graceful Gothic lines, a wide expanse of vaulted ceiling with no pillars, and beautiful stained glass windows. The windows were made by Franz Mayer and Company of Munich and were installed in 1931 at a cost of $48,000.

The altars of St. Gertrude's are pure white marble imported from Italy. The reredos behind the central altar was made from cloth woven especially for the coronation of Queen Elizabeth II of England in 1953 and acquired for the church by Msgr. J. Gerald Kealy, pastor from 1936 to 1968.

The three-manual Kilgen pipe organ has thirty ranks and has accompanied fine men and boys choirs through the years.

St. Gertrude's has a large elementary school conducted by the Sisters of Charity, B.V.M., and today has a cosmopolitan membership comprising almost every race and nationality of people.

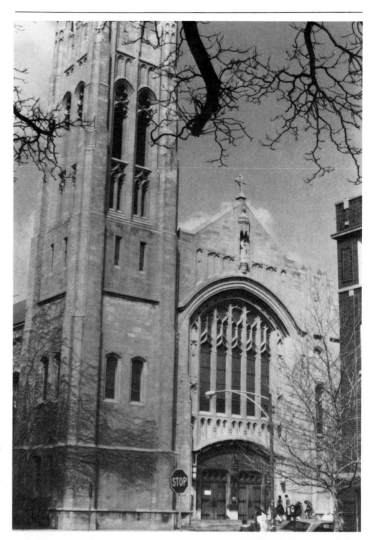

St. Pascal Church
1930-31
6149 West Irving Park Road
(4000 North)

Architects: B.J. Hotton
and Raymond Gregori
Style: Spanish Mission
Seating: 1,000

St. Pascal's is a masterpiece on a large scale of Spanish Mission style architecture.

St. Pascal's Church with its red tile roofs and 115-foot tower can be seen from blocks away, a monument of faith in the Austin—Irving neighborhood. The building is constructed of beige-colored face brick with terra cotta trim. It is cruciform in plan with the altar located in the apse at the south end of the structure. Decoration on the church is abundant; especially noteworthy is the terra cotta ornament on the gables and around the windows and doorways. There is even ornamental embossing on the copper gutters and downspouts.

One enters the vestibule through heavy, dark wooden doors, and from there proceeds into the main body of the church. The flat ceiling and the sanctuary apse are reminiscent of a basilica-style church. The ceiling appears to be constructed with wooden beams. It is actually made of steel beams covered with plaster which then was textured and painted to appear like wood.

Large areas of the half dome apse are covered with gold glass mosaic. There is an ambulatory behind the altar, and the red carpet in the sanctuary matches the red "timbered" ceiling of the nave. The altar and its furnishings have been simplified in accord with the liturgical norms of the Second Vatican Council. The wrought iron communion rail that once enclosed the altar area was removed to open this space to the congregation. The iron of the communion rail was then used to make the decorative grillwork in the alcoves flanking the apse. These spaces were previously used for side altars.

On each side of the nave is a five-column arcade with richly carved trefoil arches and stone columns having elaborate capitals. Above each arch is the name of a saint who was especially devoted to the Holy Eucharist: six male saints on the west side, six female saints on the east side. The saints featured in the stained glass windows in the clerestory, four on each side, have a similar division between males and females.

St. Pascal parish, named after the sixteenth century Franciscan brother whose life was distinguished by kindness to the poor and devotion to the Holy Eucharist, was founded in 1914. Msgr. George Heimsath began the parish, built the church, school, convent, and rectory, and served as pastor for forty-four years until his death in 1959. His successor, Rev. T. J. Neckerman, made the changes in the church called for by Vatican II. The Sisters of St. Francis of Joliet conduct the elementary school.

St. Pascal's is a large, yet warm and reverent church. The structure, furnishings, and decoration all work together to create a unified, tasteful effect, a beautiful house of worship.

**St. Bartholomew Church
1937-38
3601 North Lavergne Avenue
(5000 West)**

Architect: Gerald A. Barry
Style: American Colonial
Seating: 1,050

This American Colonial style church features a handsome facade and a beautifully simple interior.

The American Colonial style of architecture was derived from the Georgian style which in turn was based upon Renaissance forms. St. Bartholomew Church was designed in this tradition. The building is cruciform in plan. It is constructed with red face brick all the way around with limestone trim and with limestone quoins at each corner.

The church faces Lavergne Avenue and the three-door entrance is sheltered with a handsome high-columned portico. An entablature carries a Latin inscription which translates, "For the greater glory of God." Above this is a pediment with an oval window in its center. Just behind the pediment, rising up through the gable of the roof, is a square brick tower surmounted by an octagonal stone belfry with arches, columns, and ornamental urns, and then a sharply pointed spire topped with a cross.

The interior of St. Bartholomew is bright and spacious and has a simplicity of design that is characteristic of the Colonial style. The rough plaster walls and ceiling panels are divided by pilasters and arched beams. Mural decoration was entirely eliminated in the design of the nave except for the bronze stations of the cross. The altars are constructed of various kinds of marble, while the bright stained glass windows in the nave and transepts were made by the Franz Mayer Co. of Munich.

St. Bartholomew parish was founded in 1917 to serve English-speaking Catholics who lived west of St. Viator parish. Today, the congregation consists of about 3,000 families of different ethnic backgrounds.

**The Assumption
Greek Orthodox Church
1937-38
601 South Central Avenue
(5600 West)**

Architect: Peter E. Camburas
Style: Byzantine with
Romanesque elements
Seating: 550

The great central dome and the beautiful portico facing Columbus Park announce the Byzantine character of The Assumption church.

The Eisenhower motorist sees the large copper dome of The Assumption a block north of the expressway at Central Avenue, just north of Loretto Hospital. The Latin cross plan of the building, its central dome and clerestory, and the heavy emphasis on the portico are similar in composition to the eleventh century Cathedral of SS. Peter and Gorgonus in Minden, Germany. The architect's choice of materials, however, cream-colored Wisconsin Lannon stone, red clay mission-tile roof, copper trim, and oak doors, has transformed the Germanic configuration into one having the spirit and warmth of the congregation's Mediterranean culture.

The three-portal entrance on Central Avenue announces the artistic motifs of the church. The two columns with the beautifully carved Byzantine capitals are similar to the columns which support the barrel vault of the nave. All the vertical lines in the church terminate in round arches. This motif culminates in the dome, over 40 feet in diameter, which rises over the intersection of the nave and transepts. The dome is carried on pendentives in authentic Byzantine style.

The interior of The Assumption was decorated in 1945 and again in the late 1970s with authentic Byzantine iconography. The brilliant stained glass windows featuring the Repose of Mary and the saints of the Eastern church are also Byzantine in design and concept. They were executed by the F. X. Zettler Studio of Munich in 1959-60. The beautiful chandeliers which hang near the transepts of the church were donated by Balaban and Katz, the theater operators, in 1944. The church measures 75 by 150 feet.

Beneath the main body of the church is a Sunday school chapel. And just to the east of the church is the parish's Plato School.

The Greek-American community of The Assumption was established in 1925 at the terminus of the Harrison street-car line. Services were held in a frame building until the present church was opened in 1938. The official ceremony of consecration took place in 1947.

Services at The Assumption are conducted in Greek and English. Members of this congregation come from Chicago and all over the western suburbs to worship here.

**Madonna della Strada Chapel
1938-39
6525 North Sheridan Road
(at Lake Michigan)**

Architect: Andrew Rebori
Style: Modern
Seating: 725

This chapel is modern yet graceful with stress on masses, smooth surfaces, and continuous lines.

It was in September of 1924 that Rev. James J. Mertz, S.J., first conceived the idea of building a chapel for students on the Lake Shore Campus of Loyola University. With the help of personal friends, he then began a fund raising campaign that continued for several decades until the chapel and its furnishings were complete.

The basic design of the chapel, facing Lake Michigan and paralleling the Cudahy Library, was determined by that building which was also designed by Andrew Rebori. The style is modern with stress on masses, on continuous lines, and on smooth surfaces of limestone.

The tower of Madonna della Strada reaches 108 feet into the sky. Father Mertz intended the chapel to be "a haven of peace and a place of retirement and meditation." The lakeside facade of the chapel symbolizes the Blessed Sacrament held aloft in benediction. The roof over the sanctuary at the west end of the building is unique. Each of the five stone ribs carries a continuous arching band of glass brick which illuminates the altar and sanctuary with daylight.

The chapel is named in honor of Mary, the mother of Jesus, under the ancient Roman title, *Madonna della Strada*, Our Lady of the Way. St. Ignatius Loyola, the founder of the Society of Jesus, had a special devotion to Mary under this title, and the first church of the Society in Rome was that of Santa Maria della Strada. Father Mertz predicted that "the chapel of our Lady, on the great Outer Drive, will become the central pilgrimage point of those who love the Mother of God."

Inside the chapel on the west wall is a 9-by-30-foot fresco of Jesus crowning Mary as Queen of Heaven and Queen of the Society of Jesus. The painting by Mel Steinfels also portrays all the saints of the Society except the North American martyrs who have their own shrine on the south side of the chapel. Other examples of Steinfels' work are the lanterns in the nave and the stations of the cross painted around the interior of the chapel.

The windows in the chapel are made from the finest English glass. Those on the north side depict the professional departments of the university at the time the windows were installed, 1945-50. The windows on the south wall present the various apostolic works undertaken by the Society of Jesus.

Beneath the sanctuary of Madonna della Strada are six crypt chapels which form a chevet around a seventh. These chapels, like the sanctuary of the church, are constructed with the finest of marble acquired by Father Mertz from all over the world.

The organ in the chapel is a four-manual, 48-rank Wicks organ.

This lovely and stately building stands as a tribute to Mary, Our Lady of the Way, and to Father Mertz (1882-1979) who personified the finest elements of human learning, personal warmth, and Jesuit spirituality.

**Elijah Muhammad Mosque
#2**
1948-52
**7351 S. Stony Island Avenue
(1600 East)**
Architect: Christopher
Chamales
Style: Neo-Byzantine
Seating: 1,800

**The impressive structure at
74th and Stony Island contains
elements of authentic Byzantine
architecture.**

The imposing limestone structure set back on the landscaped site at the corner of 74th Street and Stony Island Avenue was built by the Greek Orthodox congregation of SS. Constantine and Helen. The building exemplifies authentic Byzantine architecture and, at the time it was built, it was the largest Greek Orthodox church in North and South America. The dome, 70 feet high and 60 feet in diameter, is styled after that of St. Sophia in Constantinople. There are twelve windows, each twelve feet high, around the base of the dome.

The interior of the church was decorated with Byzantine iconography of tenth century style and featured a marble *iconostasis* and an altar rail with mosaic icons. Most of the interior art work was removed in 1972 when the church was sold to the Black Muslims.

The parish of St. Constantine was established in 1909 at 6105 South Michigan Avenue by immigrant Greek Orthodox Christians living on the South Side. It was the second Greek Orthodox church in Chicago. The parish prospered and became one of the largest and most progressive of the Greek Orthodox Archdiocese of North and South America. The parish buildings on Michigan Avenue were

destroyed by fire in 1926 and rebuilt at the same location. In 1946 the parish moved to 74th Street and Stony Island Avenue in the South Shore area.

This church was sold to the Black Muslims for four million dollars in 1972 and the parish of SS. Constantine and Helen relocated and built a new church in suburban Palos Hills.

St. Peter's Church
1951-53
110 West Madison Street

Architects: Karl Vitzthum
and John Burns
Style: Modern Gothic
Seating: 1,500

St. Peter's is a place of spiritual refuge in the midst of skyscrapers.

St. Peter's has been called "a house of God in a valley of stone." It stands in the midst of skyscrapers. It has no resident parishioners, and yet every weekday there are fifteen Masses offered from 5:30 in the morning until evening. On holy days there are thirty-seven Masses offered at various altars with an average of 500 people attending each. Approximately 500,000 Catholic people work and shop in Chicago's Loop every day. St. Peter's offers them an opportunity to attend Mass, to receive Communion, to attend devotions, and to find a place to pray.

St. Peter's is a five-story building, measuring 170 by 80 feet, and consisting of the main church, two chapels on the second floor, an auditorium/chapel in the basement, and three floors of living space at the top for the Franciscan fathers and brothers assigned to the church.

The marble facade is dominated by a giant crucifix, Christ of the Loop, designed by the Latvian sculptor Arvid Strauss and executed by the Chicago sculptor J. Watts. The work is 18 feet tall and weighs 26 tons.

The interior of the church is paneled with highly polished Georgia pink stone. The only window in the body of the church is the Gothic stained glass window on the Madison Street facade which is dedicated to Mary, Queen of Peace. In place of windows, there are ten recessed panels, five on each side of the nave, portraying in bas-relief scenes from the life of St. Francis of Assisi. The Botticino marble panels, each 8 by 15 feet, were carved by Carlo Vinchessi, an Italian sculptor, from sketches by a Chicago artist named Louis Carraciolo. Carraciolo also painted the stations of the cross around the church.

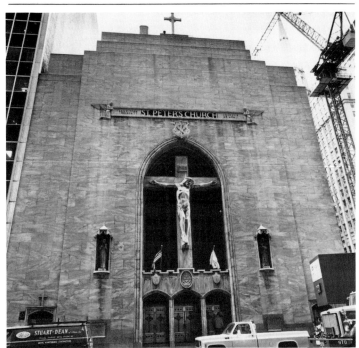

The cream-colored Botticino marble of the nave panels was also used for the main altar, the lofty reredos behind it, and the canopy above it. The crucifixion group is in white Carrara marble.

St. Peter's has a three-manual, 30-rank Reuter organ. Historically, St. Peter's was the first German Catholic parish in Chicago, founded in 1846 on Washington Street between Wells and Franklin streets. A brick church, built at the southwest corner of Clark and Polk streets in 1865, was given over to the care of the Franciscans in 1875, and remained in use until the present church was opened in 1953.

IIT Chapel
1952
3200 South Michigan Avenue
(100 East)
Architect:
 Ludwig Mies van der Rohe
Style: International
Seating: about 100

Rectangular simplicity characterizes this chapel designed by Ludwig Mies van der Rohe.

The Chapel of St. Saviour on the campus of the Illinois Institute of Technology is the sole example of church design by Mies van der Rohe, one of the acknowledged masters of modern architecture.

The overall simplicity of the chapel design and its original furnishings were meant to evoke a personal contemplation of the deity. The structure is a simple rectangle, 37 by 60 feet, constructed of brick and glass. Brick masonry bearing walls set in an English bond wrap around three sides of the chapel. On the fourth side, brick walls flank the floor-to-ceiling glass portal. A steel frame roof tops the structure and a dark terrazzo floor covers the radiant heating system.

The focal point of the chapel is a solid rectangular altar of light travertine. The altar is framed by a large silk curtain and surmounted by a six-foot chromium cross. Simple portable chairs with metal frames provide the seating in the chapel. The six glass panels and the double glass doors on the east wall create a meditation chapel which relates the world to the sacred.

The chapel was decorated in October, 1978 with textile hangings on the south wall. The tapestries depict the biblical saga of Noah, the Flood, and Reconciliation. They were made by a faculty-student team at The Art Institute of Chicago under the direction of Helen O'Rourke.

St. Saviour Chapel was sponsored by the Episcopal Diocese of Chicago and dedicated to the memory of Robert Franklin Carr, former president of Dearborn Chemical Company. In addition to regular Christian liturgy, IIT Chapel accommodates several student study and prayer groups, music and dance classes, and various ethnic and social functions. There is a certain tension between the simplicity of the original design concept and the furnishings added for liturgical celebrations.

St. Gall Church
1955-58
5500 South Kedzie Avenue
(3200 West)

Architects: Pavlecic and
Kovacevic and Ota
Style: Modern
Seating: 1,400

This modern, central plan church
anticipated many of the liturgical
reforms of Vatican II by ten
years.

It was the wish of Rev. James D. Hishen, the pastor of St. Gall's, that the new church be designed so that the congregation would feel close to the altar and be able to participate more actively in the Mass. "The altar should be the true center of the church," Father Hishen told the architects. Working with these directions, Radoslav Kovacevic created a central plan church in a quarter circle design. The freestanding altar was placed in the center of the circle and became the focal point of the church. The pews fan out around the altar. Behind the altar is a white plaster wall with gold wire mesh crosses on it. The sanctuary is flooded with light from a clerestory window above and from tall hidden windows on each side. The side walls of the church are constructed of hand-made bricks, each of which is coated with a patina green

glaze. The stations of the cross on the side walls, created by Peter Recker, are made of hand-hammered bronze. They are flat, but majestic in their height. The plaster ceiling is made up of a series of diamond patterns; it contains light and heat sources, and its lines, like those of the walls, converge on the altar.

The curving rear wall of the church is a series of alternating gray granite panels and stained glass windows. The richly veined granite was quarried in Georgia. The seven tall windows portray the seven sacraments of the Catholic church. The windows were designed by Kovacevic and executed by the Conrad Schmitt Studios of New Berlin, Wisconsin. They were made with a special process in which the lead lines or cames between the pieces of glass are painted silver on the outside so that the design in the window is visible from outside as well as from inside the church.

The main entrance to the church is on an axis with the altar. Just inside the front door is the baptistry. This is symbolic, because baptism is the sacrament of entry into the community of the church. Directly in front of the main entrance is a tall, stainless steel cross which rises above the church and can be seen from blocks away.

Many elements in the design and decoration of St. Gall Church anticipated by ten years the liturgical reforms of Vatican II.

St. Gall, named for a sixth century Irish missionary to Switzerland, was founded in 1899. The parish is very active today with a membership of more than two thousand families. Polish Americans are the largest ethnic group in the parish.

Queen of All Saints Basilica
1956-60
6284 N. Sauganash Avenue
(4700 West)

Architects: Meyer and Cook
Style: Gothic
Seating: 1,100

A Gothic masterpiece, rich in marble and mosaic decoration.

A basilica is designated as such by the pope because of its architectural, artistic, and religious importance. Queen of All Saints is one of two basilicas in Chicago, Our Lady of Sorrows is the other. When it was raised to the rank of a basilica by Pope John XXIII in 1962, it was one of only fourteen in the United States.

This monumental and beautiful church faces more than a city block of open grass field. It is constructed of rough-hewn Wisconsin Lannon stone with Indiana limestone trim. It has a Vermont slate roof. The church is 240 feet long, 80 feet wide at the transepts, and 80 feet high at the roof ridge. The tower and spire rise 140 feet above the surrounding neighborhood. Nine stone buttresses support the walls along each side of the nave creating eight bays, each containing a 28-foot double-lancet stained glass window.

Above the richly carved and decorated entrance portal, between two octagonal stone buttresses, is a great Gothic arch which announces the dominant architectural theme of the church and frames a finely traceried stained glass window.

A glass wall with a bronze grillwork screen separates the narthex from the body of the church. The nave is long, narrow, and majestic in its Gothic detailing. Stone piers and gracefully curving roof beams lead the eye upward and toward the sanctuary. The open-truss ceiling with its polychrome and gold leaf ornament is magnificent.

The sanctuary is a marble and mosaic enthronement of the Eucharist. The sanctuary is paneled with variegated marble. The altar was carved and constructed in Italy. The reredos rising behind the altar was hewn from a single piece of Sienna marble. It frames a Venetian mosaic, the Queen of All Saints, drawn by Lelio de Ranieri and executed in the Vatican galleries with more than 33,000 pieces of colored murano glass. Above the reredos is a bronze canopy surmounted by a slender tapering spire with a crucifix on the top. And above all this is a symbolic representation of the Blessed Trinity.

On the south wall of the sanctuary behind the altar and reredos is an immense Gothic-arched Florentine mosaic with a central motif of the Blessed Trinity. Within the oval medallion, God the Father is symbolized by the hand, God the Son by the lamb, and the Holy Spirit by the dove. The sunburst effect is made with alternating yellow Sienna and black Belgian marble. The larger rays further away are made of Pompeian onyx.

The stained glass windows in the basilica were designed by Leo Cartwright with the assistance of Erhard Stoettner of the Esser Company in Milwaukee. The choir window, presenting the apparitions of Mary, was made with more than 57,000 pieces of glass. It fills much of the north facade of the church.

The basilica organ is a 54-rank, four-manual Wicks organ with 3,339 pipes. Its console is located in the choir loft.

Queen of All Saints parish was founded in 1929. It is located in the Sauganash district on the far Northwest Side of Chicago. The parish school, convent, rectory, gymnasium, and religious education center, all of similar design, occupy most of a city block. The whole parish complex was built under the direction of Rev. Msgr. Francis J. Dolan, pastor from 1934 to 1969. Since the basilica is relatively new, many of the same people who built it are still members of the parish. There is no dominant ethnic group in the parish, although there are large numbers of Irish, Italians, and Poles.

Chicago Loop Synagogue
1957-58
16 South Clark Street
(100 West)

Architects: Loebl, Schlossman
and Bennett
Style: Modern
Seating: 530

Chicago's central synagogue
features tasteful design and a
brilliant stained glass window.

"Let there be light." And indeed there is, and brilliant colors as well. The east wall of this synagogue has become world-famous as a unique example of contemporary stained glass art. It is 30 by 40 feet of cosmic and Hebraic symbolism conceived and designed by the distinguished American artist Abraham Rattner. It was executed by the Barrillet Studio of Paris and installed in the autumn of 1960.

Richard Bennett's design of the synagogue itself is noteworthy. It is a very efficient solution to the problem of situating a house of worship on a narrow downtown lot.

One enters through glass doors under the "Hands of Peace" sculpture by Henri Azaz. A large carpeted lobby to the left leads to a small meditation chapel on the north side of the first floor. On the west end of the lobby are the synagogue offices and elevators. On the south wall is a ramp leading up to the sanctuary on the second floor.

One enters the sanctuary from the west. Directly ahead is the great stained glass window wall. The interior of the sanctuary is simple, peaceful, and reverent. The seating arrangement makes maximum use of the space in this narrow site. The ark containing the scrolls of the Torah is in the northeast corner of the room.

The Rattner window is a complex design of traditional Jewish symbols whirling through the universe. Flames of fire emanate from the ark, as from the burning bush. Above the ark is the brilliant star and shield of David spinning out the twelve tribes of Israel.

In the center section of the window is a great menorah poetically conceived as a seven-branched tree of life and light. Next to and below the menorah is the palm of "Shins," an ascending pattern based on the form of the first letter of the word *shaddai.* The Shin represents the name of the Lord.

The third section, on the right side of the window, portrays the planets, the sun and the moon; and below these is the star of David. Across the bottom of the entire window in *dalle de vere,* that is, glass set in concrete, is the *Shema* written in Hebrew characters, "Hear, O Israel, the Lord our God, the Lord is One."

The marble ark, the eternal light which hangs above the ark, and the "Hands of Peace" sculpture above the main entrance outside were all designed by the Israeli sculptor Henri Azaz.

The Loop Synagogue, since its founding in 1929, has been a place of worship for business and professional people who work downtown, a growing residential congregation, and thousands of Jewish visitors to the city. It is, in fact, the city's central synagogue. It offers a wide range of prayer services, liturgies, and adult education programs.

St. Pauls Church
1959
2335 North Orchard Street
(700 West)

Architect: Benjamin Franklin Olson
Style: Neo-Gothic
Seating: 1,150

This Neo-Gothic church in the Lincoln Park neighborhood possesses beautiful art glass windows and a magnificent organ.

The magnificent Aeolian-Skinner organ in St. Pauls United Church of Christ is called "The Phoenix." In a way the church itself might be called a phoenix because the present structure was built after fire completely destroyed the old church on Christmas night, 1955.

"We are a community of faith," says the parish literature, "surrounded by the city. We want to share the joys, challenges and fellowship of the Christian life-style with others."

The large, masonry church faces Orchard Street. Its lofty spire rises above the Lincoln Park neighborhood. The building is longitudinal in plan on an east-west axis with seven bays of double windows on each side of the nave.

The narthex of St. Pauls has a vaulted ceiling; this vestibule serves as a greeting place of fellowship for the congregation.

The intricate and beautiful stained glass windows in St. Pauls were created by the Chicago firm of Giannini and Hilgart. The large clerestory windows depict scenes from the life of Christ from the Nativity to the Ascension, with the addition of a window in honor of St. Paul. The lower windows along the side aisles present great Christian artists, musicians, reformers, missionaries and martyrs, as well as saints and prophets of the New and Old Testaments.

The hand-carved woodwork in the chancel area is especially beautiful. The lectern and the pulpit stand on either side of the chancel. The choir pews face each other and flank the altar. Behind and above the altar is the beautiful traceried wood reredos with symbols of the Trinity near the top.

The principal components of St. Pauls' organ and its console are also located in the chancel. This organ is a four-manual instrument of 109 stops and 92 ranks made up of 5,362 individual pipes ranging in length from 6 inches to 32 feet. The antiphonal organ is located on the west wall of the church above the balcony. In the center of this organ are the gleaming pipes of the fanfare trumpet projecting horizontally into the church.

St. Pauls was founded by German immigrants to Chicago in 1843. It was a mixed congregation of Lutherans and Reformed Christians under the leadership of Rev. August Selle.

Selle was a strict Lutheran, and eventually the more liberal members of the congregation wanted a more liberal pastor. They found him in Rev. J. A. Fischer and split from First St. Paul's in 1848.

St. Pauls has done significant benevolent work throughout the years. Shortly before the Civil War it founded an orphanage, Uhlich Children's Home. In 1920 it founded St. Pauls House for the elderly and in 1974 the Grace Convalescent Home.

The large parish house-community center is used regularly by the neighborhood as well as the congregation. One service each Sunday is still held in the German language.

Old St. Mary Church
1959-61
25 East Van Buren Street
(400 South)

Architects: Belli & Belli
Style: Modern
Seating: 600

The oldest Catholic church in Chicago, once the cathedral, is rich in ecclesiastical and architectural history.

Old St. Mary's, organized in 1833 and originally known as St. Mary of the Assumption, was the first Catholic church in Chicago. It has an illustrious ecclesiastical history serving as the cathedral church, 1843 to 1875, for the first five bishops of the Chicago diocese.

But St. Mary's architectural history is equally significant. Augustine Deodat Taylor and his brother Anson planned and built the first St. Mary's church on a canal lot on the south side of Lake Street just west of State in the summer of 1833. This little frame church, 36 feet long, 24 feet wide, and 12 feet high, was the first balloon frame building ever constructed. Veteran builders, suspecting it would not be as strong as a heavier frame house or a log cabin, predicted it would collapse in the first high wind. The little church not only withstood the wind but revolutionized the building industry. It became the model for most of the houses built in Chicago for years to come.

The balloon frame building became popular because lumber was so plentiful and this type of structure with its light timber frame and clapboard siding could be erected by two men in a matter of days. They used pre-cut boards and machine-made nails. This process did not require the services of a skilled carpenter to fashion the joints. The idea for the balloon frame building is attributed to George W. Snow; the execution of it to the Taylor brothers; the first example, Old St. Mary's Church.

St. Mary's second church was a brick building in the Colonial style at the southwest corner of Madison and Wabash. Mass was first celebrated there on Christmas Day, 1843. This building was the cathedral church of the diocese of Chicago until it was destroyed in the Great Fire of 1871. The bishops, however, began using the new and larger Holy Name Church on the North Side for larger diocesan events from the middle 1850s.

After the Chicago Fire destroyed St. Mary's and Holy Name, Bishop Foley purchased the former Plymouth Congregational Church at the southeast corner of 9th and Wabash and rededicated it as St. Mary's Procathedral on October 9, 1872, the anniversary of the Fire. This handsome brick church with an Illinois limestone facade had been designed by Gurdon P. Randall; its cornerstone was laid in 1865; it had been dedicated in 1867. This famous old church, designated a Chicago landmark in 1965, was sold by the Archdiocese to the Standard Oil Company in June of 1970.

Four months later the 103-year-old edifice was razed for a parking lot.

Since October 1970, all the functions of St. Mary's parish have been held in the modern church building at the southwest corner of Van Buren and Wabash. This building was opened in 1961 as a chapel of Old St. Mary Church.

The Paulist fathers from New York City took charge of this parish in November 1903 and have served it ever since. St. Mary's was the home of the famous Paulist Choir, founded in 1904. Rev. Eugene F. O'Malley, C.S.P., served as director of the choir from 1928 until it was disbanded in 1967.

St. Mary's parish boundaries encompass the whole downtown area and a portion of the Near South Side. Worshipers include a wide variety of merchants, business people, shoppers, tourists, and a growing number of residential parishioners.

St. Luke Evangelical Lutheran Church 1960
1500 West Belmont Avenue (3200 North)

Architect: Harold A. Stahl
Style: Modern
Seating: 1,000

Majestic height and artistic furnishings make this church a liturgical and architectural masterpiece.

Dr. Adalbert Kretzmann was first called to St. Luke's in 1927. For more than 50 years as pastor, teacher, and liturgical arts advisor, he has served as consultant in the design and furnishing of hundreds of churches. St. Luke's is his own church, and its planning reflects his expertise, sensitivity, and reverence.

Initial plans were for an octagonal church on the northwest corner of Belmont and Greenview. But zoning ordinances and a city planning commission required that the church be moved 33 feet west of its proposed site. The new church was also to complement and be connected with the existing five-story school building. With these factors determining the height, area, and volume of the building, the architect then selected the materials and specified the proportions.

In its own way, the resulting church approaches the ideal of Gothic verticality. A great stained glass window forms the north wall of the church. Towering laminated wooden arches rise 65 feet from floor to ceiling along the walls of the nave. And the south wall is graced with the pipes of a great three-manual Schlicker organ.

St. Luke's is constructed of red face brick, inside and out, with Wisconsin Lannon stone trim. The nave is 185 feet long. The floor is terrazzo. The pews and pulpits in the church are made of African mahogany. The great window of the north wall, made by Giannini and Hilgart of Chicago, speaks of Christ as "the Light of the World" and "the Son of Righteousness arising with healing in His wings." The clerestory windows contain only tinted glass and they fill the auditorium with natural light.

The choir balcony at the rear of the nave stands 27 feet from the south wall. As a result, upon entering the vestibule, one experiences immediately the full height of the church and finds on the south wall the beautiful *Christus* figure flanked by tall ornamental stained glass windows.

The *Christus* figure as well as the 27-foot cross behind the altar, the seven candlesticks, the baptismal font, and the panels decorating the two pulpits, were all done in cloisonné enamel by Harold Martin.

The Evangelical Lutheran Church of St. Luke was founded in 1884 by former members of St. James Lutheran Church. When the parish school was dedicated in 1905, it was considered to be Chicago's first fireproof school building. Sunday and midweek services at St. Luke's are held in German and English.

**St. Jane de Chantal Church
1962-64
5251 S. McVicker Avenue
(6034 West)**
Architects: Pavlecic and
Kovacevic
Style: Modern
Seating: 700

Contemporary design here
eloquently serves the purposes of
Christian worship.

The basic materials of this church are brick, glass, and wood. The shape is a diagonally placed square, or diamond. The design concept is contemporary, where form is the product of function. The function here is the celebration of Mass. So the altar is the focal point and the pews converge upon it. The four free-standing buff-colored brick walls of the structure terminate short of the corners and short of the roof; then plate glass, mostly clear glass, continues up to the roof and on to the corners. This makes the interior bright and attractive, even without electric lighting.

The roof of St. Jane's is serrated and placed diagonally over the building. The main peak of the roof is supported by a 32-ton laminated wooden beam which was transported from Washington State on three railroad flatcars, and was reported to be the longest laminated beam ever fabricated.

The front of the church houses a two-story narthex and balcony. The baptistry is placed just inside the entrance to symbolize that it is through baptism that a person enters the Christian community. On the opposite corner of the diamond, on the same axis, is the sanctuary and altar.

The color scheme of the church is black and white. This motif is only broken by the bold orange and red mosaic of the altar panel and the brilliantly colored faceted glass at the corners of the building. Sr. Miriam Gordon, O.P., designed and executed the mosaics and the stations of the cross. The faceted glass work was done by Richard O'Brien of Barrington, Illinois.

This modern, functional church was built under the direction of Rev. John A. Ward who founded the parish in 1954. St. Jane's operates a school and sponsors many parish organizations.

**North Shore Congregation
Israel   1962-64**
1185 Sheridan Road
Glencoe, Illinois

Architects: Minoru Yamasaki
with Friedman, Alschuler
and Sincere
Style: Modern
Seating: 1,200

This graceful, modern synagogue
on the shores of Lake Michigan
has been called an architecture of
light.

As the visitor enters the sanctuary of this synagogue, even on a cloudy day, the whole impact is light, shaped and sculptured in graceful forms. Minoru Yamasaki called his design for North Shore Congregation Israel an "architecture of light." Concrete and glass were used to achieve a sculptured, reverent effect, conducive to prayer and inspiration.

The sanctuary ceiling is unique. It consists of eight pairs of huge poured-in-place concrete vaults; each pair weighs 90 tons. Each vault begins as a stem-like pier at ground level, fans out as it rises to the ceiling, and cantilevers gracefully over the auditorium, narrowing again as it approaches the ridge line of the roof.

But the ceiling itself is mainly a skylight system. For between each of the vaults and bordering each of the side wall panels is a panel of amber-tinted glass. Taken all together, these panels bathe the sanctuary with soft daylight and make the whole place a spectacle of light.

The east and west walls of the sanctuary, that is, the front and back walls of the room, are styled in a modified ogee arch which lends its shape to the sixteen ceiling vaults. The side walls are formed of precast concrete panels paired alongside each pier. These are shaped to suggest hands in prayer; and at the bottom of each panel, at eye level, are ogee-shaped windows which permit a view of trees and lawns and the lake outside.

The central feature of the auditorium is the ark which contains the scrolls of the Torah, the first five books of the Bible. The ark is made of teakwood covered with gold leaf. The ark rests on a white marble bema or altar and is sheltered by a rising form which symbolizes the traditional Jewish prayer shawl. In front of the ark hangs a golden lamp, the eternal light, which was first kindled here when the building was dedicated in 1964. To the left or north of the ark is a graceful menorah, the seven-branched candlestick, and behind it on the wall are the two stone tablets containing the Ten Commandments. On the wall to the right of the ark are the Hebrew words of the prophet Micah: "What doth the Lord require of thee? Only to do justice and to love mercy and to walk humbly with thy God." From ancient times these words have been called the essence of Judaism.

At the rear of the auditorium above the entrance is the choir balcony and above this, a shining assembly of pipes for the three-manual 46-rank Casavant organ which was especially designed for this synagogue.

Just outside and to the west of the sanctuary is Memorial Hall which provides space for lectures, meetings, and social gatherings after services. But the hall has sliding doors which when opened can provide seating for another six hundred people to participate in the services.

Flanking Memorial Hall are two wings connected by a glass-enclosed arcade. The south wing contains the rabbi's study, caretaker's quarters, and rest rooms. In the north wing are a youth lounge, offices, and storage facilities. Connected to the north wing is a two-story school building with eighteen classrooms.

Services of worship are held each Friday evening at 8:00 and Saturday morning at 10:15. The temple is open to visitors Monday through Thursday during the day.

Emmanuel Presbyterian
Church 1965
1850 South Racine Avenue
(1200 West)
Architects: Edward D. Dart
and Associates
Style: Modern
Seating: about 250

This small, modern church designed by Edward Dart is rich in symbolism.

In the very heart of the old Pilsen neighborhood, Emmanuel Presbyterian Church lifts up its modern, angular bell tower. The area was once Bohemian; it is now mostly Spanish-speaking. Services are held in Spanish and English for the predominantly Mexican-American congregation which comes to worship here from various parts of the city.

This small brick church is an example of irregular, free-flowing space designed to suggest welcome and shelter. The entranceway adjoins the bell tower, and just inside is the chancel with the pews fanning out to the right. The walls are all plain brick, modern in character, but suggesting a medieval monastery as well. The walls are bathed in light from recessed lamps and hidden windows. This is like our experience of God who shows us only reflections of himself while he remains hidden from our sight.

The main body of the church is wider than it is deep in order to keep the congregation close to the service. The pews are placed so that people are gathered close to the Lord's Supper. The floor level is the same throughout the chapel; this suggests the availability of Christ to all the people. Only the pulpit is raised, not to exalt the preacher, but to exalt the Word of God. The baptismal font is located just inside the entrance to the chapel to remind the worshipers that baptism is the means by which each one enters Christ's church. And the chancel is central; the walls converge on it, the ceiling rises to exalt it.

Beneath the chapel, downstairs, are rooms for Sunday school classes and for coffee gatherings after services. The church has operated a day care center in an annex since 1974.

Emmanuel Presbyterian Church was formed in 1960 by the merger of three congregations. When this church was built, the congregation was half Anglo and half Spanish-speaking. Today it is almost entirely Spanish-speaking, but the services are bilingual.

**Congregation Bnei Ruven
1967-68
6350 North Whipple Street
(3034 West)**
Architects: I. Moses and
Associates
Style: Modern Biblical
Seating: 400

The round column, symbolic of
and housing the scrolls of the
Torah, is the central feature of
this synagogue.

In its 1968 Distinguished Buildings awards, the Chicago Chapter of the American Institute of Architects cited Bnei Ruven as, "A bold, consistent design in brick and wood with a plan that seems to suit its function very well. Compatible in scale to its neighborhood." The plan of this synagogue is centered upon a massive round column of brick that rises up in the sanctuary, ascends through the ceiling, and emerges as the central core of a three-tiered tower. The column, a symbol of strength, contains in a compartment near its base the scrolls of the Torah, the Word of God. From the outside, the three-tiered tower itself looks like the top of a scroll.

The walls of Bnei Ruven, inside and out, are constructed of brown Canadian clinker brick, a face brick that was specially chosen for its color and texture. The brick is laid up with a random pattern of king and queen closers; that is, with certain bricks jutting out from the surface. This form of rustication gives the synagogue an affinity with older structures, especially those built with rough-faced stone.

The auditorium emerges from the "Torah column" in an elliptical shape with the seating arranged in a semi-circular pattern on two levels. In Orthodox Jewish congregations women are required to sit apart from men during prayer services. Instead of providing a section for women at the rear of the structure, as is often done in other synagogues, the architect designed a separate raised area on the south side of the room that runs the length of the synagogue.

The massing of forms involved in the design of this building is dramatic. The area where the rabbi sits, just to the left of the great column, is cantilevered over a broad stairway that leads down to the fellowship hall beneath the sanctuary. One half of the outermost wall of the brick tower is carried on a round steel beam that is cantilevered over the sanctuary. The intermediate wall of the brick tower is carried entirely on another round steel beam.

The ceiling of this synagogue is wood and is supported by open laminated wooden beams. The auditorium is carpeted and furnished with beige upholstered individual seats. The combination of brick and wood in the sanctuary gives the space a feeling of antiquity and modernity that is very appealing.

Bnei Ruven in West Rogers Park is the largest Orthodox Jewish congregation in Chicago. It consists of young and old and many professional people.

**Seventeenth Church
of Christ, Scientist 1968
55 East Wacker Drive
(300 North)**

Architects: Harry Weese
and Associates
Style: Modern
Seating: 800

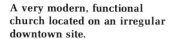

A very modern, functional
church located on an irregular
downtown site.

From its founding in 1924 until this structure was completed in 1968, Seventeenth Church of Christ, Scientist, met in rented quarters. They met from 1944 to 1968 in Orchestra Hall on Michigan Avenue. After a long search in the late 1940s and early 1950s, the membership voted in 1956 to purchase the seven-sided lot at the corner of Wabash Avenue and Wacker Drive. Thirty-four architects were screened and Harry Weese was selected to design the new church building.

The dramatic, marble-clad structure was designed to fit the site and to accommodate the services of the Christian Science assembly. Weese felt that the church should be modern in design, individual, and visually strong so as not to be dwarfed by the surrounding "high rises" of brick and mortar. The church is constructed of reinforced concrete faced with travertine marble quarried in Italy.

The interior of this church consists of 800 seats arranged in semi-circular, ascending rows around an elevated podium. Below the reading stand is the organ console and above that the gleaming ranks of organ pipes. The interior walls of the auditorium are covered with the same travertine marble used on the exterior. The interior woodwork is walnut throughout, and the hardware is bronze. The windows and doors are all fitted with non-glare solar bronze glass, and the carpeting and seat covers are moss green.

The organ of Seventeenth Church is a three-manual and pedal Aeolian-Skinner pipe organ with 45 registers, 57 stops, 59 ranks, with a total of 3,316 pipes. All the pipes in the displayed facade are speaking pipes.

The Sunday service centers on a Bible lesson-sermon, comprised of readings from the Bible and from the denominational textbook, *Science and Health with Key to the Scriptures* by Mary Baker Eddy. Wednesday meetings include testimonies of healing offered by those present. For this there is a specially designed sound system with a microphone located next to every other seat in the auditorium. Each meeting includes both congregational and silent prayer plus the singing of several hymns.

Behind the main body of the church are seven levels of offices and meeting rooms. Access to the church is through a handsome lower-level, glass-enclosed lobby. Sunday school classrooms and a children's room are located beneath ground level and they open onto a sunken atrium. The Sunday school meets at the same hour as the worship service.

This church was designed to be dignified, vital, spacious, and comfortable. It demonstrates a very efficient use of space in a high-density, city center location.

**St. Simeon Mirotocivi
Serbian Orthodox Church
1968-69
3737 East 114th Street**

Architects: Pavlecic and
Kovacevic and R. Markovich
Style: Morava School of
Serbian Byzantine
architecture
Capacity: about 350

**An authentic reproduction of a
fifteenth century Serbian
monastery.**

St. Simeon Mirotocivi on
Chicago's far Southeast Side
is a modern reproduction of
the fifteenth century Serbian
monastery of *Kalenich* in
what is now southern
Yugoslavia. The original
monastery, which is still
standing, was constructed of
white stone with red brick
courses. St. Simeon's was
built entirely of brick on a
steel frame. Beige-colored
brick takes the place of the
stone in the original, but the
stripes and checkerboard
patterns are all the same.

This church is built on a
beautifully landscaped site
with lawn and flowers, trees
and shrubs all around it. Its
dome, rising 66 feet above
ground level, is a dominant
feature of the landscape.
There are no pews in the
church, as the people are
accustomed to stand or kneel
during the services which are
conducted in the Old Slavonic
language.

St. Simeon's was built by a
community of 300 Serbian-
American families, most of
whom work in the steel mills.
The design of the church and
the services held there
provide the parishioners a
link with their Serbian
heritage and homeland. These
people fled Communism in
Yugoslavia after World War II.

Just to the south of the church
is a community hall and pic-
nic pavilion which serve as
educational, cultural, and
social centers for the
community.

St. Procopius Abbey Church
1968-70
5601 College Road
Lisle, Illinois

Architect: Edward D. Dart
Style: Modern
Seating: 800

"A religious complex endowed with inspired simplicity . . . yet rich in meaning."

Seen from a distance, the St. Procopius Abbey Church is a dramatic statement in brick and glass on a wooded Illinois hillside. Its plan is equally dramatic and gives the visitor a sense of discovery as he or she walks through a labyrinthine spiral of spaces on the way to the sanctuary. One enters the building from the left moving to the right, from the low, wide narthex, through a narrow brick corridor, then into the soaring openness of the nave.

The church itself is designed as a room within a room with one area for the monastic choir and sanctuary, illumi-nated from above by a 13-by-90-foot clerestory, and another larger area to the north for visitors having three banks of pews converging on the altar.

The American Institute of Architects selected St. Procopius Abbey Church and Monastery as one of twelve outstanding buildings in the United States in 1973. The citation read as follows:

"St. Procopius is for many members of the jury and for many reasons the most satisfying of all the projects submitted.

"A religious complex endowed with inspired simplicity, devoid of mannerism, yet rich in meaning, it possesses the character of the religious teachings of Benedictine monasticism without overstating the purpose.

"There is a great flow of space from church to monks' rooms, a great consistency and restraint in the use of materials and of scale.

"Interior and exterior are well related to each other and to the environment.

"Here the architect has created a special environment and at the same time given greater meaning to all the surrounding area."

214

A 17-foot cedar cross near the main entrance is the only exterior symbol of the monastery's religious nature. All of the interior and exterior walls are made of Chicago common brick. Floors are made of reddish brown tile, carpeted in certain areas; and the ceilings are Douglas fir on laminated beams. The whole has a noble simplicity which inspires peace, serenity, and contemplation.

Very much integrated with the worshiping space is a 35-rank, three-manual Möller organ containing over 2,000 pipes, most of which are visible immediately above and behind the choir.

The main worshiping area is spacially related to the St. Mary Chapel which accommodates about forty persons for weekday services, and to the Blessed Sacrament Chapel which seats about twenty. The whole complex is conceived as a volute or spiral working out from the main entrance. This is also true of the monastery which spirals left from the entrance and houses sixty-five monks, many of whom conduct the nearby Illinois Benedictine College and Benet Academy.

In 1973, Rembert G. Weakland, then abbot primate of the international Benedictine federation called St. Procopius Abbey "A noble and masculine building [which] symbolizes the inner vitality and leadership of the Lisle Benedictine community and its optimistic, forward-looking attitude."

St. Procopius was an eleventh century monk who founded a monastery and school in Bohemia. The St. Procopius

Benedictine community was founded in 1885 in the Pilsen neighborhood on Chicago's Lower West Side. The college and boys' high school moved to Lisle in 1901; the abbey in 1914. St. Procopius parish continued at 18th and Allport streets where the Benedictines served Czechs, Slovaks, and in recent years a Spanish-speaking community. The parish was transferred to the care of the Chicago diocesan clergy in 1980.

First St. Paul's
Evangelical Lutheran Church
1969-70
1301 North LaSalle Drive
(150 West)

Architect: Edward D. Dart
Style: Modern
Seating: 400

Chicago's oldest Lutheran church
worships in a modern, functional
sanctuary.

First St. Paul's is "an old church in a new day." It is Chicago's oldest Lutheran church, dating from 1846, and the "cradle of the Missouri Synod" which grew out of historic meetings held here in 1847.

The new church building at the corner of LaSalle and Goethe stands in dramatic simplicity in the middle of Carl Sandburg Village. The high portion of the building along LaSalle Drive contains the worship space, while the low portion to the east houses the administration wing, a multi-purpose room, a church parlor, kitchen facilities, and the narthex. The tall, curving brick wall facing Goethe Street contains the chancel. A high, clerestory window facing north allows natural light to spill across the entire chancel area. The interior as well as the exterior of the church is brick.

Lutheran worship revolves around Word and Sacrament. This is expressed in the chancel by the pulpit, the chief visual symbol of the Word, and the table, symbolic of the Sacrament of Holy Communion. The pews in the nave are placed so that the center aisle leads directly to the table. The raised area at the rear of the nave contains the organ and seating for the choir. There is a chaste simplicity about this church, very little in the way of ornament; everything focuses on the pulpit and the table.

The ten-rank Schlicker organ in First St. Paul is a powerful instrument in an excellent acoustic setting.

The Near North Side of Chicago is a fascinating center of modern urban life and culture. People of all racial and national backgrounds live here and a cross section of them worship at First St. Paul's. The neighborhood has been highly transient and cosmopolitan. Until recently, 80 percent of the membership of this parish has been single people. As Sandburg Village becomes condominium, some new families are joining the church. Through many phases of urban change, this church and its pastor since 1949, Dr. James Manz, proclaim the gospel of Jesus Christ. It is a very special ministry in a very secular setting.

Midwest Buddhist Temple
1971
**435 West Menomonee Street
(1800 North)**

Architect: Hideaki Arao
Style: Neo-Japanese Temple
Seating: 175

An authentic Japanese Buddhist temple in the Old Town Triangle district.

It might be situated anywhere in Japan, but the Midwest Buddhist Temple is unique in Chicago. It is the only Japanese style house of worship in the area. The temple is located next to a rolling, landscaped park in the middle of the Old Town Triangle district. The building is constructed of concrete, wood, and plaster. It was erected by second and third generation Japanese Americans whose parents and grandparents came to Chicago during and after the Second World War.

The broad eaves and low profile of the temple are typically Japanese. The lower part of the building houses classrooms, meeting rooms, and a social hall. The temple itself is upstairs. It is known as the "Temple of Enlightenment" and is done in simple, contemporary Japanese styling. The focal point of the temple is the beautiful altar which was dedicated in 1972.

The Midwest Buddhist Temple holds regular religious services on Sunday mornings. It also sponsors an annual Ginza holiday which attracts people from all over Illinois and neighboring states. The temple conducts a Sunday school, youth programs, sports programs, and senior citizen activities.

When it was dedicated in 1971, Mayor Richard J. Daley hailed the new temple as a Chicago landmark. The building and its people have made a distinct contribution to the ethnic and cultural diversity of Chicago.

**Holy Resurrection
Serbian Orthodox Cathedral
1973-75
5701 North Redwood Drive
(8024 West)**

Architect: Radoslav Kovacevic
Style: Modern Byzantine
Seating: 450

Holy Resurrection, alongside the
Kennedy, captures the spirit of
Serbian churches in a
contemporary building.

Holy Resurrection Cathedral is the prominent Neo-Byzantine church which the Kennedy motorist sees on the south side of the expressway just east of Cumberland Avenue. The architect, Radoslav Kovacevic, wished to create a design that would capture the spirit of Serbian churches in a contemporary building. "The new church," he wrote, "had to be free of cumbersome ornamentation, clear in concept, simple in detail." Kovacevic chose to use a single Byzantine element, the rounded arch, throughout the structure. A Serbian element in the design is the five-dome roof, a large central dome with four smaller ones at the corners of the building.

Holy Resurrection is constructed on a steel frame with dark beige brick and limestone arches. The arches, seven on each side and three at the front and back, frame beautiful stained glass windows.

The stained glass was done by the Conrad Schmitt Studios of New Berlin, Wisconsin. These windows picture saints of the Eastern church in authentic Byzantine style. Very little paint is used on the glass. The design is carried out almost exclusively with the lead lines and the colored glass. A special feature of these windows is that the design pattern is apparent from the outside as well as from the inside of the church. This has been done by applying gold leaf to the outside surfaces of the cames or lead strips that hold the pieces of glass

together. The effect is a brilliant outline of the artwork clearly visible on the exterior.

Inside, Holy Resurrection has a terrazzo floor and a marble *iconostasis* with brilliant mosaics by Sirio Tonelli of Chicago. The altar is of Carrara marble and was imported from Italy.

The Serbian-American people who make up this worshiping community come from all over the North Side of Chicago and the suburbs. The parish moved to this location from the Wicker Park area around 1960. The church is located on a beautifully landscaped site and has a large community and social hall across the street to the south.

SS. Volodymyr and Olha Church 1973-75
739 North Oakley Boulevard
(2300 West)

Architect: Jaroslaw Korsunsky
Style: Byzantine
Seating: 800

The splendid dome, the mosaics, frescoes, and icons of this modern church aptly express the ethnic heritage of the Ukrainian people.

The congregation of SS. Volodymyr and Olha consists of eleven hundred Ukrainian Catholic families who were originally members of the neighboring Cathedral of St. Nicholas. They separated from the cathedral parish in 1968 when the cathedral changed from the Julian to the Gregorian calendar. The people of SS. Volodymyr and Olha wanted to follow the Julian calendar which observes Christmas on January 7-9. The new parish was established with the consent of the local Ukrainian Catholic bishop. The people follow all of the old-country traditions and are committed to the preservation of their ethnic heritage and the Eastern Rite in the Catholic church.

The church itself, 121 by 89 feet, is constructed of light brown rusticated brick with smooth face brick of the same color for decorative trim. Copper downspouts recessed in the walls add distinctive vertical lines to the exterior of the church. The body of the church is in the form of a Greek cross. A large aluminum gold anodized dome rises 70 feet above the center of the building and four smaller domes stand at each corner of the roof.

The church is elevated and set back on its site and the visitor approaches the front entrance from a broad landscaped patio which extends out to the sidewalks both on Oakley and Superior streets. Above the three-door main entrance to the church is a huge mosaic executed by Hordynsky, Makarenko, and Baransky showing St. Volodymyr the Great baptizing the people of Kiev in the Dnipro River in 988 A.D. This event marked the conversion of the Ukrainian people to Christianity.

The interior of the church is brilliantly painted in traditional Byzantine iconography. The composition and content of the icons, representing Christ, the Holy Virgin, and the saints, are strictly prescribed. It took Ivan Diky, the Ukrainian artist-painter, five years to finish the paintings, from 1975 to 1980.

The sanctuary is divided from the body of the church by a hand-carved oak *iconostasis*, a separating wall with holy icons on it. The marble in the sanctuary was imported from Italy. Hanging in the center of the church is a great chandelier that was made in Greece. The stained glass windows were created by the Baransky Studios in Yonkers, New York.

Below the sanctuary is a parish auditorium and social center. It contains a kitchen and full facilities for the meetings and social events of the parish.

SS. Volodymyr and Olha is a very active parish. It has two choirs, a drama group, a youth association, and five religious organizations. The church owns a bookstore, a printing shop, publishes a biweekly newspaper, and broadcasts a weekly radio program. The parish is administered by an elected council headed by the pastor, Rev. Marion Butrynsky.

St. Joseph's Ukrainian Catholic Church   1975-77
5000 North Cumberland Avenue   (8400 West)

Architect: Zenon Mazurkevich
Style: Ukrainian modified Byzantine
Seating: 300

"An example of old country architectural tradition with a modern, progressive expression."

St. Joseph's is "an example of old country architectural tradition with a modern, progressive expression," says Rev. Joseph Shary, the pastor and founder of the parish. Like the ancient cathedral of Kiev, St. Joseph's has thirteen domes symbolizing Christ and the twelve apostles. The three interior stories of the church correspond to the three persons of the Blessed Trinity. The ground floor is shaped in the form of a Jerusalem cross, the second floor as a Coptic cross, and the third in the form of a St. Vladimir cross.

The multiplication of domes and half domes together with the streaming interplay of light is reminiscent of St. Sophia in Istanbul. The altar, icons, and liturgy are all derived from the ancient Byzantine traditions.

And yet the building is constructed with space-age materials and technology— concrete, steel, glass, and fiberglass. It is 100 feet square at the base and rises 116 feet high. Seventy-five percent of the exterior walls is glass, 12,700 square feet of one-quarter inch solar bronze glass. As of 1975, this was one of the largest bent glass projects in the United States.

The effect is a bright, cheerful environment filled with light and open to the outside. The seemingly endless space symbolizes God's presence everywhere, unconfined by walls.

Architect Mazurkevich chose concrete for the church because it has the touch of man. "Humble people have raised concrete to the level of a palace," he said. Originally the major dome, like the minor domes, was to be made of fiberglass. The Chicago Fire Department, however, would not permit it. So the major dome was constructed of

concrete precast in twelve pieces on the site. The entire construction, 2,200 cubic yards of concrete with a poured-in-place ring beam supporting the dome, took approximately fourteen months to complete.

The decoration and furnishing of St. Joseph's are continuing projects. Specially baked ceramic mosaics of Christ and his mother by Marko Zubar of Philadelphia will soon be put in place. A large mural of Our Lady of Vladimir and the Eastern Fathers of the Church was painted in the south entranceway by Susan Brooks.

St. Joseph's parish was founded in 1956 from St. Nicholas Cathedral for those Ukrainian Catholics living on the far Northwest Side. Two hundred and fifty families raised funds to build the church for the glory of God and for future generations.

St. Joseph's is the house of God rising above the houses of men. It is a friendly building, the doors are open, and visitors are welcome. The church is surrounded by homes, traffic rushes by in front, and the church, according to Mazurkevich, is as accessible as a shopping center. Services are held in Ukrainian and English.

Appendices

Ceiling detail
John A. Mallin Co., interior decoration
St. Thomas Aquinas Church
Karl M. Vitzthum, architect

Alphabetical Index

The churches and synagogues in this book
with mailing addresses
and telephone numbers.

North Shore Congregation Israel   208-9
1185 Sheridan Road
Glencoe, 60022   Chicago phone: 273-3474

Notre Dame Church   55
1335 West Harrison Street
Chicago, 60607   243-7400

Olivet Baptist Church   38-39
405 East 31st Street
Chicago, 60616   842-1081

Operation PUSH   170
930 East 50th Street
Chicago, 60615   373-3366

Our Lady of Lourdes Church   138
4640 North Ashland Avenue
Chicago, 60640   561-2141

Our Lady of Mount Carmel Church   132-33
690 West Belmont Avenue
Chicago, 60657   525-0453

Our Lady of Sorrows Basilica   66-67
3121 West Jackson Boulevard
Chicago, 60612   638-5800

St. Pascal Church   190-91
3935 North Melvina Avenue
Chicago, 60634   725-7641

St. Patrick Church   22-23
718 West Adams Street
Chicago, 60606   782-6171

St. Paul Church   76-77
2127 West 22nd Place
Chicago, 60608   847-7622

St. Pauls Church   204
655 West Fullerton Parkway
Chicago, 60614   348-3829

St. Peter's Church   197
110 West Madison Street
Chicago, 60602   372-5111

St. Philip Neri Church   181
2132 East 72nd Street
Chicago, 60649   363-1700

Pilgrim Baptist Church   64-65
3301 South Indiana Avenue
Chicago, 60616   842-5830

Presentation Church   108
758 South Springfield Avenue
Chicago, 60624   533-2820

St. Procopius Abbey Church   214-15
5601 College Road
Lisle, 60532   969-6410

Queen of All Saints Basilica   200-1
6280 North Sauganash Avenue
Chicago, 60646   736-6060

Quigley Preparatory Seminary North,   150-51
St. James Chapel
103 East Chestnut Street
Chicago, 60611   787-9343

Quinn Chapel A.M.E. Church   68
2401 South Wabash Avenue
Chicago, 60616   791-1846

Rockefeller Memorial Chapel   182-83
University of Chicago
Special Activities Office
5801 South Ellis Avenue
Chicago, 60637   753-4429

St. Sabina Church   180
1210 West 78th Place
Chicago, 60620   483-4300

Second Presbyterian Church   32-33
1936 South Michigan Avenue
Chicago, 60616   225-4951

Seventeenth Church of Christ, Scientist   212
55 East Wacker Drive
Chicago, 60601   236-4671

St. Simeon Mirotocivi   213
Serbian Orthodox Church
3737 East 114th Street
Chicago, 60617   731-2925

St. Stanislaus Kostka Church   42-43
1351 West Evergreen Avenue
Chicago, 60622   278-2470

Temple Sholom   186-87
3480 North Lake Shore Drive
Chicago, 60657   525-4707

St. Thomas the Apostle Church   164-65
5472 South Kimbark Avenue
Chicago, 60615   324-2626

St. Thomas Aquinas Church   168-69
5112 West Washington Boulevard
Chicago, 60644   287-0206

Trinity Episcopal Church   34-35
125 East 26th Street
Chicago, 60616   842-7545

United Church of Hyde Park   59
1448 East 53rd Street
Chicago, 60615   363-1620

Unity Temple   116-17
The Unitarian Universalist Church in Oak Park
875 Lake Street
Oak Park, 60302   848-7123

Architects

The architects in this book with their other churches and synagogues in Chicago. Addresses indicate the fronts of buildings.

Adler, Dankmar and Sullivan, Louis H.

Pilgrim Baptist Church   1890-91
formerly K.A.M. Temple
3301 South Indiana Avenue   (200 East)

Dankmar Adler   (1844-1900)

Ebenezer Baptist Church   1898-99
formerly Temple Isaiah
4501 South Vincennes Avenue   (500 East)

Louis Sullivan   (1856-1924)

Holy Trinity Cathedral   1903
1121 North Leavitt Street   (2200 West)

Ahlschlager, Frederick   (1858-1905)

Holy Cross Lutheran Church   1886
3120 South Racine Avenue   (1200 West)

First Immanuel Lutheran Church   1888
1124 South Ashland Avenue   (1600 West)

Concordia Ev. Lutheran Church   1892-93
2649 West Belmont Avenue   (3200 North)

Pillar's Rock Baptist Church   1893
formerly Anshe Emet Synagogue
1363 North Sedgwick Street   (400 West)

Alschuler, Alfred S.   (1876-1940)

Anshe Emet Synagogue   1910-11
formerly Temple Sholom
3760 North Pine Grove Avenue   (700 West)

Mt. Pisgah Missionary Baptist Church   1910-12
formerly Sinai Temple
4600 South Martin Luther King Drive   (400 East)

Greater Bethesda Baptist Church   1913-14
formerly B'nai Sholom Temple Israel
5301 South Michigan Avenue   (100 East)

K.A.M.—Isaiah Israel Temple   1923-24
originally Temple Isaiah
5045 South Greenwood Avenue   (1100 East)

Alschuler, John   (1918-   )

Chapel addition, K.A.M.—Isaiah Israel Temple   1973
5045 South Greenwood Avenue   (1100 East)
See also Friedman, Alschuler and Sincere

Arao, Hideaki   (1921-   )

Midwest Buddhist Temple   1971
435 West Menomonee Street   (1800 North)

Barnett, George D. of St. Louis

St. Clement Church   1917-18
646 West Deming Place   (2534 North)

Barry, Gerald A.   (1894-1966)

Our Lady Help of Christians Church   1926-27
5104 West Iowa Street   (900 North)

St. Bartholomew Church   1937-38
3601 North Lavergne Avenue   (5000 West)

St. Nicholas of Tolentine Church   1937-39
6204 South Lawndale Avenue   (3700 West)

St. Rose of Lima Church   1939-40
1546 West 48th Street

Our Lady of the Angels Church   1939-41
3804 West Iowa Street   (900 North)

St. Andrews Temple   1942
formerly St. Mary of Mount Carmel Church
1735 West Marquette Road   (6700 South)

Barry and Kay

Our Lady of the Cross Mission Church   1947-48
2849 West Chase Avenue   (7300 North)

St. Ferdinand Church   1956-59
3101 North Mason Avenue   (5932 West)

St. Priscilla Church   1957-59
6955 West Addison Street   (3600 North)

St. Thomas More Church   1957-59
8106 South California Avenue   (2800 West)

Our Lady of Mercy Church   1958-61
4428 North Troy Street   (3132 West)

St. Mark Church   1962-63
1050 North Campbell Avenue   (2500 West)

St. Cajetan Church   1962-64
2441 West 112th Street

St. Cornelius Church   1964-65
5430 West Foster Avenue   (5200 North)

St. Denis Church   1964-66
3454 West 83rd Place

Bauer, Augustus: See Carter and Bauer

Becker, Louis A. of Mainz, Germany

St. Martin Church   1894-95
5848 South Princeton Avenue   (300 West)
See also Henry J. Schlacks

Bell, Theodore N. and Swift, Frank R.

Antioch Missionary Baptist Church   1889-90
formerly Englewood Baptist Church
6234 South Stewart Avenue   (400 West)

Belli & Belli

St. William Church   1958-60
7007 West Wrightwood Avenue   (2600 North)

St. Thaddeus Church   1959-60
9550 South Harvard Avenue   (332 West)

Old St. Mary Church   1959-61
25 East Van Buren Street   (400 South)

Immaculate Conception Church   1963-66
4403 South California Avenue   (2800 West)

St. John Bosco Church   1964-66
2305 North McVicker Avenue   (6034 West)

Beman, Solon S.   (1853-1914)

The Greenstone Church   1882
Pullman United Methodist Church
11201 South St. Lawrence Avenue   (600 East)

Metropolitan Community Church   1889
formerly 41st Street Presbyterian Church
and First Presbyterian Church
4100 South Martin Luther King Drive   (400 East)

Holy Rosary Church   1890
11302 South Martin Luther King Drive   (400 East)

Grant Memorial A.M.E. Church   1897
formerly First Church of Christ, Scientist
4017 South Drexel Boulevard   (900 East)

Second Church of Christ, Scientist   1899
2700 North Pine Grove Avenue   (530 West)

Fifth Church of Christ, Scientist   1904
4840 South Dorchester Avenue   (1400 East)

Roseland Presbyterian Church   1910
11200 South State Street

Sixth Church of Christ, Scientist   1910-11
11321 South Prairie Avenue   (300 East)

Bennett, Richard   (1907-   ):
See Loebl, Schlossman and Bennett

Beretta, Giuseppe

Assumption B.V.M. Church   1884-86
319 West Illinois Street   (500 North)

Bernham, Felix: See Newhouse and Bernham

Bettinghofer, Josef

St. Alphonsus Church   1889-97
2950 North Southport Avenue   (1400 West)
See also Adam Boos and Schrader and Conradi

Boos, Adam

St. Alphonsus Church   1889-97
2950 North Southport Avenue   (1400 West)
See also Josef Bettinghofer and Schrader and Conradi

Bourgeois, Louis J.   (1856-1930) of Canada

Baha'i House of Worship   1920-53
100 Linden Avenue, Wilmette, Illinois

Architects

Brinkman, William J. (1874-1911)

St. James Temple AOH Church of God   1896-1901
formerly St. Nicholas Church
11330 South State Street

St. Josaphat Church   1900-1902
2301 North Southport Avenue   (1400 West)

Our Lady of Sorrows Basilica   1890-1902   (interior)
3101 West Jackson Boulevard   (300 South)
See also Henry Engelbert and John F. Pope

St. Patrick Church   1902-3
9515 South Commercial Avenue   (3000 East)

St. George Church   1903-4
9554 South Ewing Avenue   (3634 West)

St. Francis of Assisi Church   (rebuilt 1904-5)
815 West Roosevelt Road   (1200 South)

St. Dominic Church   1905-6
869 North Sedgwick Street   (400 West)

St. Leo Church   1905-6
7750 South Emerald Avenue   (732 West)

St. Michael Church   1907-9
83rd Street and South Shore Drive   (3132 East)

Holy Cross Church   1909-10
836 East 65th Street

Burling, Edward J. (1819-92)

The Cathedral of St. James   1856-57
65 East Huron Street   (700 North)

Burling and Bacchus

The Cathedral of St. James   (reconstruction, 1875)
65 East Huron Street   (700 North)

Burling and Whitehouse

Church of the Epiphany   1885
201 South Ashland Avenue   (1600 West)

St. Pius V   (upper church, 1892-93)
1901 South Ashland Avenue   (1600 West)

Burnham, D.H. (1846-1912) **and Root, John W.** (1850-91)

St. Gabriel Church   1887-88
4501 South Lowe Avenue   (632 West)

Lake View Presbyterian Church   1887-88
3600 North Broadway   (700 West)

Burns, James

St. Columbanus Church   1923-25
315 East 71st Street

St. Kevin Church   1925-26
10501 South Torrence Avenue   (2634 East)

Our Lady of Guadalupe Church   1928
3204 East 91st Street

St. Gertrude Church   1930-31
6204 North Glenwood Avenue   (1400 West)

Burns, John J. (1886-1956)

St. Peter's Church   1951-53
110 West Madison Street
See also Karl M. Vitzthum

Byrne, Francis Barry (1883-1967)

St. Thomas the Apostle Church   1922-24
5476 South Kimbark Avenue   (1300 East)

Camburas, Peter E. (1892-   )

The Assumption Greek Orthodox Church   1937-38
601 South Central Avenue   (5600 West)

Camburas & Theodore

St. Andrew's Greek Orthodox Church   1955-56
5649 North Sheridan Road   (1000 West)

Carter, Asher (1805-77) **and
Bauer, Augustus** (1827-94)

Old St. Patrick Church   1852-56
140 South Desplaines Street   (700 West)

Chamales, Christopher (1907-   )

Elijah Muhammad Mosque #2   1948-52
formerly SS. Constantine and Helen
Greek Orthodox Church
7351 South Stony Island Avenue   (1600 East)

Cochrane, John C. (1833-1887)

All Saints Episcopal Church   1882-84
4552 North Hermitage Avenue   (1734 West)

Comes, Perry, and McMullen of Pittsburgh

St. Gregory the Great Church   1924-26
5533 North Paulina Street   (1700 West)

Coolidge, Charles A. (1858-1936) of Boston
and Hodgdon, Charles (1864-1953) of Chicago

Bond Chapel   1925-26
1050 East 59th Street

**Coolidge and Hodgdon with
Loebl, Schlossman and Demuth**

Temple Sholom   1928-30
3480 North Lake Shore Drive   (500 West)

Cram, Ralph Adams (1863-1942) of Boston

Fourth Presbyterian Church   1912-14
876 North Michigan Avenue   (100 East)
See also Howard Van Doren Shaw

Dart, Edward D. (1922-75) **and Associates**

Emmanuel Presbyterian Church   1965
1850 South Racine Avenue   (1200 West)

Augustana Lutheran Church of Hyde Park   1967-68
1151 East 55th Street

St. Procopius Abbey Church   1968-70
5601 College Road, Lisle, Illinois

First St. Paul's Ev. Lutheran Church   1969-70
1301 North LaSalle Drive   (150 West)

Davis, Zachary T.   (1872-1946)

St. Ambrose Church   1906-26
1002 East 47th Street

St. James Chapel   1917-20
Quigley Preparatory Seminary North
831 North Rush Street   (75 East)
See also Gustave Steinback

Dillenburg, John and **Zucher** of Milwaukee

Holy Family Church   1857-60
1080 West Roosevelt Road   (1200 South)

Dokas, N.

The Annunciation Cathedral   1910
1017 North LaSalle Drive   (150 West)

Druiding, Adolphus

St. John Cantius Church   1893-98
821 North Carpenter Street   (1032 West)

St. Hedwig Church   1899-1901
2100 West Webster Avenue   (2200 North)

Drummond, William E.   (1876-1946)

Greater Holy Temple, Church of God in Christ   1908-9
originally First Congregational Church of Austin
5701 West Midway Park   (500 North)
See also Guenzel and Drummond

Egan, James J.   (1839-1914)

St. Pius V   (lower church, 1885)
1901 South Ashland Avenue   (1600 West)

St. Vincent de Paul Church   1895-97
1004 West Webster Avenue   (2200 North)

Holy Angels Church   1896-97
605 East Oakwood Boulevard   (3940 South)

Egan & Prindeville

St. Agatha Church   1904-6
3151 West Douglas Boulevard   (1330 South)

St. Bridget Church   1905-6
2940 South Archer Avenue   (1500 West)

St. Andrew Church   1912-13
3550 North Paulina Street   (1700 West)

Our Lady of Mount Carmel Church   1913-14
700 West Belmont Avenue   (3200 North)

See also Charles H. Prindeville

Engelbert, Henry of Detroit

St. Mary of Perpetual Help Church   1889-92
1035 West 32nd Street

Our Lady of Sorrows Basilica   1890-1902
3101 West Jackson Boulevard   (300 South)
See also John F. Pope and William J. Brinkman

Faulkner, Charles D.

United Church of Hyde Park
(interior renovation, 1923-24)
1440 East 53rd Street

St. Luke Missionary Baptist Church   1927-31
originally Eighteenth Church of Christ, Scientist
7262 South Coles Avenue   (2500 East)

Fischer, Albert and **Gaul, Hermann J.**

Immaculate Conception Church   1908-10
3101 South Aberdeen Street   (1100 West)
See also Hermann J. Gaul

Friedman, Alschuler and Sincere

Sinai Temple   1948-50
5350 South Shore Drive   (1800 East)

The Old Landmark Church of God
Holiness in Christ   1952-54
formerly South Shore Temple
7201 South Jeffery Boulevard   (2000 East)

North Shore Congregation Israel   1962-64
1185 Sheridan Road, Glencoe, Illinois
See also Minoru Yamasaki

Fugard, John R.   (1886-1968)

The Moody Memorial Church   1924-25
1630 North Clark Street   (100 West)

Garden, Hugh M. G.   (1873-1961)

Metropolitan Missionary Baptist Church   1899
formerly Third Church of Christ, Scientist
2151 West Washington Boulevard   (100 North)

Gaul, Hermann J.   (1869-1949)

St. Matthias Church   1915-16
2336 West Ainslie Street   (4900 North)

St. Raphael Church   1915-16
6001 South Justine Street   (1532 West)

St. Benedict Church   1917-18
2201 West Irving Park Road   (4000 North)

St. Philomena Church   1922-23
4130 West Cortland Street   (1900 North)

Sacred Heart Church   1925-27
7003 South May Street   (1132 West)

St. Francis Xavier Church   1927-29
3035 North Francisco Avenue   (2900 West)

See also Albert Fischer

Architects

Goodhue, Bertram G. (1869-1924) of New York

St. Andrew Chapel in St. James Cathedral   1913
65 East Huron Street   (700 North)

Rockefeller Memorial Chapel   1926-28
1160 East 59th Street

Gubbins, William F. (1876-1937)

Presentation Church   1903-9
750 South Springfield Avenue   (3900 West)

St. Therese Chinese Mission   1904
formerly Santa Maria Incoronata Church
214 West Alexander Street   (2246 South)

St. Agnes Church   1905-6
2650 West Pershing Road   (3900 South)

Precious Blood Church   1907-8
2401 West Congress Parkway   (500 South)

Maternity B.V.M. Church   1910-11
3643 West North Avenue   (1600 North)

Guenzel and Drummond

Park Manor Christian Church   1914-15
originally Lorimer Memorial Baptist Church
600 East 73rd Street
See also William E. Drummond

Guenzel, Louis H. (1860-1956)

Our Lady of Lourdes Church   1931-32
4206 West 15th Street

Hansen, Christian O. (1842-1930)

LaSalle Street Church   1882-86
originally Trinity Evangelical Lutheran Church
1136 North LaSalle Drive   (150 West)

St. Jerome Croatian Church   1885
formerly Salem Lutheran Church
2819 South Princeton Avenue   (300 West)

Holabird, William (1854-1923) **and
Roche, Martin** (1855-1927)

The Chicago Temple   1922-24
First United Methodist Church
77 West Washington Street   (100 North)

Hotton, Bartholomew J. with **Raymond Gregori**

St. Pascal Church   1930-31
6149 West Irving Park Road   (4000 North)

Hull, Denison Bingham (1897-   )

First Unitarian Church of Chicago   1929-31
5650 South Woodlawn Avenue   (1200 East)

Kallal and Molitor

St. Vitus Church   1896-97
1820 South Paulina Street   (1700 West)
See also Joseph Molitor

Keely, Patrick C. (1816-1896)

Holy Name Cathedral   1874-75
735 North State Street

St. James Church   1875-80
2940 South Wabash Avenue   (50 East)

Nativity of Our Lord Church   1876-85
655 West 37th Street

St. Stanislaus Kostka Church   1877-81
1327 North Noble Street   (1400 West)

Korsunsky, Jaroslaw (1933-   ) of Minneapolis

SS. Volodymyr and Olha Church   1973-75
739 North Oakley Boulevard   (2300 West)

Kovacevic, Radoslav

Holy Resurrection Serbian Orthodox Cathedral   1973-75
5701 North Redwood Drive   (8024 West)
See also Pavlecic & Kovacevic

Krieg, William (1874-1944)

Holy Trinity Church   1905-6
1120 North Noble Street   (1400 West)
See also Olszewski

Levy, Alexander

St. Basil Greek Orthodox Church   1910
formerly Anshe Sholom
733 South Ashland Avenue   (1600 West)

Lloyd & Pearce of Detroit

Trinity Episcopal Church   1873-74
125 East 26th Street

Loebl, Schlossman and Bennett

Congregation Emanuel   1953-55
5941 North Sheridan Road   (1000 West)

Chicago Loop Synagogue   1957-58
16 South Clark Street   (100 West)

Loebl, Schlossman and Demuth

Temple Sholom   1928-30
3480 North Lake Shore Drive   (500 West)
See also Coolidge and Hodgdon

McCarthy, Joe W. (1884-1965)

Corpus Christi Church   1914-16
4900 South Martin Luther King Drive   (400 East)

St. Thomas of Canterbury Church   1916-17
4815 North Kenmore Avenue   (1038 West)

St. Justin Martyr Church   1917-18
7037 South Honore Street   (1832 West)

St. Catherine of Genoa Church 1923-24
11762 South Lowe Avenue (632 West)

Our Lady of Peace Church 1924-35
2002 East 79th Street

St. Sabina Church 1925-33
7821 South Throop Street (1300 West)

St. Basil Church 1925-26
1840 West Garfield Boulevard (5500 South)

St. Timothy Church 1926
6330 North Washtenaw Avenue (2700 West)

St. Philip Neri Church 1926-28
2126 East 72nd Street

Our Lady of Lourdes Church
(interior renovation, 1929)
1601 West Leland Avenue (4700 North)

St. Andrew Church (renovation, 1931-32)
3550 North Paulina Street (1700 West)

St. Jerome Church (expansion and renovation, 1934)
1701 West Lunt Avenue (7000 North)

St. Angela Church 1949-52
1306 North Massasoit Avenue (5732 West)

McCarthy, Smith & Eppig

St. Kilian Church 1931-37
1115 West 87th Street

Our Lady of Grace Church 1934-35
2450 North Ridgeway Avenue (3732 West)

St. Maurice Church 1936-37
3601 South Hoyne Avenue (2100 West)

Blessed Sacrament Church 1937-38
3604 West Cermak Road (2200 South)

St. Francis de Paula Church 1937-38
1028 East 78th Street

St. Margaret Mary Church 1937-38
2322 West Chase Avenue (7300 North)

St. Edward Church 1938-40
4356 West Sunnyside Avenue (4500 North)

Queen of Angels Church 1938-40
2334 West Sunnyside Avenue (4500 North)

St. Genevieve Church 1939-41
2453 North Lamon Avenue (4900 West)

St. Wenceslaus Church 1940-42
3656 West Roscoe Street (3400 North)

McCarthy and Associates

St. Richard Church 1959-60
4404 West 50th Street

St. Rene Goupil Church 1960-62
6340 South New England Avenue (6900 West)

McCarthy, Hundreiser and Associates

St. Barnabas Church 1968-69
10140 South Longwood Drive (1900 West)

St. Robert Bellarmine Church 1969-70
4650 North Austin Avenue (6000 West)

Mazurkevich, Zenon (1944-   ) of Philadelphia

St. Nicholas Ukrainian Catholic Cathedral
(renovation, 1974-77)
2238 West Rice Street (824 North)

St. Joseph's Ukrainian Catholic Church 1975-77
5000 North Cumberland Avenue (8400 West)

Meyer and Cook

St. Adrian Church 1929-30
7006 South Washtenaw Avenue (2700 West)

St. Peter Canisius Church 1935-36
5101 West North Avenue (1600 North)

St. Therese of the Infant Jesus 1951-52
(Little Flower) Church
1957 West 80th Street

Our Lady of Fatima Mission Church 1956-57
3051 North Christiana Avenue (3332 West)

Queen of All Saints Basilica 1956-60
6284 North Sauganash Avenue (4700 West)

Immaculate Conception Church 1961-63
7201 West Talcott Avenue (5800 North)

St. Thecla Church 1962-63
6352 North Oak Park Avenue (6800 West)

Our Lady Mother of the Church 1967-68
4720 North Oakview Avenue (8650 West)

Mies Van der Rohe, Ludwig (1886-1969)

IIT Chapel 1952
3200 South Michigan (100 East)

Molitor, Joseph

St. Laurence Church 1911-12
7142 South Dorchester Avenue (1400 East)

SS. Cyril and Methodius Church 1912-13
5001 South Hermitage Avenue (1734 West)

St. Joseph Church 1913-14
1729 West 48th Street

Holy Cross Church 1913-15
1736 West 46th Street

Providence of God (lower church, 1914)
1800 South Union Avenue (700 West)
See also Leo Strelka

See also Kallal and Molitor

Moses, I. and Associates

Congregation Bnei Ruven 1967
6350 North Whipple Street (3034 West)

Architects

Murphy, C. F. Associates

Holy Name Cathedral   (renovation, 1968-69)
735 North State Street

Newhouse, Henry L. and Bernham, Felix M.

Independence Boulevard Seventh Day
Adventist Church   1921-26
formerly Anshe Sholom
748 South Independence Boulevard   (3800 West)

Operation PUSH   1923-24
formerly K.A.M. Temple
4945 South Drexel Boulevard   (900 East)

Norman, Andrew E.

Ebenezer Lutheran Church   1904-12
1650 West Foster Avenue   (5200 North)

Olson, Benjamin Franklin   (1888-   )

St. Pauls Church   1959
2335 North Orchard Street   (700 West)

Olszewski (Von Herbulis) of Washington, D.C.

Holy Trinity Church   1905-6
1120 North Noble Street   (1400 West)
See also William Krieg

Otis, William Augustus   (1855-1929)

St. Peter's Episcopal Church   1894-95
615 West Belmont Avenue   (3200 North)

Hull Memorial Chapel   1896-97
First Unitarian Church of Chicago
5650 South Woodlawn Avenue   (1200 East)

Pavlecic, William P.   (1920-   ) **and
Kovacevic, Radoslav**   (1923-

St. Jane de Chantal Church   1962-64
5251 South McVicker Avenue   (6034 West)

Pavlecic & Kovacevic with **R. Markovich**

St. Simeon Mirotocivi
Serbian Orthodox Church   1968-69
3737 East 114th Street

Pavlecic & Kovacevic with **Jack Ota**

St. Gall Church   1955-58
5500 South Kedzie Avenue   (3200 West)

See also Radoslav Kovacevic

Pope, John F.

Our Lady of Sorrows Basilica   1890-1902
3101 West Jackson Boulevard   (300 South)
See also Henry Engelbert and William J. Brinkman

Prindeville, Charles H.   (1868-1947)

St. Jerome Church   1914-16
1701 West Lunt Avenue   (7000 North)

See also Egan & Prindeville

Randall, Gurdon P.   (1821-84)

First Baptist Congregational Church   1869-71
60 North Ashland Avenue   (1600 West)

Rebori, Andrew   (1886-1966)

Madonna della Strada Chapel   1938-39
6525 North Sheridan Road   (at Lake Michigan)

Renwick, James   (1818-95)   of New York

Second Presbyterian Church   1872-74
1936 South Michigan Avenue   (100 East)

Rogers, James Gamble   (1867-1947)

Hyde Park Union Church   1904-6
formerly Hyde Park Baptist Church
5600 South Woodlawn Avenue   (1200 East)

Root, John Wellborn: See Burnham and Root

Schlacks, Henry J.   (1868-1938)

St. Martin Church   1894-95
5848 South Princeton Avenue   (300 West)
See also Louis A. Becker

St. Paul Church   1897-99
2234 South Hoyne Avenue   (2100 West)

St. Boniface Church   1902-4
1348 West Chestnut Street   (860 North)

Angel Guardian Mission   1905-6
formerly St. Henry Church
6360 North Ridge Avenue   (1845 West)

St. Adalbert Church   1912-14
1656 West 17th Street

All Saints—St. Anthony Church   1913-15
2849 South Wallace Street   (600 West)

St. Mary of the Lake Church   1913-17
4200 North Sheridan Road   (1000 West)

St. Ignatius Church   1916-17
6555 North Glenwood Avenue   (1400 West)

Resurrection Church   1916-18
5084 West Jackson Boulevard   (300 South)

Our Lady of Solace Church   1917
935 West 62nd Street

St. John of God Church   1918-20
1238 West 52nd Street

St. Clara—St. Cyril Church   1923-27
originally St. Clara Church
6401 South Woodlawn Avenue   (1200 East)

St. Ita Church   1924-27
5500 North Broadway   (1200 West)

St. Henry Church   1928-29
6329 North Hoyne Avenue   (2100 West)

Schrader and Conradi of St. Louis

St. Alphonsus Church   1889-97
2950 North Southport Avenue   (1400 West)
See also Adam Boos and Josef Bettinghofer

Shaw, Howard Van Doren   (1869-1926)

Second Presbyterian Church
(interior restoration, 1900)
1936 South Michigan Avenue   (100 East)

Fourth Presbyterian Church   1912-14
876 North Michigan Avenue   (100 East)
See also Ralph Adams Cram

Howard Van Doren Shaw and **Henry K. Holsman**

University Church of Disciples of Christ   1923
5655 South University Avenue   (1144 East)

Sherer, J. J. of Milwaukee

Blair Chapel   1971
Fourth Presbyterian Church
876 North Michigan Avenue   (100 East)

Smith, George S.

Our Lady of Hungary Church   1929-30
9242 South Kimbark Avenue   (1300 East)

St. Joachim Church   (expansion and renovation, 1933)
708 East 91st Street

St. Bernard Church   1935
formerly St. Bernard Lyceum
6550 South Harvard Avenue   (332 West)

St. Daniel the Prophet Church   1947-55
6604 West 54th Street

St. Felicitas Church   1951-56
8356 South Blackstone Avenue   (1500 East)

Holy Innocents Church   (restoration, 1962-63)
735 North Armour Street   (1500 West)

Stahl, Harold A.   (1910-   )

St. Michael Lutheran Church   1955-56
8200 West Addison Street   (3600 North)

St. Luke Evangelical Lutheran Church   1960
1500 West Belmont Avenue   (3200 North)

Steinbach, J. G.

St. John Berchmans Church   1906-7
2519 West Logan Boulevard   (2600 North)

St. Callistus Church   1926
2169 West Bowler Street   (900 South)

All Saints Cathedral   1930
2018 West Dickens Avenue   (2100 North)

See also Worthmann and Steinbach

Steinback, Gustave of New York

St. James Chapel   1917-20
Quigley Preparatory Seminary North
831 North Rush Street   (75 East)
See also Zachary Davis

Straka, Paul   (1939-   )

St. James Church   (restoration, 1974-76)
2940 South Wabash Avenue   (50 East)

Corpus Christi Church   (renovation, 1976)
4900 South Martin Luther King Drive   (400 East)

St. Clara—St. Cyril Church   (restoration, 1977-80)
6401 South Woodlawn Avenue   (1200 East)

Strelka, Leo

Providence of God   (upper church, 1926-27)
1800 South Union Avenue   (700 West)
See also Joseph Molitor

St. Bronislava Church   1928-29
8716 South Colfax Avenue   (2600 East)

St. Ladislaus Church   1953-57
3343 North Long Avenue   (5400 West)

Sullivan, Louis H.:   See Adler and Sullivan

Tallmadge, Thomas E.   (1876-1940) **and
Watson, Vernon S.**   (1879-1950)

Trinity Episcopal Church   (interior, 1920)
125 East 26th Street

Rogers Park Baptist Church   1918-19
(rebuilt 1935-36)
1900 West Greenleaf Avenue   (7032 North)

St. James United Methodist Church   1925-27
formerly St. James Methodist Episcopal Church
4611 South Ellis Avenue   (1000 East)

First Presbyterian Church   1927-28
6400 South Kimbark Avenue   (1300 East)

Grace Episcopal Church   1927-28
(closed, not functioning)
1442 South Indiana Avenue   (200 East)

Tilton, John   (1860-1921)

Church of the Ascension   1882-87
1133 North LaSalle Drive   (150 West)
See also Albert Wilcox

Van Osdel, John M.   (1811-91)

Holy Family Church   1857-60 (tower and interior)
1080 West Roosevelt Road   (1200 South)

Vigeant, Gregory A.   (1853-1918)

St. Charles Lwanga Church   1875-80
originally St. Anne Church
155 West Garfield Boulevard   (5500 South)

Notre Dame Church   1887-92
1336 West Flournoy Street   (700 South)

Architects

United Church of Hyde Park   1889
formerly Hyde Park Presbyterian Church
1448 East 53rd Street

Vitzthum, Karl M.   (1880-1967)

St. Thomas Aquinas Church   1923-25
5120 West Washington Boulevard   (100 North)

St. Peter's Church   1951-53
110 West Madison Street
See also John J. Burns

Walcott, Chester H.   (1883-1947)

St. Chrysostom's Church   1925-26
1424 North Dearborn Parkway   (50 West)

Wallace, Charles L. of Joliet

St. Mel—Holy Ghost Church   1910-11
originally St. Mel Church
4301 West Washington Boulevard   (100 North)

St. Anselm Church   1924-25
6049 South Michigan Avenue   (100 East)

St. Margaret of Scotland Church   1926-28
1256 West 99th Street

St. Viator Church   1927-29
4160 West Addison Street   (3600 North)

St. Dorothy Church   1928-29
440 East 78th Street

St. Clotilde Church   1929-30
8400 South Calumet Avenue   (344 East)

Wallbaum, August

St. Michael Church   1866-69, 1873
455 West Eugenie Street   (1700 North)

Warren, Clinton J.   (1860-   )

Church of Our Saviour   1888-89
530 West Fullerton Parkway   (2400 North)

Weese, Harry and Associates

Seventeenth Church of Christ, Scientist   1968
55 East Wacker Drive   (300 North)

Whitehouse, Francis M.   (1848-1938):
See Burling and Whitehouse

Wilcox, Albert

Church of the Ascension   1882-87
1133 North LaSalle Drive   (150 West)
See also John Tilton

Willcox, William H. and Miller, Charles C.

Olivet Baptist Church   1875-76
formerly First Baptist Church
3101 South Martin Luther King Drive   (400 East)

Worthmann, Henry   (1857-1946)

New Mt. Hope Missionary Baptist Church   1902-3
formerly Our Redeemer Lutheran Church
6034 South Princeton Avenue   (300 West)

Worthmann and Steinbach

Holy Innocents Church   1911-12
735 North Armour Street   (1500 West)

First Lutheran Church of the Trinity   1912-13
643 West 31st Street

St. Barbara Church   1912-14
2855 South Throop Street   (1300 West)

St. Nicholas Ukrainian Catholic Cathedral   1913-15
2238 West Rice Street   (824 North)

Our Lady of Lourdes Church   1913-16
1601 West Leland Avenue   (4700 North)

Jehovah Lutheran Church   1914-15
3736 West Belden Avenue   (2300 North)

St. Mary of the Angels Church   1914-20
1850 North Hermitage Avenue   (1734 West)

St. James Lutheran Church   1916-17
2048 North Fremont Street   (900 West)

St. Hyacinth Church   1917-21
3635 West George Street   (2900 North)

Greater Mt. Vernon Baptist Church   1922-23
formerly Our Redeemer Lutheran Church
6430 South Harvard Avenue   (332 West)

Our Lady of Pompeii Church   1923-25
1224 West Lexington Street   (732 South)

Worthmann and Steinbach with **C. L. Piontek**

St. Casimir Church   1917-19
3035 West Cermak Road   (2200 South)

See also J. G. Steinbach

Wright, Frank Lloyd   (1867-1959)

Unity Temple   1906-9
The Unitarian Universalist Church in Oak Park
875 Lake Street at Kenilworth

Yamasaki, Minoru (1912-   ) in association with
Friedman, Alschuler and Sincere

North Shore Congregation Israel   1962-64
1185 Sheridan Road, Glencoe, Illinois

Zucher: See Dillenburg and Zucher

Ethnic Churches

Churches in this book plus those mentioned in the preceding architects list. Addresses indicate the fronts of buildings. Irish list: predominantly Irish parishes founded in the nineteenth century. German list: parishes founded from 1852 to 1904.

Belgian

St. John Berchmans Church   1906-7
2519 West Logan Boulevard   (2600 North)

Black

Quinn Chapel A.M.E. Church   1891-94
2401 South Wabash Avenue   (50 East)

St. Thaddeus Church   1959-60
9550 South Harvard Avenue   (332 West)

Bohemian

St. Vitus Church   1896-97
1820 South Paulina Street   (1700 West)

SS. Cyril and Methodius Church   1912-13
5001 South Hermitage Avenue   (1734 West)

Our Lady of Lourdes Church   1931-32
4206 West 15th Street

French

Notre Dame Church   1887-92
1336 West Flournoy Street   (700 South)

German

St. Michael Church   1866-69, 1873
455 West Eugenie Street   (1700 North)

Holy Cross Lutheran Church   1886
3120 South Racine Avenue   (1200 West)

First Immanuel Lutheran Church   1888
1124 South Ashland Avenue   (1600 West)

St. Alphonsus Church   1889-97
2950 North Southport Avenue   (1400 West)

Concordia Evangelical Lutheran Church   1892-93
2649 West Belmont Avenue   (3200 North)

St. Martin Church   1894-95
5848 South Princeton Avenue   (300 West)

St. Nicholas Church   1896-1901
now St. James Temple AOH Church of God
11330 South State Street

St. Paul Church   1897-99
2234 South Hoyne Avenue   (2100 West)

St. Boniface Church   1902-4
1348 West Chestnut Street   (860 North)

St. Francis of Assisi Church   (reconstructed, 1904-5)
815 West Roosevelt Road   (1200 South)

St. Henry Church   1905-6
now Angel Guardian Mission
6360 North Ridge Avenue   (1845 West)

Immaculate Conception Church   1908-10
3101 South Aberdeen Street   (1100 West)

Jehovah Lutheran Church   1914-15
3736 West Belden Avenue   (2300 North)

First Lutheran Church of the Trinity   1912-13
643 West 31st Street

St. Anthony Church   1913-15
now All Saints—St. Anthony Church
2849 South Wallace Street   (600 West)

St. Matthias Church   1915-16
2336 West Ainslie Street   (4900 North)

St. Raphael Church   1915-16
6001 South Justine Street   (1532 West)

St. James Lutheran Church   1916-17
2048 North Fremont Street   (900 West)

St. Benedict Church   1917-18
2201 West Irving Park Road   (4000 North)

St. Philomena Church   1922-23
4130 West Cortland Street   (1900 North)

St. Gregory the Great Church   1924-26
5533 North Paulina Street   (1700 West)

Sacred Heart Church   1925-27
7003 South May Street   (1132 West)

St. Francis Xavier Church   1927-29
3035 North Francisco Avenue   (2900 West)

St. Pauls Church   1959
2335 North Orchard Street   (700 West)

St. Luke Evangelical Lutheran Church   1960
1500 West Belmont Avenue   (3200 North)

Greek

The Annunciation Cathedral   1910
1017 North LaSalle Drive   (150 West)

The Assumption Greek Orthodox Church   1937-38
601 South Central Avenue   (5600 West)

SS. Constantine and Helen Greek Orthodox
Church   1948-52
now Elijah Muhammad Mosque #2
7351 South Stony Island Avenue   (1600 East)

St. Andrew's Greek Orthodox Church   1955-56
5649 North Sheridan Road (1000 West)

Hungarian

Our Lady of Hungary Church   1929-30
9242 South Kimbark Avenue   (1300 East)

Ethnic List

Irish

Old St. Patrick Church   1852-56
140 South Desplaines Street   (700 West)

Holy Family Church   1857-60
1080 West Roosevelt Road   (1200 South)

Holy Name Cathedral   1874-75
735 North State Street

St. Anne Church   1875-80
now St. Charles Lwanga Church
155 West Garfield Boulevard   (5500 South)

St. James Church   1875-80
2940 South Wabash Avenue   (50 East)

Nativity of Our Lord Church   1876-85
655 West 37th Street

St. Pius V Church   1885-93
1901 South Ashland Avenue   (1600 West)

St. Gabriel Church   1887-88
4501 South Lowe Avenue   (632 West)

Holy Rosary Church   1890
11302 South Martin Luther King Drive   (400 East)

Our Lady of Sorrows Basilica   1890-1902
3101 West Jackson Boulevard   (300 South)

St. Vincent de Paul Church   1895-97
1004 West Webster Avenue   (2200 North)

Holy Angels Church   1896-97
605 East Oakwood Boulevard   (3940 South)

Presentation Church   1903-9
750 South Springfield Avenue   (3900 West)

St. Patrick Church   1902-3
9515 South Commercial Avenue   (3000 East)

St. Agatha Church   1904-6
3151 West Douglas Boulevard   (1330 South)

St. Agnes Church   1905-6
2650 West Pershing Road   (3900 South)

St. Bridget Church   1905-6
2940 South Archer Avenue   (1500 West)

St. Leo Church   1905-6
7750 South Emerald Avenue   (732 West)

Holy Cross Church   1909-10
836 East 65th Street

St. Mel Church   1910-11
now St. Mel—Holy Ghost Church
4301 West Washington Boulevard   (100 North)

St. Laurence Church   1911-12
7142 South Dorchester Avenue   (1400 East)

St. Andrew Church   1912-13
3550 North Paulina Street   (1700 West)

Our Lady of Mount Carmel Church   1913-14
700 West Belmont Avenue   (3200 North)

Our Lady of Lourdes Church   1913-16
1601 West Leland Avenue   (4700 North)

St. Jerome Church   1914-16
1701 West Lunt Avenue   (7000 North)

Italian

Assumption B.V.M. Church   1884-86
319 West Illinois Street   (500 North)

Santa Maria Incoronata Church   1904
now St. Therese Chinese Mission
214 West Alexander Street   (2246 South)

Our Lady of Pompeii Church   1923-25
1224 West Lexington Street   (732 South)

St. Callistus Church   1926
2169 West Bowler Street   (900 South)

St. Mary of Mount Carmel Church   1942
now St. Andrews Temple
1735 West Marquette Road   (6700 South)

Japanese

Midwest Buddhist Temple   1971
435 West Menomonee Street   (1800 North)

Jewish

K.A.M. Temple   1890-91
now Pilgrim Baptist Church
3301 South Indiana Avenue   (200 East)

Anshe Emet Synagogue   1893
now Pillar's Rock Baptist Church
1363 North Sedgwick Street   (400 West)

Temple Isaiah   1898-99
now Ebenezer Baptist Church
4501 South Vincennes Avenue   (500 East)

Anshe Sholom   1910
now St. Basil Greek Orthodox Church
733 South Ashland Avenue   (1600 West)

Temple Sholom   1910-11
now Anshe Emet Synagogue
3760 North Pine Grove Avenue   (700 West)

Sinai Temple   1910-12
now Mt. Pisgah Missionary Baptist Church
4600 South Martin Luther King Drive   (400 East)

B'nai Sholom Temple Israel   1913-14
now Greater Bethesda Baptist Church
5301 South Michigan Avenue   (100 East)

Anshe Sholom   1921-26
now Independence Boulevard Seventh Day
Adventist Church
748 South Independence Boulevard   (3800 West)

K.A.M. Temple   1923-24
now Operation PUSH
4945 South Drexel Boulevard   (900 East)

Temple Isaiah   1923-24
now K.A.M.—Isaiah Israel Temple
5045 South Greenwood Avenue   (1100 East)

Temple Sholom   1928-30
3480 North Lake Shore Drive   (500 West)

Sinai Temple   1948-50
5350 South Shore Drive   (1800 East)

South Shore Temple   1952-54
now The Old Landmark Church of God
Holiness in Christ
7201 South Jeffery Boulevard   (2000 East)

Congregation Emanuel   1953-55
5941 North Sheridan Road   (1000 West)

Chicago Loop Synagogue   1957-58
16 South Clark Street   (100 West)

North Shore Congregation Israel   1962-64
1185 Sheridan Road, Glencoe, Illinois

Congregation Bnei Ruven   1967
6350 North Whipple Street   (3034 West)

Lithuanian

Holy Cross Church   1913-15
1736 West 46th Street

Providence of God Church   1914-27
1800 South Union Avenue   (700 West)

Immaculate Conception Church   1963-66
4403 South California Avenue   (2800 West)

Mexican

Our Lady of Guadalupe Church   1928
3204 East 91st Street

Polish

St. Stanislaus Kostka Church   1877-81
1327 North Noble Street   (1400 West)

St. Mary of Perpetual Help Church   1889-92
1035 West 32nd Street

St. John Cantius Church   1893-98
821 North Carpenter Street   (1032 West)

St. Hedwig Church   1899-1901
2100 West Webster Avenue   (2200 North)

St. Josaphat Church   1900-1902
2301 North Southport Avenue   (1400 West)

Holy Trinity Church   1905-6
1120 North Noble Street   (1400 West)

St. Michael Church   1907-9
83rd Street and South Shore Drive   (3132 East)

Holy Innocents Church   1911-12
735 North Armour Street   (1500 West)

St. Barbara Church   1912-14
2855 South Throop Street   (1300 West)

St. Adalbert Church   1912-14
1656 West 17th Street

St. Joseph Church   1913-14
1729 West 48th Street

St. Mary of the Angels Church   1914-20
1850 North Hermitage Avenue   (1734 West)

St. Casimir Church   1917-19
3035 West Cermak Road   (2200 South)

St. Hyacinth Church   1917-21
3635 West George Street   (2900 North)

St. John of God Church   1918-20
1238 West 52nd Street

St. Bronislava Church   1928-29
8716 South Colfax Avenue   (2600 East)

All Saints Cathedral   1930
2018 West Dickens Avenue   (2100 North)

St. Wenceslaus Church   1940-42
3656 West Roscoe Street   (3400 North)

St. Ladislaus Church   1953-57
3343 North Long Avenue   (5400 West)

Our Lady of Fatima Mission Church   1956-57
3051 North Christiana Avenue   (3332 West)

Russian

Holy Trinity Cathedral   1903
1121 North Leavitt Street   (2200 West)

Serbian

St. Simeon Mirotocivi Serbian Orthodox
Church   1968-69
3737 East 114th Street

Holy Resurrection Serbian Orthodox Cathedral   1973-75
5701 North Redwood Drive   (8024 West)

Slovene

St. George Church   1903-4
9554 South Ewing Avenue   (3634 East)

Swedish

Salem Lutheran Church   1885
now St. Jerome Croatian Church
2819 South Princeton Avenue   (300 West)

Ebenezer Lutheran Church   1904-12
1650 West Foster Avenue   (5200 North)

Ukrainian

St. Nicholas Ukrainian Catholic Cathedral   1913-15
2238 West Rice Street   (824 North)

SS. Volodymyr and Olha Church   1973-75
739 North Oakley Boulevard   (2300 West)

St. Joseph's Ukrainian Catholic Church   1975-77
5000 North Cumberland Avenue   (8400 West)

Architectural Styles

Addresses indicate the fronts of buildings.

American Colonial

St. Bartholomew Church   1937-38
3601 North Lavergne Avenue   (5000 West)

Basilica

St. Adalbert Church   1912-14
1656 West 17th Street

St. Mary of the Lake Church   1913-17
4200 North Sheridan Road   (1000 West)

Byzantine

St. Nicholas Ukrainian
Catholic Cathedral   1913-15
2238 West Rice Street   (824 North)

K.A.M.—Isaiah Israel Temple   1923-24
5045 South Greenwood Avenue   (1100 East)

St. Basil Church   1925-26
1840 West Garfield Boulevard   (5500 South)

Temple Sholom   1928-30
3480 North Lake Shore Drive   (500 West)

The Assumption Greek Orthodox Church   1937-38
601 South Central Avenue   (5600 West)

Elijah Muhammad Mosque #2   1948-52
7351 South Stony Island Avenue   (1600 East)

St. Simeon Mirotocivi
Serbian Orthodox Church   1968-70
3737 East 114th Street

Holy Resurrection
Serbian Orthodox Cathedral   1973-75
5701 North Redwood Drive   (8024 West)

SS. Volodymyr and Olha Church   1973-75
739 North Oakley Boulevard   (2300 West)

St. Joseph's Ukrainian
Catholic Church   1975-77
5000 North Cumberland Avenue   (8400 West)

Chicago School

Pilgrim Baptist Church   1890-91
3301 South Indiana Avenue   (200 East)

Georgian

Ebenezer Baptist Church   1898-99
4501 South Vincennes Avenue   (500 East)

Anshe Emet Synagogue   1910-11
3760 North Pine Grove Avenue   (700 West)

Gothic

Holy Family Church   1857-60
1080 West Roosevelt Road   (1200 South)

First Baptist Congregational Church   1869-71
60 North Ashland Avenue   (1600 West)

Olivet Baptist Church   1875-76
3101 South Martin Luther King Drive   (400 East)

LaSalle Street Church   1882-86
1136 North LaSalle Drive   (150 West)

St. Alphonsus Church   1889-97
2950 North Southport Avenue   (1400 West)

St. Paul Church   1897-99
2234 South Hoyne Avenue   (2100 West)

Ebenezer Lutheran Church   1904-12
1650 West Foster Avenue   (5200 North)

St. Michael Church   1907-9
83rd Street and South Shore Drive   (3132 East)

St. Peter's Church   1951-53
110 West Madison Street

Queen of All Saints Basilica   1956-60
6284 North Sauganash Avenue   (4700 West)

French Gothic

Church of the Ascension   1882-87
1133 North LaSalle Drive   (150 West)

Quigley Preparatory Seminary North,
St. James Chapel   1917-20
831 North Rush Street   (75 East)

The Chicago Temple
First United Methodist Church   1922-24
77 West Washington Street   (100 North)

St. Ita Church   1924-27
5500 North Broadway   (1200 West)

Norman Gothic

St. Gregory the Great Church   1924-26
5533 North Paulina Street   (1700 West)

English Gothic

Second Presbyterian Church   1872-74
1936 South Michigan Avenue   (100 East)

Trinity Episcopal Church   1873-74
125 East 26th Street

Fourth Presbyterian Church   1912-14
876 North Michigan Avenue   (100 East)

Our Lady of Mount Carmel Church   1913-14
700 West Belmont Avenue   (3200 North)

Greater Mt. Vernon Baptist Church   1922-23
6430 South Harvard Avenue   (332 West)

St. Thomas Aquinas Church   1923-25
5120 West Washington Boulevard   (100 North)

Bond Chapel   1925-26
1050 East 59th Street

St. Chrysostom's Church   1925-26
1424 North Dearborn Parkway   (50 West)

St. Sabina Church   1925-33
7821 South Throop Street   (1300 West)

St. Philip Neri Church   1926-28
2126 East 72nd Street

First Presbyterian Church   1927-28
6400 South Kimbark Avenue   (1300 East)

St. Viator Church   1927-29
4160 West Addison Street   (3600 North)

First Unitarian Church of Chicago   1929-31
5650 South Woodlawn Avenue   (1200 East)

St. Gertrude Church   1930-31
6204 North Glenwood Avenue   (1400 West)

German Gothic

St. Martin Church   1894-95
5848 South Princeton Avenue   (300 West)

Victorian Gothic

The Cathedral of St. James   1856-57, 1875
65 East Huron Street   (700 North)

Holy Name Cathedral   1874-75
735 North State Street

St. James Church   1875-80
2940 South Wabash Avenue   (50 East)

First Immanuel Lutheran Church   1888
1124 South Ashland Avenue   (1600 West)

Quinn Chapel A.M.E. Church   1891-94
2401 South Wabash Avenue   (50 East)

Neo-Gothic

St. James Lutheran Church   1916-17
2048 North Fremont Street   (900 West)

Rockefeller Memorial Chapel   1926-28
1160 East 59th Street

St. Pauls Church   1959
2335 North Orchard Street   (700 West)

Greek Revival

Grant Memorial A.M.E. Church   1897
4017 South Drexel Boulevard   (900 East)

Metropolitan Missionary Baptist Church   1899
2151 West Washington Boulevard   (100 North)

St. Basil Greek Orthodox Church   1910
733 South Ashland Avenue   (1600 West)

Operation PUSH   1923-24
4945 South Drexel Boulevard   (900 East)

International

IIT Chapel   1952
3200 South Michigan Avenue   (100 East)

Modern

St. Thomas the Apostle Church   1922-24
5476 South Kimbark Avenue   (1300 East)

Madonna della Strada Chapel   1938-39
6525 North Sheridan Road   (at Lake Michigan)

St. Gall Church   1955-58
5500 South Kedzie Avenue   (3200 West)

Chicago Loop Synagogue   1957-58
16 South Clark Street   (100 West)

Old St. Mary Church   1959-61
25 East Van Buren Street   (400 South)

St. Luke Evangelical Lutheran Church   1960
1500 West Belmont Avenue   (3200 North)

St. Jane de Chantal Church   1962-64
5251 South McVicker Avenue   (6034 West)

North Shore Congregation Israel   1962-64
1185 Sheridan Road   Glencoe, Illinois

Emmanuel Presbyterian Church   1965
1850 South Racine Avenue   (1200 West)

Congregation Bnei Ruven   1967
6350 North Whipple Street   (3034 West)

Seventeenth Church of Christ, Scientist   1968
55 East Wacker Drive   (300 North)

St. Procopius Abbey Church   1968-70
5601 College Road   Lisle, Illinois

First St. Paul's
Evangelical Lutheran Church   1969-70
1301 North LaSalle Drive   (150 West)

Neo-Japanese Temple

Midwest Buddhist Temple   1971
435 West Menomonee Street   (1800 North)

Prairie School

Unity Temple   1906-9
The Unitarian Universalist Church in Oak Park
875 Lake Street at Kenilworth
Oak Park, Illinois

Greater Holy Temple,
Church of God in Christ   1908-9
5701 West Midway Park   (500 North)

Architectural Styles

Renaissance

St. Stanislaus Kostka Church   1877-81
1327 North Noble Street   (1400 West)

Assumption B.V.M. Church   1884-86
319 West Illinois Street   (500 North)

Our Lady of Sorrows Basilica   1890-1902
3101 West Jackson Boulevard   (300 South)

St. John Cantius Church   1893-98
821 North Carpenter Street   (1032 West)

St. Hedwig Church   1899-1901
2100 West Webster Avenue   (2200 North)

Presentation Church   1903-9
750 South Springfield Avenue   (3900 West)

Holy Trinity Church   1905-6
1120 North Noble Street   (1400 West)

The Annunciation Cathedral   1910
1017 North LaSalle Drive   (150 West)

Mt. Pisgah Missionary Baptist Church   1910-12
4600 South Martin Luther King Drive   (400 East)

St. Andrew Church   1912-13
3550 North Paulina Street   (1700 West)

SS. Cyril and Methodius Church   1912-13
5001 South Hermitage Avenue   (1734 West)

Holy Cross Church   1913-15
1736 West 46th Street

Corpus Christi Church   1914-16
4900 South Martin Luther King Drive   (400 East)

St. Jerome Church   1914-16
1701 West Lunt Avenue   (7000 North)

St. Mary of the Angels Church   1914-20
1850 North Hermitage Avenue   (1734 West)

St. Ignatius Church   1916-17
6555 North Glenwood Avenue   (1400 West)

St. Hyacinth Church   1917-21
3635 West George Street   (2900 North)

St. Clara—St. Cyril Church   1923-27
6401 South Woodlawn Avenue   (1200 East)

Romanesque

Old St. Patrick Church   1852-56
140 South Desplaines Street   (700 West)

St. Michael Church   1866-69, 1873
455 West Eugenie Street   (1700 North)

The Greenstone Church   1882
Pullman United Methodist Church
11201 South St. Lawrence Avenue   (600 East)

Notre Dame Church   1887-92
1336 West Flournoy Street   (700 South)

Church of Our Saviour   1888-89
530 West Fullerton Parkway   (2400 North)

United Church of Hyde Park   1889
1440 East 53rd Street

Antioch Missionary Baptist Church   1889-90
6234 South Stewart Avenue   (400 West)

St. Vitus Church   1896-97
1820 South Paulina Street   (1700 West)

St. Josaphat Church   1900-1902
2301 North Southport Avenue   (1400 West)

St. Boniface Church   1902-4
1348 West Chestnut Street   (860 North)

St. Mel—Holy Ghost Church   1910-11
4301 West Washington Boulevard   (100 North)

St. Joseph Church   1913-14
1731 West 48th Street

All Saints—St. Anthony Church   1913-15
2849 South Wallace Street   (600 West)

St. Benedict Church   1917-18
2201 West Irving Park Road   (4000 North)

The Moody Memorial Church   1924-25
1630 North Clark Street   (100 West)

Romanesque, Lombard

St. Bridget Church   1905-6
2940 South Archer Avenue   (1500 West)

Romanesque, French

St. Vincent de Paul Church   1895-97
1004 West Webster Avenue   (2200 North)

Holy Angels Church   1896-97
605 East Oakwood Boulevard   (3940 South)

St. Agatha Church   1904-6
3151 West Douglas Boulevard   (1330 South)

Romanesque, Spanish

St. John Berchmans   1906-7
2519 West Logan Boulevard   (2600 North)

Holy Innocents Church   1911-12
735 North Armour Street   (1500 West)

Our Lady of Lourdes Church   1913-16
1601 West Leland Avenue   (4700 North)

Romanesque, Richardsonian

Church of the Epiphany   1885
201 South Ashland Avenue   (1600 West)

St. Gabriel Church   1887-88
4501 South Lowe Avenue   (632 West)

Metropolitan Community Church   1889
4100 South Martin Luther King Drive   (400 East)

Hyde Park Union Church   1904-6
5600 South Woodlawn Avenue   (1200 East)

Romanesque, Byzantine

St. Mary of Perpetual Help Church   1889-92
1035 West 32nd Street

St. Clement Church   1917-18
646 West Deming Place   (2534 North)

Russian Provincial

Holy Trinity Cathedral   1903
1121 North Leavitt Street   (2200 West)

Shingle

All Saints Episcopal Church   1882-84
4552 North Hermitage Avenue   (1734 West)

Lake View Presbyterian Church   1887-88
3600 North Broadway   (700 West)

Spanish Mission

St. Pascal Church   1930-31
6149 West Irving Park Road   (4000 North)

Suggested Tours

Downtown Chicago

Seventeenth Church of Christ, Scientist
55 East Wacker Drive   (300 North)

The Chicago Temple
First United Methodist Church
77 West Washington Street   (100 North)

Chicago Loop Synagogue
16 South Clark Street   (100 West)

St. Peter's Church
110 West Madison Street

Old St. Mary Church
25 East Van Buren Street   (400 South)

Near South Side

Second Presbyterian Church
1936 South Michigan Avenue   (100 East)

Quinn Chapel A.M.E. Church
2401 South Wabash Avenue   (50 East)

Trinity Episcopal Church
125 East 26th Street

St. James Church
2940 South Wabash Avenue   (50 East)

IIT Chapel
3200 South Michigan Avenue   (100 East)

Pilgrim Baptist Church
3301 South Indiana Avenue   (200 East)

Olivet Baptist Church
3101 South Martin Luther King Drive   (400 East)

Oakland—Grand Boulevard

Grant Memorial A.M.E. Church
4017 South Drexel Boulevard   (900 East)

Holy Angels Church
605 East Oakwood Boulevard   (3940 South)

Metropolitan Community Church
4100 South Martin Luther King Drive   (400 East)

Ebenezer Baptist Church
4501 South Vincennes Avenue   (500 East)

Mt. Pisgah Missionary Baptist Church
4600 South Martin Luther King Drive   (400 East)

Corpus Christi Church
4900 South Martin Luther King Drive   (400 East)

Kenwood—Hyde Park

Operation PUSH
4945 South Drexel Boulevard   (900 East)

K.A.M.—Isaiah Israel Temple
5045 South Greenwood Avenue (1100 East)

Suggested Tours

United Church of Hyde Park
1440 East 53rd Street

Congregation Rodfei Zedek
5200 South Hyde Park Boulevard   (1700 East)

Sinai Temple
5350 South Shore Drive   (1800 East)

St. Thomas the Apostle Church
5476 South Kimbark Avenue   (1300 East)

Augustana Lutheran Church of Hyde Park
1151 East 55th Street

Hyde Park Union Church
5600 South Woodlawn Avenue   (1200 East)

First Unitarian Church of Chicago
5650 South Woodlawn Avenue   (1200 East)

University Church of Disciples of Christ
5655 South University Avenue   (1144 East)

Bond Chapel
1050 East 59th Street

Rockefeller Memorial Chapel
1160 East 59th Street

Woodlawn—South Shore—South Chicago

St. Clara—St. Cyril Church
6401 South Woodlawn Avenue   (1200 East)

First Presbyterian Church
6400 South Kimbark Avenue   (1300 East)

St. Philip Neri Church
2126 East 72nd Street

Elijah Muhammad Mosque #2
7351 South Stony Island Avenue   (1600 East)

St. Michael Church
83rd Street and South Shore Drive   (3132 East)

Pullman—East Side

The Greenstone Church
Pullman United Methodist Church
11201 South St. Lawrence Avenue   (600 East)

Holy Rosary Church
11302 South Martin Luther King Drive   (400 East)

St. Simeon Mirotocivi Serbian Orthodox Church
3737 East 114th Street

Bridgeport

All Saints—St. Anthony Church
2849 South Wallace Street   (600 West)

St. Bridget Church
2940 South Archer Avenue   (1500 West)

St. Barbara Church
2855 South Throop Street   (1300 West)

Holy Cross Lutheran Church
3120 South Racine Avenue   (1200 West)

Immaculate Conception Church
3101 South Aberdeen Street   (1100 West)

St. Mary of Perpetual Help Church
1035 West 32nd Street

St. George Church
902 West 33rd Street

Nativity of Our Lord Church
655 West 37th Street

First Lutheran Church of the Trinity
643 West 31st Street

Canaryville—Back of the Yards

St. Gabriel Church
4501 South Lowe Avenue   (632 West)

Holy Cross Church
1736 West 46th Street

St. Joseph Church
1729 West 48th Street

SS. Cyril and Methodius Church
5001 South Hermitage Avenue   (1734 West)

Nativity Ukrainian Catholic Church
4952 South Paulina Street   (1700 West)

St. Augustine Church
5037 South Laflin Street   (1500 West)

St. Martini Lutheran Church
1624 West 51st Street

St. John of God Church
1238 West 52nd Street

St. Basil Church
1840 West Garfield Boulevard   (5500 South)

Englewood

St. Charles Lwanga Church
155 West Garfield Boulevard   (5500 South)

Visitation Church
845 West Garfield Boulevard   (5500 South)

St. Martin Church
5848 South Princeton Avenue   (300 West)

Antioch Missionary Baptist Church
6248 South Stewart Avenue   (400 West)

Greater Mount Vernon Baptist Church
6430 South Harvard Avenue   (332 West)

Auburn—West Highland

St. Leo Church
7750 South Emerald Avenue   (732 West)

St. Sabina Church
7821 South Throop Street   (1300 West)

St. Therese of the Infant Jesus
(Little Flower) Church
1957 West 80th Street

Southwest Side

St. Gall Church
5500 South Kedzie Avenue   (3200 West)

St. Jane de Chantal Church
5251 South McVicker Avenue   (6034 West)

Near West Side

Old St. Patrick Church
140 South Desplaines Street   (700 West)

First Baptist Congregational Church
60 North Ashland Avenue   (1600 West)

Church of the Epiphany
201 South Ashland Avenue   (1600 West)

St. Basil Greek Orthodox Church
733 South Ashland Avenue   (1600 West)

First Immanuel Lutheran Church
1124 South Ashland Avenue   (1600 West)

Notre Dame Church
1336 West Flournoy Street   (700 South)

Holy Family Church
1080 West Roosevelt Road   (1200 South)

Lower West Side

St. Adalbert Church
1656 West 17th Street

St. Vitus Church
1820 South Paulina Street   (1700 West)

St. Matthew Lutheran Church
2104 West 21st Street

St. Paul Church
2234 South Hoyne Avenue   (2100 West)

Emmanuel Presbyterian Church
1850 South Racine Avenue   (1200 West)

West Side

Metropolitan Missionary Baptist Church
2151 West Washington Boulevard   (100 North)

Our Lady of Sorrows Basilica
3101 West Jackson Boulevard   (300 South)

St. Mel—Holy Ghost Church
4301 West Washington Boulevard   (100 North)

St. Thomas Aquinas Church
5120 West Washington Boulevard   (100 North)

The Assumption Greek Orthodox Church
601 South Central Avenue   (5600 West)

Greater Holy Temple, Church of God in Christ
5701 West Midway Park   (500 North)

Unity Temple
875 Lake Street
Oak Park, Illinois

Independence Boulevard—Douglas Boulevard

Presentation Church
750 South Springfield Avenue   (3900 West)

Independence Boulevard Seventh Day Adventist Church
748 South Independence Boulevard   (3800 West)

Old Douglas Boulevard Synagogue District

St. Agatha Church
3151 West Douglas Boulevard   (1330 South)

Near North Side

Assumption B.V.M. Church
319 West Illinois Street   (500 North)

The Annunciation Cathedral
1017 North LaSalle Drive   (150 West)

Church of the Ascension
1133 North LaSalle Drive   (150 West)

LaSalle Street Church
1136 North LaSalle Drive   (150 West)

First St. Paul's Evangelical Lutheran Church
1301 North LaSalle Drive   (150 West)

The Moody Memorial Church
1630 North Clark Street   (100 West)

Gold Coast

The Cathedral of St. James
65 East Huron Street (700 North)

Holy Name Cathedral
735 North State Street

Quigley Preparatory Seminary North
St. James Chapel
831 North Rush Street   (75 East)
(not open to the public)

Fourth Presbyterian Church
876 North Michigan Avenue   (100 East)

St. Chrysostom's Church
1424 North Dearborn Parkway (50 West)

Old Town—De Paul

St. Michael Church
455 West Eugenie Street   (1700 North)

Midwest Buddhist Temple
435 West Menomonee Street   (1800 North)

St. James Lutheran Church
2048 North Fremont Street   (900 West)

Suggested Tours

St. Vincent de Paul Church
1004 West Webster Avenue   (2200 North)

St. Josaphat Church
2301 North Southport Avenue (1400 West)

Lincoln Park

Church of Our Saviour
530 West Fullerton Parkway   (2400 North)

St. Pauls Church
2335 North Orchard Street   (700 West)

St. Clement Church
646 West Deming Place   (2534 North)

New Town—Uptown

Our Lady of Mount Carmel Church
700 West Belmont Avenue   (3200 North)

Temple Sholom
3480 North Lake Shore Drive   (500 West)

Lake View Presbyterian Church
3600 North Broadway   (700 West)

Anshe Emet Synagogue
3760 North Pine Grove Avenue   (700 West)

St. Mary of the Lake Church
4200 North Sheridan Road   (1000 West)

Edgewater—Rogers Park

St. Ita Church
5500 North Broadway   (1200 West)

St. Gertrude Church
6200 North Glenwood Avenue   (1400 West)

St. Ignatius Church
6555 North Glenwood Avenue   (1400 West)

Madonna della Strada Chapel
6525 North Sheridan Road   (at Lake Michigan)

St. Jerome Church
1701 West Lunt Avenue   (7000 North)

Lake View—North Center

St. Alphonsus Church
2950 North Southport Avenue   (1400 West)

St. Luke Evangelical Lutheran Church
1500 West Belmont Avenue   (3200 North)

St. Andrew Church
3550 North Paulina Street   (1700 West)

St. Benedict Church
2201 West Irving Park Road   (4000 North)

Ravenswood—Summerdale

All Saints Episcopal Church
4552 North Hermitage Avenue   (1734 West)

Our Lady of Lourdes Church
1601 West Leland Avenue   (4700 North)

Ebenezer Lutheran Church
1650 West Foster Avenue   (5200 North)

St. Gregory the Great Church
5533 North Paulina Street   (1700 West)

Near Northwest Side

St. John Cantius Church
821 North Carpenter Street   (1032 West)

Holy Innocents Church
735 North Armour Street   (1500 West)

St. Boniface Church
1348 West Chestnut Street   (860 North)

Holy Trinity Church
1120 North Noble Street   (1400 West)

St. Stanislaus Kostka Church
1327 North Noble Street   (1400 West)

St. Mary of the Angels Church
1850 North Hermitage Avenue   (1734 West)

St. Hedwig Church
2100 West Webster Avenue   (2200 North)

St. John Berchmans Church
2519 West Logan Boulevard   (2600 North)

St. Hyacinth Church
3635 West George Street   (2900 North)

Ukrainian Village

SS. Volodymyr and Olha Church
739 North Oakley Boulevard   (2300 West)

St. Nicholas Ukrainian Catholic Cathedral
2238 West Rice Street   (824 North)

Holy Trinity Cathedral
1121 North Leavitt Street   (2200 West)

Jefferson Park—Portage Park

St. Viator Church
4160 West Addison Street   (3600 North)

St. Bartholomew Church
3601 North Lavergne Avenue   (5000 West)

St. Pascal Church
6149 West Irving Park Road   (4000 North)

Far Northwest Side

St. Joseph's Ukrainian Catholic Church
5000 North Cumberland Avenue   (8400 West)

Holy Resurrection Serbian Orthodox Cathedral
5701 North Redwood Drive   (8024 West)

West Rogers Park—Sauganash

Congregation Bnei Ruven
6350 North Whipple Street   (3034 West)

Queen of All Saints Basilica
6284 North Sauganash Avenue   (4700 West)

North Suburban

Baha'i House of Worship
100 Linden Avenue
Wilmette, Illinois

North Shore Congregation Israel
1185 Sheridan Road
Glencoe, Illinois

West Suburban

St. Procopius Abbey Church
5601 College Road
Lisle, Illinois

Stained Glass

Manufacturers and their Chicago installations. Chicago firms unless otherwise noted. Addresses indicate the fronts of buildings.

Artmaier, Joseph

St. Mary of Perpetual Help Church
1035 West 32nd Street

St. George Church
902 West 33rd Street

Baransky Studios,   Yonkers, New York

SS. Volodymyr and Olha Church
739 North Oakley Boulevard   (2300 West)

Barrillet Studio,   Paris, France

Chicago Loop Synagogue
16 South Clark Street   (100 West)

Burne-Jones, Sir Edward (1833-98): See William Morris

Clinton Glass Company

Our Lady of Sorrows Basilica   (north facade windows)
3101 West Jackson Boulevard   (300 South)

Blessed Agnes Church
2655 South Central Park Avenue   (3600 West)

Connick Studios, Charles J.,   Boston, Massachusetts

The Cathedral of St. James   (Randall memorial window)
65 East Huron Street   (700 North)

Hyde Park Union Church
5600 South Woodlawn Avenue   (1200 East)

Fourth Presbyterian Church
876 North Michigan Avenue   (100 East)

Bond Chapel
1050 East 59th Street

St. Chrysostom's Church
1424 North Dearborn Parkway   (50 West)

First Unitarian Church of Chicago   (rose window)
5650 South Woodlawn Avenue   (1200 East)

Daprato Studios

St. Gabriel Church
4501 South Lowe Avenue   (632 West)

St. John Bosco Church
2305 North McVicker Avenue   (6034 West)

D'Ogier Studios,   New Hope, Connecticut

St. Thomas the Apostle Church
5476 South Kimbark Avenue   (1300 East)

Stained Glass

Drehobl Brothers Art Glass Company

Assumption B.V.M. Church   (nave windows)
319 West Illinois Street (500 North)

Anshe Emet Synagogue
3760 North Pine Grove Avenue   (700 West)

Felician Sisters' Infirmary Chapel
3800 West Peterson Avenue   (6000 North)

Immaculate Heart of Mary Church
3307 West Byron Street   (3900 North)

Luther Memorial Church
2500 West Wilson Avenue   (4600 North)

Queen of the Universe Church
7130 South Hamlin Avenue   (3800 West)

St. John United Church of Christ
2442 West Moffat Street   (1832 North)

Temple Shaare Tikvah
5800 North Kimball Avenue   (3400 West)

Esser Company,   Milwaukee, Wisconsin

Queen of All Saints Basilica
6284 North Sauganash Avenue   (4700 West)

Blair Chapel
Fourth Presbyterian Church
876 North Michigan Avenue   (100 East)

Flanagan and Biedenweg

St. Vincent de Paul Church   (transept windows)
1004 West Webster Avenue   (2200 North)

Frei, Emil Art Glass Company,   St. Louis, Missouri

St. Ignatius Church
6555 North Glenwood Avenue   (1400 West)

K.A.M.—Isaiah Israel Temple
5045 South Greenwood Avenue   (1100 East)

St. Viator Church
4160 West Addison Street   (3600 North)

Gawin Company,   Milwaukee, Wisconsin

St. John Cantius Church
821 North Carpenter Street   (1032 West)

Giannini and Hilgart

The Chicago Temple
First United Methodist Church
77 West Washington Street   (100 North)

St. Angela Church
1306 North Massasoit Avenue   (5732 West)

St. Pauls Church
2335 North Orchard Street   (700 West)

St. Luke Evangelical Lutheran Church
1500 West Belmont Avenue   (3200 North)

Messiah Evangelical Lutheran Church
6201 West Peterson Avenue   (6000 North)

Our Lady of Grace Church
2450 North Ridgeway Avenue   (3732 West)

St. Sabina Church
7821 South Throop Street   (1300 West)

Hardman, John and Company,   London, England

Holy Angels Church
605 East Oakwood Boulevard   (3940 South)

Healy & Millet

Second Presbyterian Church   (Cast Thy Garment . . .)
1936 South Michigan Avenue (100 East)

Ingrand, Max,   Paris, France

Quigley Preparatory Seminary South
7740 South Western Avenue   (2400 West)

St. Mary of the Woods Church
7000 North Moselle Avenue   (6000 West)

Kinsella, John J. Company

St. John Berchmans Church
2519 West Logan Boulevard   (2600 North)

St. James Lutheran Church
2048 North Fremont Street   (900 West)

Quigley Preparatory Seminary North
St. James Chapel
831 North Rush Street   (75 East)

LaFarge, John   (1835-1910)

Second Presbyterian Church (Angel in the Lilies)
1936 South Michigan Avenue (100 East)

Lloyd & Pearce: See Wells Brothers

McCully & Miles

Second Presbyterian Church   (Beside the Still Waters)
1936 South Michigan Avenue   (100 East)

MacKay, Joseph Evan

United Church of Hyde Park   (Lily window)
1400 East 53rd Street

Maumejean Freres,   France

St. Ita Church
5500 North Broadway   (1200 West)

Mayer & Company,   Munich, Germany

St. Michael Church
455 West Eugenie Street   (1700 North)

St. Alphonsus Church
2950 North Southport Avenue   (1400 West)

St. Vincent de Paul Church
1004 West Webster Avenue   (2200 North)

St. Josaphat Church   (apse windows)
2301 North Southport Avenue   (1400 West)

St. Benedict Church
2201 West Irving Park Road   (4000 North)

St. Gertrude Church
6204 North Glenwood Avenue   (1400 West)

St. Bartholomew Church
3601 North Lavergne Avenue   (5000 West)

Michaudel, Arthur Studio

Holy Cross Church
1736 West 46th Street

Millet, Louis J.   (1856-1923): See Healy & Millet

Morris, William   (1834-96)

Second Presbyterian Church   (narthex windows)
1936 South Michigan Avenue   (100 East)

Munich Studio,   Chicago, Illinois

Our Lady of Sorrows Basilica   (choir balcony window)
3101 West Jackson Boulevard   (300 South)

Presentation Church
750 South Springfield Avenue   (3900 West)

St. Veronica Church
3316 North Whipple Street   (3032 West)

St. Agnes Church
2650 West Pershing Road   (3900 South)

St. Bridget Church
2940 South Archer Avenue   (1500 West)

St. Dominic Church
869 North Sedgwick Street   (400 West)

St. Leo Church
7750 South Emerald Avenue   (732 West)

St. Bride Church   *(Mary of the Gael)*
7801 South Coles Avenue   (2600 East)

SS. Cyril and Methodius Church
5001 South Hermitage Avenue   (1734 West)

St. Nicholas Ukrainian Catholic Cathedral
2238 West Rice Street   (824 North)

St. Philip's Lutheran Church
6232 South Eberhart Avenue   (500 East)

St. Margaret Mary School
2302 West Chase Avenue   (7300 North)

St. Margaret of Scotland Church
1256 West 99th Street

O'Brien, Richard

St. Jane de Chantal Church
5251 South McVicker Avenue   (6034 West)

O'Duggan, John Terrence

St. Philip Neri Church
2126 East 72nd Street

O'Shaughnessy, Thomas A.   (1870-1958)

Old St. Patrick Church
140 South Desplaines Street   (700 West)

St. Benedict Chapel
Illinois Benedictine College
5700 College Road, Lisle, Illinois

St. Stephen's Episcopal Church   (over the altar)
3533 North Albany Avenue   (3100 West)

Madonna della Strada Chapel   (small west windows)
6525 North Sheridan Road   (at Lake Michigan)

Reynolds, Francis and Rohnstock,   Boston, Massachusetts

Church of the Ascension   (west nave window)
1133 North LaSalle Drive   (150 West)

Salano Company,   Milan, Italy

Holy Name Cathedral
735 North State Street

Schmitt, Conrad Studios,   New Berlin, Wisconsin

St. Vincent de Paul Church   (south rose window)
1004 West Webster Avenue   (2200 North)

St. Gall Church
5500 South Kedzie Avenue   (3200 West)

St. William Church
7007 West Wrightwood Avenue   (2600 North)

Holy Resurrection Serbian Orthodox Cathedral
5701 North Redwood Drive   (8024 West)

Shaw, Howard Van Doren   (1869-1926)

Second Presbyterian Church   (Arts and Crafts window)
1936 South Michigan Avenue   (100 East)

Temple Art Glass Company

Unity Temple
875 Lake Street at Kenilworth
Oak Park, Illinois

Tiffany, Louis C.   (1848-1933), New York, New York

Second Presbyterian Church   (14 nave windows)
1936 South Michigan Avenue   (100 East)

Church of Our Saviour
530 West Fullerton Parkway   (2400 North)

Hyde Park Union Church
5600 South Woodlawn Avenue   (1200 East)

Stained Glass

Von Gerichten Art Glass Company, Columbus, Ohio

Holy Family Church   (figure windows)
1080 West Roosevelt Road   (1200 South)

Wells Brothers

Trinity Episcopal Church   (chancel and north facade windows)
125 East 26th Street

Willett Studio, Philadelphia, Pennsylvania

Church of the Ascension   (four nave windows)
1133 North LaSalle Drive   (150 West)

St. Sylvester Church
2159 North Humboldt Boulevard   (3000 West)

First Presbyterian Church   (reredos window)
6400 South Kimbark Avenue   (1300 East)

Church of St. Paul and the Redeemer   (south transept and narthex)
4949 South Dorchester Avenue   (1400 East)

Wright, R. Toland, Cleveland, Ohio

First Presbyterian Church   (nave windows)
6400 South Kimbark Avenue   (1300 East)

Greater Mt. Vernon Baptist Church
formerly Our Redeemer Lutheran Church
6430 South Harvard Avenue   (332 West)

Zettler, F. X., Royal Bavarian Art Institute
Munich, Germany

St. Stanislaus Kostka Church
1327 North Noble Street   (1400 West)

St. Paul Church
2234 South Hoyne Avenue   (2100 West)

St. Josaphat Church   (nave windows)
2301 North Southport Avenue   (1400 West)

St. Boniface Church
1348 West Chestnut Street   (860 North)

St. Agatha Church
3151 West Douglas Boulevard   (1330 South)

Hyde Park Union Church   (south nave window)
5600 South Woodlawn Avenue   (1200 East)

St. Michael Church
83rd Street and South Shore Drive   (3132 East)

St. John the Baptist Church
905 West 50th Place

St. Mel—Holy Ghost Church
4301 West Washington Boulevard   (100 North)

St. Adalbert Church
1656 West 17th Street

All Saints—St. Anthony Church
2849 South Wallace Street   (600 West)

St. Mary of the Lake Church
4200 North Sheridan Road   (1000 West)

Corpus Christi Church
4900 South Martin Luther King Drive   (400 East)

St. Benedict Church
2201 West Irving Park Road   (4000 North)

St. Hyacinth Church
3635 West George Street   (2900 North)

St. Clara—St. Cyril Church
6401 South Woodlawn Avenue   (1200 East)

The Assumption Greek Orthodox Church
601 South Central Avenue   (5600 West)

Glossary

acanthus   decoration of the Corinthian capital based on the leaf of the acanthus plant

acroterion   a small foliate ornament rising up at the center or at the extremities of a pediment in classical architecture

aisle   a passageway, the part of a church that runs parallel to the nave and is separated from it by piers or columns

altar   a tablelike construction used in a church for the celebration of the Eucharist

ambulatory   a sheltered space or passageway around and behind the altar

apse   a projecting part of a church, usually semicircular and vaulted

arcade   a series of arches with the columns that support them

arch   a curved structural member which spans an opening and serves as a support to the weight above

architrave   the lowest part of an entablature which rests immediately on the capital of the column

ashlar   hewn or squared stone

baldachin or **baldachino**   an ornamental canopy that is supported by columns over an altar

baluster   a short column, often with a molded vaselike outline; often one of a series

balustrade   a series of balusters

baroque   a style of art and architecture marked by dynamic opposition and energy and by the use of elaborate ornamentation

barrel vault   a semicircular ceiling vault having the same section throughout

basilica   a rectangular building with a broad nave flanked by colonnaded aisles and ending in a semicircular apse

bas-relief   sculptural relief in which the projection is slight and no part of the modeled form is undercut

battlement   a parapet that consists of alternate solid parts and open spaces; it is used on castles for defense and on churches for decoration

bay   the rectangular area between four piers

belfry   a bell tower

bema   a raised platform at the front of a church or synagogue that contains the altar, ark, and seats for the principal ministers of the service

blank arcading   a series of ornamental arches flat against a wall, with no openings

bond   the systematic laying of brick in a wall

boss   an ornamental projecting block used at the intersection of ribs in Gothic vaulting or at the centers of ceiling panels

bracket   a carved or sculptured overhanging member that projects from a wall and serves to support a load or strengthen an angle; it is sometimes merely decorative

broken pediment   a pediment with a gap in its center

buttress   a projecting structure of stone or wood used to support a wall but sometimes serving principally for ornament

Byzantine   a style of architecture developed in the Byzantine Empire in the fifth and sixth centuries and having as its central structural feature the dome carried on pendentive arches over a square base

campanile   a bell tower, usually freestanding

capital   the top, head, or uppermost part of a column or pilaster

casement window   a window that opens on hinges fastened to the sides of the frame

cathedral   the church of a bishop, derived from *cathedra*, the bishop's official seat

Celtic cross   a cross having basically the form of a Latin cross with a ring around the intersection of the crossbar and the upright shaft

chalice   a cup for the wine of the Eucharist

chancel   that part of a church which contains the altar, pulpit, and lectern and is usually on a higher level than the nave

choir   a place for singers in a church, sometimes located between the nave and the sanctuary

choir loft   a gallery for a choir

choir stall   a seat in the choir of a church which is often covered and may be elaborately carved

cinquefoil   a conventionalized figure of a flower with five petals or leaves

clerestory   an outside wall of a church, carried above an adjoining roof and pierced with windows

cloister   a covered passage usually having one side walled and the other side open with an arcade or colonnade; it usually connects different buildings of a group or runs around an open court, especially of a monastery

coffer   a recessed panel which usually with other panels forms a continuous pattern in a ceiling or vault

colonnade   a series of columns placed at regular intervals, usually with an architrave

console   the desk from which an organ is played which contains the keyboards, pedal board, and other controlling mechanisms

corbel   an architectural member which projects from within a wall and supports a weight that is stepped upward and outward from a vertical surface

Glossary

corbel table a projecting course, usually masonry, which rests on a horizontal row of corbels

corbiestep one of a series of steps which rise toward the top of a building and terminate the upper part of a gable wall

Corinthian the lightest and most ornate of the three Greek orders; it is characterized by its bell-shaped capital surrounded with acanthus leaves

cornice the typically molded and projecting horizontal member which is the uppermost member of a classical entablature

course a continuous horizontal range of brick or masonry throughout a wall

crocket projecting carved foliage, used to decorate gables and pinnacles and similar elements in Gothic architecture

cruciform in the shape of a cross

crypt a vault or other chamber wholly or partly underground, as under the main floor of a church

cupola a small structure built on top of a roof or dome to provide interior lighting or simply for ornamental purposes

curvilinear consisting of curved lines

dentil cornice a cornice with tooth-like ornamentation

dome a vaulted circular roof or ceiling

Doric the oldest and simplest of the Greek architectural orders characterized by a fluted shaft with no base and with a simple capital

eave or **eaves** the lower part of a roof that overhangs the wall

engaged column a column which is partly embedded in a wall

English bond a masonry bond in which courses consist alternately of headers and stretchers

entablature that part of a wall consisting of the architrave, the frieze, and the cornice, which rests upon the capitals of the columns and supports the pediment or roof plate

escutcheons an area shaped like a shield on which armorial bearings are displayed

facade the front of a building that is given emphasis by special architectural treatment

face brick brick made especially for use in the face of a wall

festoon a carved, molded, or painted ornament representing a festoon, a decorative chain of flowers or leaves hanging in a curve between two points

filigree very delicate ornamental work, basically with fine wire

finial an ornament, usually foliated, which forms the top of a pinnacle or gable; any capping or terminating ornament

flèche a slender spire which rises above the intersection of the nave and transepts of a church

Florentine mosaic a mosaic of semiprecious stones inlaid in a background of black or white marble

fluting vertical channels on the shaft of a column or pilaster

fresco the art of painting on moist plaster

frieze a sculptured or richly ornamented band as on a building

gable the triangular portion of the end of a building from the cornice or eaves to the ridge of the roof

gargoyle a spout often having the form of a grotesque figure or animal which projects from a roof gutter and throws rain water clear of the building

garth or **cloister garth** a small yard or enclosure, an open court surrounded by cloisters, especially in a monastery or college

Gothic the architectural style that originated in northern France which features pointed arches and vaults, large amounts of glass in the walls, and an overall feeling of height

Gothic arch a pointed arch with a joint rather than a keystone at its apex

Gothic Revival an artistic style of the eighteenth and nineteenth centuries inspired by and imitating the Gothic style

Greek Revival a style of architecture in the first half of the nineteenth century marked by the use or imitation of Greek orders

grisaille a coating of glasswork with white to produce an opalescent effect

hammer beam the short horizontal beams which project from opposite walls and support the ceiling beams for a Gothic roof

header a brick laid with its end toward the face of the wall

hip roof a roof having sloping ends and sloping sides

icon, also **ikon** a sacred image venerated in churches of Eastern Christianity depicting Christ, the Virgin Mary, a saint, or some other religious subject in the conventional manner of Byzantine art and typically painted on a small wooden panel

iconostasis a screen or partition with doors decorated with icons that separates the bema from the nave in Eastern churches

Ionic   the order of architecture that is lighter and more graceful than Doric and is characterized by the special volutes of its capital

keystone   the central stone at the top of an arch

lancet window   a high narrow window with a sharply pointed head

lectern   a reading desk in a church from which Scripture is read during worship

lintel   a horizontal architectural member, usually above a doorway, which spans and carries the load above the opening

lunette   the surface at the upper part of a wall that is partly surrounded by a vault and is often filled by a window or a mural painting

mansard roof   a roof having two slopes on all sides with the lower slope steeper than the upper one; after the French architect Francois Mansart (1598-1666)

manual   a keyboard for the hands, specifically one of the several keyboards of a pipe-organ console

medallion   a large medal, or something like a large medal, as a tablet in a wall or window bearing a figure shown in relief

minaret   a slender tower attached to a mosque from which a muezzin summons people to prayer

molding   a continuous narrow contoured surface, usually projecting, which is used for decorative effect

mosaic   a surface decoration of colored marble or glass chips set in cement to form pictures or patterns

mullion   the narrow vertical pier used to divide the panels of glass in a window

narthex   the vestibule leading to the nave of a church

nave   the main part of the interior of a church, the long narrow central hall in a cruciform church

ogee   a pointed arch

opalescent   having a milky iridescence; having a smooth colored surface that gives the effect of cloudiness and diffusion of light

organ   a wind instrument consisting of sets of pipes sounded by compressed air, controlled by manual and pedal keyboards, and capable of producing a variety of musical tones

organ case   the ornamental box or screen which contains the organ pipes, often beautifully carved and often decorated with imitation, non-speaking pipes

oriel   a large bay window projecting from the face of a wall and supported by a corbel or bracket

Palladian window   an architectural unit consisting of a central window with an arched head and on each side a usually narrower window with a square head; after the Italian architect Andrea Palladio (1508-80)

parapet   a low wall, especially one which protects the edge of a roof

pedestal   the base of an upright structure, as of a statue or vase

pediment   a triangular architectural element which forms the gable of a two-pitched roof; it is also used as a decoration, over doors, porticoes, and windows in classical architecture

pendentive arches   spherical triangles, standing on their apexes, which form the structural transition between the circular base of a dome and the square base of the supporting masonry

Perpendicular Gothic   a medieval English Gothic style of architecture in which vertical lines predominate

pier   a pillar, post, or other structural member that supports the end of an arch or lintel

pilaster   an upright, rectangular architectural member that functions as a pier but is treated as a column with base, shaft, and capital, and usually projects one-third of its width or less from the wall; it may be load-bearing or simply decorative

pinnacle   an upright architectural member usually ending in a small spire and used in Gothic construction to give additional weight to a buttress

polychrome   made or decorated with various colors

portal   the whole architectural composition around and including the doorways of a church

portico   an open porch consisting of a pediment or entablature carried on columns, usually at the entrance of a building

pulpit   an elevated platform or a high reading desk used for preaching

quoins   the slightly projecting stones at the corners of a building, usually laid so their faces are alternately large and small

rafter   one of the sloping timbers of a roof

rank   a series or set of organ pipes of the same construction and quality

register   a set of pipes of the same quality in a pipe organ; a stop

reredos   an ornamental screen or wall of wood or stone located behind an altar

retable   a raised shelf or ledge behind an altar on which are placed the altar cross, lights, and vases of flowers; also, an elaborate framework rising behind the altar and enclosing a panel decorated with painting or sculpture

Glossary

rococo interior decoration prevalent during the eighteenth century, chiefly characterized by an elaborate use of curved spatial forms, often fantastic curved lines

Romanesque the architectural style that has the round arch and the round vault as its characteristic features

rood a large crucifix at the entrance of the chancel of a church

rose window a circular window filled with tracery

sacristy a room in or attached to a church where the sacred utensils and vestments are kept

sanctuary a consecrated place, the most sacred part of any religious building, the part of a Christian church in which the altar is placed

scagliola an imitation marble which consists of finely ground gypsum mixed with glue and polished, it is used for floors and columns

sconce a bracket candlestick or group of candlesticks projecting from a plaque on a wall

screen a nonbearing partition that may be solid or pierced and is often ornamental

sedile, pl. **sedilia** one of usually three seats in the chancel of a church used by officiating clergy during intervals in a service

soffit the underside of a part of a building, as of an overhang, ceiling, staircase, cornice, or entablature

spandrel an ornamental wall panel between the exterior curve of an arch and the enclosing right angle

spire a steeply tapering roof which surmounts a tower

steeple a tall structure composed of diminishing stories which is topped with a spire

stop a graduated set of organ pipes of like kind and tone quality

stop knob one of the handles by which the player of an organ opens or shuts off a particular stop

stretcher a brick laid with its length parallel to the face of the wall

stringcourse a horizontal band of masonry running around a building, usually on the outside

"swallow's nest" organ an organ hung from the wall like a swallow's nest

tabernacle a small, locked box, specially ornamented, which contains the consecrated elements of the Eucharist

terrazzo a mosaic flooring made by embedding small pieces of marble or granite in fresh mortar; after hardening, the surface is ground and polished

tessera a small piece of marble, glass or tile which is used in mosaic work

tracery decorative carved stonework

tracker action a completely mechanical linkage between the keys and valves in a pipe organ

transept the transverse part of a cruciform church that crosses the nave at right angles

transom window a window above a door or other window built on and commonly hinged to a transom

trefoil a three-leafed conventionalized flower in Gothic tracery

triptych a picture consisting of a central panel and two flanking panels of half its size that fold over it

turret a little tower, specifically, an ornamental structure at one of the angles of a larger structure

Tuscan one of the classical orders of architecture that is of Roman origin and is very plain in style

tympanum the sculptural area enclosed by the arch above the doors of a church

vault an arched structure of masonry, usually forming a ceiling or roof

Venetian mosaic pieces of glass from Venice inlaid in plaster

wainscoting the lower three or four feet of an interior wall when finished differently from the rest of the wall, as with wood or marble panels

Illuminating Angel
Presentation Church
William Gubbins, architect